HARVARD HISTORICAL MONOGRAPHS

XXXVII

Published under the direction of the Department of History
from the income of The Robert Louis Stroock Fund

The Renaissance Idea of Wisdom

By
EUGENE F. RICE Jr.

CAMBRIDGE, MASSACHUSETTS
HARVARD UNIVERSITY PRESS
1958

Published in Great Britain by
Oxford University Press, London

LIBRARY OF CONGRESS CATALOG CARD NUMBER 58-12973

Made and printed in Great Britain by William Clowes and Sons Ltd,
London and Beccles

To my Parents

Preface

I have tried in this book to sketch out a history of the idea of wisdom in the two and a half centuries between Petrarch's "De sapientia" in the *De Remediis utriusque fortunae* and Pierre Charron's *De la Sagesse*. My immediate aims were two: first, to give a detailed analysis of what a selected number of fifteenth- and sixteenth-century theorists thought wisdom was; second, to relate these individual conceptions to each other in an intelligible pattern of historical change.

My greatest problem was that of selection. Anything like a complete treatment of such a subject is impossible. Virtually everyone who put pen to paper had something to say about wisdom. I chose as my principal sources the major treatises *de sapientia* (those of Cusanus, Bovillus, Sir Thomas Elyot, Cardanus and Pierre Charron) and several smaller works such as Petrarch's "De sapientia" or Vives' *Praelectio in sapientiam*. I supplemented these explicit, topical discussions of wisdom with material both from writers who defined *sapientia* at some length, though in more general contexts (like Salutati or Cardinal Sadoleto), and from others (Ficino and Pico della Mirandola, for example) whose treatment of the subject is fragmentary and often not as closely related to the central problems of their thought as I should have wished. In selecting this supplementary material I have tried to assemble as representative a collection of texts as my knowledge of the sources and the obscurer workings of personal preference allow. That the selection is really satisfactorily representative is to claim too much. But I hope it is not tendentious.

This is a deliberately limited study tracing one narrow band in the spectrum of human activity. Yet a history of the idea of wisdom does, I think, help clarify several more general problems.

It is often said, for example, that the Renaissance was a period of secularization, secularization in personal and collective behavior, political and economic attitudes, in men's ideas. I have been interested not so much in testing the general truth of such statements—properly defined and limited they seem to me obviously true—as in making the notion of secularization itself more precise by illustrating it in the history of a single important idea. I am convinced, of course, that the idea of wisdom was in fact secularized; and I hope I have collected enough evidence to make a fact of the working hypothesis with which I began. But I have been more interested in asking several specific questions. What does it mean to say that an idea has been secularized? What is the process by which secularization took place in the Renaissance? When and how did it happen?

This analysis of the varieties of wisdom is also a study in humanism. The Renaissance idea of wisdom (even using the word Renaissance, as I have tried to do, in a purely periodic sense) is largely synonymous with the humanist idea of wisdom; and a history of it can not only make more precise an important cultural aspiration of the movement, but also, perhaps, make a few familiar problems more tractable for having been looked at in its special perspective. How uniform, for example, were humanist definitions of *sapientia*? What was the relation of these humanist definitions to antique and medieval ones? How, in this particular case, was antique thought used and understood? Is there a concrete and definable relation between *sapientia* and *humanitas* and does this suggest that humanism has some sort of doctrinal content similar to the literal meaning of the word?

A history of the idea of wisdom in the Renaissance inevitably touches on the central problem of the period: that of historical change in a transitional age, more particularly that of the changing meanings of familiar words. The meaning of the word *sapientia*, and its vernacular equivalents, changed fundamentally. What happened can best be understood as the moralization of a metaphysical idea, what Ronsard called the "transformation of contemplation into action." One can see this as the object of wisdom shifts from divine things, to things divine and human and their causes, then to

human things alone. One sees it in the increasing emphasis on history
and experience as sources of wisdom; in efforts to tie wisdom more
closely to civic virtue and active political and business life; in the
gradual replacement of speculation about quiddities with what
Salutati called "a new type of speculation and the study of a true
and moral philosophy which is called wisdom." These are important changes which sum up the main transformations of the idea of
wisdom in this period. For the process by which *sapientia*, traditionally one of the central ideas of metaphysics and theology, became
a term with primarily ethical meanings is both a secularizing one—
as wisdom is drained of its specifically Christian meanings—and a
humanizing one—as wisdom comes to concern itself with human
things. This development suggests, perhaps, something about the
changed direction of European thought generally.

I owe particular thanks to Myron Gilmore under whose direction
this book, in its original form, was written as a doctoral disserta-
tion. The late Theodor Mommsen read the manuscript and gave
me much helpful advice.

The bulk of the writing was done while I was a *pensionnaire
étranger* at the Ecole Normale Supérieure. I am profoundly grateful
to the directors of that admirable institution and to Harvard for
the Sheldon Travelling Fellowship which made those years
possible.

The librarians of Harvard, the Bibliothèque Nationale, and the
British Museum were, as always, generous and helpful at every
stage.

My greatest obligation is to my wife, for her unshakeable interest
and encouragement.

Eugene F. Rice, Jr.

Contents

Illustrations

following page 128

The Renaissance Idea of Wisdom

Chapter 1

The Medieval Idea of Wisdom

Wisdom was a virtue highly and consistently prized in antiquity, the Middle Ages, and the Renaissance. "Happy is the man that findeth wisdom," exclaimed the author of Proverbs, "For the merchandise of it is better than the merchandise of silver, and the gain thereof than fine gold. She is more precious than rubies: and all the things thou canst desire are not to be compared to her. Length of days is in her right hand; and in her left hand riches and honour. Her ways are ways of pleasantness, and all her paths are peace." Plato called wisdom the "highest of human things," a "treasure," and the "most valuable of our possessions." For Seneca its possession was equivalent to blessedness. St. Augustine and St. Thomas said that it was man's highest good. In the Renaissance, Leonardo da Vinci described it as the highest happiness men are capable of, and Pierre Charron, in *De la Sagesse*, called it the naturally acquired "perfection of man as man."

Definitions of wisdom were various and tenacious. As verbal formulas they were invented by the Greek philosophers; and each important classical definition was known and repeated by medieval and Renaissance thinkers. Plato, for example, said that wisdom was a contemplation of eternal, immutable, and intelligible Ideas; Augustine that it was the contemplation of an infinite treasury of invisible and intelligible things; Cardinal Sadoleto that it was the contemplation of divine and immutable things, of things in the divine realm above the generation, change, and conflicting elements of the sublunar world. Aristotle defined wisdom as a knowledge of the first causes and principles of things and called it a "divine science"; St. Thomas defined it as knowledge of the first cause or of the highest and most noble causes and principles; Leonardo Bruni as a knowledge of first principles and the consequences which flow from them.

The Stoics widened the meaning of the term. For them wisdom was not simply the knowledge of divine things only, as it was for Plato and Aristotle, but of both human and divine things. Augustine began a discussion of wisdom in the *Contra Academicos* by repeating this: *sapientia est rerum humanarum divinarumque scientia.* Renaissance humanists like Coluccio Salutati, Reuchlin, Guillaume Budé, Bovillus, Conrad Celtis, Sir Thomas Elyot, Louis Le Caron, and Bacon rediscovered the same definition. Cicero and Seneca, finally, often spoke of wisdom as an *ars vivendi*, understood it as a moral rather than an intellectual virtue, identified it with prudence, and defined it as an imitation of reason and nature. Alexander of Hales echoed curiously these ethical preoccupations when he distinguished *scientia*, which is a speculative knowledge of the true, from *sapientia*, a perfection of the will moving it toward the good. The learned man knows the truth; the wise man loves and does the good. Petrarch, Erasmus, and Jerome Cardan in their turn revived wisdom as a moral, prudential, and active virtue; while Charron, consciously following Seneca, called the wise man a follower of "our great mother Nature."

But if the various definitions of wisdom invented by the Greek philosophers remained verbally intact from Plato's *Phaedrus* and Aristotle's *Metaphysics* to the *De la Sagesse* of Charron, their meanings changed profoundly. Wisdom was an ideal of twenty-two centuries. It described the highest knowledge men were capable of and the most desirable patterns of human behavior. It mirrored man's conception of himself, of the world, and of God. The history of such an idea is inevitably a continual repenetration of traditional formulas with new values and new assumptions. Word and definition remain static; the idea itself is transformed by the changing needs and aspirations of successive epochs, centuries, and even generations.

Two periods saw rapid, crucial changes in the idea of wisdom: the age of the great Church Fathers and the fifteenth and sixteenth centuries. In the first, wisdom was transformed from a pagan and naturally acquired human virtue to an attribute of the Christian God and a human participation, made possible by grace, in His light, truth, and goodness. Wisdom was identified with the Second Person of the Trinity, and understood as a fundamentally Christian insight radically opposed to the wisdom of the pagans and the profane knowledge of mere human or natural things. In the Renaissance the process was reversed: the idea was gradually secularized, drained, that is, of its religious meanings and disassociated from Christian Revelation by a conscious return to the antique. By the end of the sixteenth century it was commonly maintained that wisdom was a naturally acquired human perfection, man's self-formation to universal knowledge or his active commitment to virtue. Like the Church Fathers and the medieval Scholastics, the humanists repeated its traditional classical definitions. But they reappropriated—this was their originality—many of the original meanings of those verbal formulas. Augustine tied *sapientia* and Christianity together with knots which held a thousand years. The Renaissance patiently loosed them, and restored wisdom to its old autonomy and its purely human dignities.

I

The Patristic metamorphosis of the classical idea of wisdom was a process of selection and transformation dictated by the novel commitments and assumptions of an intransigent piety. The problem of classical philosophy had been to make the world intelligible in its own terms. It called its explanations wisdom. Religious philosophy explained the world in terms of a divinely revealed *principium* known by faith. It too called its explanations wisdom; and it opposed them to those of the philosophers. "For it is written, I will destroy the wisdom of the wise, and will bring to nothing the understanding of the prudent.... Hath not God made foolish the wisdom of this world? ... the Greeks seek after wisdom: But we preach Christ crucified, unto the Jews a stumbling-block, and unto the Greeks foolishness; But unto them which are called, both Jews and Greeks, Christ the power of God, and the wisdom of God." (I Cor. 1:19–24)

Yet, although Christians opposed their own wisdom to that of the philosophers and thought that pagan wisdom was foolish in the eyes of God, they found it useful to appropriate its definitions. They naturally selected for emphasis definitions compatible with their own revelational, other-worldly perspective. But even those definitions they selected were given meanings as opposed to their original ones as Christianity was opposed to paganism. The result was a wisdom, pagan in formula, but which in no way betrayed the spirit of the opening paragraphs of Paul's First Letter to the Corinthians.

Augustine's rethinking of the meaning of wisdom illustrates this transformation of a classical conception and its permeation by Christian assumptions and ends particularly well.[1] In the *Contra Academicos* he quotes a familiar definition: wisdom is a *rerum humanarum divinarumque scientia.*[2] This reproduces exactly the early Stoic definition of wisdom, that reported by Sextus, for example.[3] But he alters its meaning by splitting it into two parts, distinguishing the knowledge of divine things from human things and limiting the object of wisdom to the divine. Knowledge of human things is *scientia.* Wisdom is the knowledge of divine things.[4] Or, again, *sapientia* is an intellectual cognition of eternal things and *scientia* a

---

[1] For further discussion of Augustine's idea of wisdom see E. Gilson, *Introduction à l'étude de Saint Augustin*, 3rd ed. (Paris, 1949), 140–163; H. I. Marrou, *Saint Augustin et la fin de la culture antique* (Paris, 1937), 368–376 and 561–569; M. Schmaus, *Die psychologische Trinitätslehre des hl. Augustinus, Münsterische Beiträge zur Theologie*, XI (1927), 285–291; and F. Edward Cranz, "Saint Augustine and Nicholas of Cusa in the Tradition of Western Thought," *Speculum*, XXVIII (1953), 306–310.

[2] *Contra Academicos*, I, vi, 16: *Corpus scriptorum ecclesiasticorum latinorum*, LXIII (P. Knöll, ed., 1922), 16. Cf. H. A. Wolfson, *Philo: The Foundations of Religious Philosophy in Judaism, Christianity and Islam* (Harvard University Press, 1947), I, 148. The pages which follow owe much to this book.

[3] *Adversus Physicos*, I, 13.

[4] *De Trinitate*, XIV, i, 3: *PL*, XLII, 1037. "Disputantes autem de sapientia, definierunt eam dicentes: Sapientia est rerum humanarum divinarumque scientia. . . . ista definitio dividenda est, ut rerum divinarum scientia proprie sapientia nuncupetur, humanarum autem proprie scientiae nomen obtineat."

rational cognition of temporal things.[5] For Augustine, characteristically depreciating the temporal, human, and scientific, wisdom thus became knowledge of divine things only; while for the Stoic it had been an encyclopedic knowledge of all things divine and human.

Augustine then asks what divine things are; and he answers that they are those things which pertain to the life of blessedness. In this sense, God is the object of wisdom.[6] God is wise; man is a seeker of wisdom who tries to become wise. An achieved knowledge of divine things is the wisdom of God; the effort to get such knowledge is the wisdom of man. God is happy in the possession of wisdom. Man is made happy by the search for it.[7] Wisdom, finally, is knowledge of the truth, which is man's *summum bonum* and his naturally desired end. For before we are happy the notion of happiness is etched on our minds, and by this we know without the shadow of a doubt that we want to be happy. Similarly, before we are wise we know that we want to be wise by the notion of wisdom impressed on our minds. All men, therefore, wish to be wise and happy. They become so by perceiving, loving, and firmly holding that truth which is their supreme good.[8] This is *sapientia: id est*

[5] *De Trinitate*, XII, xv, 25: *PL*, XLII, 1012. "...haec est sapientiae et scientiae recta distinctio, ut ad sapientiam pertineat aeternarum rerum cognitio intellectualis; ad scientiam vero, temporalium rerum cognitio rationalis."

[6] *Enarratio in Psalmum* CXXXV, 8: *Corpus Christianorum*, XL (E. Dekkers and I. Fraipont, eds., 1956), 1962. "...non incongruenter intelligimus sapientiam in cognitione et dilectione eius quod semper est, atque incommutabiliter manet, quod Deus est."

[7] *Contra Academicos*, I, viii, 23: *Corpus script. eccl. lat.*, LXIII, 20–21. "etenim ut iam ipse explicem definitione quod sentio, sapientia mihi uidetur esse rerum humanarum et diuinarum, quae ad beatam uitam pertineant, non scientia solum, sed etiam diligens inquisitio. quam descriptionem si partiri uelis, prima pars, quae scientiam tenet, dei est, haec autem, quae inquisitione contenta est, hominis. illa igitur deus, hac autem homo beatus est."

[8] *De Libero arbitrio*, II, ix, 26: *Corpus script. eccl. lat.*, LXXIV (W. M. Green, ed., 1956), 61–62. "Num aliam putas esse sapientiam nisi veritatem in qua cernitur et tenetur summum bonum?...In quantum igitur omnes homines appetunt vitam beatam, non errant....Ut ergo constat nos beatos esse velle, ita nos constat esse velle sapientes, quia nemo sine sapientia beatus est. Nemo enim beatus est nisi summo bono, quod in ea veritate quam sapientiam vocamus cernitur et tenetur."

contemplatio veritatis, pacificans totum hominem, et suscipiens similitudinem Dei.[9]

Taken separately each affirmation of this statement is a classical commonplace. By limiting the object of wisdom to divine things Augustine distorted the Stoic definition; but the result is a definition equally traditional and classical. For Plato's wisdom had been an intellectual and contemplative virtue, a knowledge of divine, eternal, and immutable things;[10] while in the *Metaphysics* Aristotle had defined it as any science which deals with "divine objects" or with "remarkable, admirable and divine things."[11] The notion that wisdom is peculiarly an attribute of God also has Platonic and Aristotelian parallels. Wisdom, Aristotle had said, "must be in two ways most divine. For the science which it would be most fitting for God to have is a divine science, and so is any science which deals with divine objects; and this science alone has both these qualities; for God is thought to be among the causes of all things and to be a first principle and such a science either God alone can have, or God above all others."[12] Plato's similar insight led him to consider it arrogance to call man wise. God is wise; man is a lover of wisdom who tries to become wise.[13] From Plato, too, no doubt, derives the related idea that, by becoming wise, man becomes like God. To acquire wisdom, Plato had said, the soul must ascend from the visible to the invisible, from relative to absolute, from the many to the one, or from sensible, mutable, temporal things to the intelligible, immutable, eternal, and divine. "Therefore we ought to fly away from earth to heaven as quickly as we can; and to fly away is to become like God, as far as this is possible; and to become like him is to become holy, just, and wise."[14] Augustine is again following common classical precedents when he goes on to say that man has an innate notion of wisdom in his mind and a natural desire for it:

---

[9] *De Sermone Domini in monte*, I, iii, 10: *PL*, XXIV, 1234.

[10] *Repub.*, V, xxii, 478 E– 480 A; VII, iii, 517 B–C; *Protagoras*, 352 D.

[11] *Eth. Nic.*, VI, vii, 1141b, 6.

[12] *Metaph.*, I, ii, 983a, 6–7.

[13] *Phaedrus*, 278 D; *Symposium*, 203 E– 204 C; *Apology*, 23 A–B.

[14] *Theatetus*, 176 A–B.

the doctrine of innate ideas behind the parable of the midwife in the *Theatetus* and Aristotle's conviction of man's natural passion to know. Seneca, finally, and he too was repeating commonplaces, had already identified wisdom and blessedness, equated the search for wisdom with the search for truth, and called *sapientia* the "perfect good of the human mind." [15]

Yet Augustine's idea of wisdom is a radical metamorphosis of the antique conception. Like any creative thinker he used the past as a storehouse to be plundered; and he mastered it by the familiar double process of omission and positive reinterpretation. He selected from among the varieties of ancient wisdom those definitions he thought useful for his own purpose. The rest he rejected. What he rejected is as revealing as what he did with what he took.

When he quoted the Stoic definition, for example—*Sapientia est rerum humanarum divinarumque scientia*—he was not only establishing a point of departure for his own definition; he was also choosing one of two Stoic formulas. The second, influenced no doubt by the casual preoccupations of the Aristotelians, had defined wisdom as the knowledge of all things divine and human and their causes. Augustine omits this definition, although he knew it from Cicero.[16] Why he omitted it is suggested by his remarks in the *Enchiridion* on Virgil's *Felix qui potuit rerum cognoscere causas*: "Now then, when we find acceptable that verse of Maro's . . . we must not imagine that it is essential to the attainment of happiness to know the causes of the world's great physical phenomena hidden away in the most secret recesses of nature. . . . But we ought to know the causes of good and evil so far as it is given to man to know them in this life replete with mistakes and miseries, in order that we may be able to avoid them." [17]

Yet, to know the causes of good and evil, to achieve a "practical knowledge of things to be sought for and of things to be avoided," had defined another characteristic variety of pagan wisdom, a

---

[15] *Ep. Moral.*, LXXXIX, 4. Cf. *De Beneficiis*, IV, vi, 6.

[16] *De Off.*, II, ii, 5. Cf. *Tusc. Disp.*, IV, xxvi, 57 and Seneca, *Ep. Moral.*, LXXXIX, 4-5.

[17] *Enchiridion*, v, 16 (Louis A. Arand, tr.).

"moral" wisdom indistinguishable from Aristotle's prudence. Until Socrates, said Cicero, to explain this transformation of wisdom from an intellectual to a moral virtue, "philosophy dealt with numbers and movements, with the problem whence all things came or whither they returned, and zealously inquired into the size of the stars, the spaces between them, their courses, and all celestial phenomena. Socrates, on the other hand, was the first to call philosophy down from the heavens and set her in the cities of men and bring her also into their homes and compel her to ask questions about life and morality and things good and evil...."[18] In this perspective wisdom became an *ars vivendi*;[19] or, as Seneca says, a firm pursuit of virtue, a devotion to the good, a blessedness got by an imitation of nature: *Hoc est enim sapientia in naturam converti.* Its source is the law of nature, its content is to love and do the good, its fruit tranquillity and happiness.[20]

Augustine minimizes this moral wisdom as he neglected that wisdom which searched for causes. Again the *Enchiridion* suggests his reasons. Such a wisdom is a wisdom of this world, but has "God not made foolish the wisdom of this world?" It is a wisdom open to the natural man, but "just as no one can exist of himself, so neither can anyone be wise of himself, but needs to be enlightened by Him of whom it is written: All wisdom is from God." It is a wisdom, finally, of the cardinal virtues, while for man "true wisdom consists in piety." Piety is "true worship, and God is truly worshipped only by faith, hope and charity," the theological virtues.[21]

Augustine, indeed, fails to mention any definition of wisdom which implies mere skill or extensive information, any utilitarian wisdom of a practical, worldly cast, any wisdom coined into moral maxims which are simply generalizations from experience or rules which the natural man can carry out. He quotes Old Testament verses, for example, which say that all wisdom is from God, or that wisdom is piety, or that wisdom is a great good; but he is reluctant

---

[18] *Tusc. Disp.*, V, lv, 10–11.
[19] *De Finibus*, I, xiii, 42.
[20] *Ep. Moral.*, XCIV, 69; CXVIII, 11–13; *De Vita beata*, II, 2–3.
[21] *Enchiridion*, i, 1–3.

to note that in *Exodus* it describes the professional skill of craftsmen, pilots, and snake charmers, that Solomon's wisdom ranges from diplomatic acumen and legal skill to the solution of riddles and an encyclopedic knowledge of botany and zoology, that Israel's sages, like their Egyptian predecessors, taught sapiential maxims which stressed the value of wealth, the necessity of diligence and hard work to acquire it, or the ease with which it could be lost by riotous living or standing surety for another.[22] Among the pagans, similarly, he quotes the congenial Platonists but neglects the seven wise men, whose maxims had distilled the meaning of wisdom for the less sophisticated from the beginning of Greek intellectual life to the end of the Roman period: Solon, who urged all men to watch life's end; Cleobulus, who advised moderation in all things; Thales who pointed out that when you put up security for somebody loss is near; Pittacus who urged men to choose the opportune moment for their enterprises; or Chilon (although many attributed the maxim to Solon, to Socrates or Apollo), who recommended the saying "know thyself," preserved on a column at Delphi.[23]

Now this is a petty and often tiresomely uplifting wisdom, rooted in the urban and commercial life of the ancient world. But its precepts, designed to equip man for a fruitful and harmonious communal life, illuminate the essential characteristics of ancient wisdom. Moderation, self-knowledge and self-control, intellectual and moral cultivation, worldly success are its defining virtues. It is open wholly to the natural man and enables him to master life in its vulgar and great demands. It denotes any deep and human insight into the meaning and interrelationships of life and nature and the moral attitude, flowing from these insights, which man should adopt before external reality.[24] Fortified by wisdom, he is fundamentally committed to life, yet emotionally detached from it. He remembers

[22] Robert H. Pfeiffer, *Introduction to the Old Testament* (New York, 1948), 34–40.

[23] Ausonius, *Ludus Septem Sapientum*, lines 64, 82–87, 138–139, 144–145, 152, 173–174, 178–179, 181, 190, 203–206, 216, 221–223.

[24] H. Leisegang, "Sophia," Pauly-Wissowa, *Real-Encyclopädie der classischen Altertumswissenschaft*, 2. Reihe, V (Stuttgart, 1927), col. 1019.

the ineluctability of death, stands above the shifts of fortune, and submits to fate. His wisdom is an imperturbable virtue, a heart ever conscious of right, an achieved nobility in which, as it is well put by an aphorism of the Pseudo-Ausonius, the "useful and the upright are never separated."[25] It is an autonomous, self-created perfection and an ethical commitment to man and the world.

It is precisely this commitment which Augustine rejected. This is why even the classical definitions of wisdom he did accept take on entirely different meanings. Verbal identities only emphasize these differences. For, by "divine things" or "eternal and immutable things," by *summum bonum* and beatitude, by the statement that God alone is wise and man a lover of wisdom, by the distinction of *scientia* and *sapientia*, by the idea that a notion of wisdom is innate in man—by each of these things Augustine meant something profoundly different from what the same words, distinctions, and statements had meant in their original contexts.   Reordered around the divinely revealed and firmly believed *principium* of the Trinity and understood in terms of the often very different statements about wisdom in the revealed Scriptural texts, they took on new and original Christian meanings. When Augustine, in his *Commentary* on the One hundred and thirty-fifth Psalm, defined wisdom as a knowledge of God, he did not quote Plato or Aristotle. He quoted Job 28:28—*Ecce pietas est sapientia*—and defined *pietas* as the worship of God.[26] When he called wisdom a knowledge of "divine

[25] Ausonius, *Œuvres en vers et en prose*, Max Jasinski, ed. (Paris, Classiques Garnier, n.d.), II, 290, line 22.

[26] *Enarratio in Psalmum CXXXV*, 8. The phrase "pietas est sapientia" as such does not occur in the Vulgate, although the idea behind it is a Biblical commonplace (for example, Ps. 110:10; Prov. 1:7; Ecclus. 1:16). Its source is the Septuagint and St. Jerome, whose initial revision of the Latin text of the Old Testament translates θεοσέβεια as *pietas*: "Dixit autem homini: Ecce pietas est sapientia, abstinere vero a malis, scientia." (*PL*, XXIX, 95). Augustine translates the word in the same way: "Hominis autem sapientia pietas est. Habes hoc in libro sancti Job: nam ibi legitur, quod ipsa Sapientia dixerit eo loco pietatem, distinctius in graeco reperies θεοσέβειαν, qui est Dei cultus" (*Enchiridion*, ii: *PL*, XL, 231). Augustine quotes Job 28:28 in this form and with the same explanation several times. These texts are conveniently listed by Marrou, *Saint Augustin et la fin de culture antique*, 366–367. Cf.

things," he was not referring to metaphysical abstractions—to Plato's divine Ideas, the Good, the Beautiful, and Being itself or to Aristotle's first causes and principles of things[27]—but to the Trinity and the Credo. He was defining wisdom as the knowledge that Christ died and was resurrected for man's salvation. When he used the words "eternal things," he meant the divine Ideas, but Ideas which were ends and exemplary causes in the mind of a Christian God. When he said that only God should properly be called wise, it was not because he had read the *Phaedrus*, or even Plotinus, but because he had incorporated wisdom into the Trinity, made it one of the divine names and that attribute of divine substance by which all things were created, and identified it with the Second Person of the Trinity. His texts were not classical, but several helpful passages from the Book of Wisdom, the opening verses of the Gospel of John and I Corinthians 1:24 where Paul called Christ the "wisdom of God."[28] When, finally, he said that man was a lover of wisdom, he in fact replaced philosophical by Christian supremacy. For Plato and Seneca the philosopher was an *amator sapientiae*; for Augustine the Christian, the man who loved and believed in Christ.

Augustine's wisdom is thus a fundamentally Christian insight indistinguishable from religion.[29] Its core is faith in the Trinity, which then becomes the centrally seized *principium* for a total reorganization of thought and morals and a radical reordering of loves.[30] To say then that wisdom is man's *summum bonum* and his highest

---

De Civitate Dei, XIV, xxviii: *Corpus Christianorum*, XLVII (B. Dombart and A. Kalb, eds., 1955), 452: ". . . in hac autem nulla est hominis sapientia nisi pietas, qua recte colitur uerus Deus, id expectans praemium in societate sanctorum non solum hominum, uerum etiam angelorum, *ut sit Deus omnia in omnibus*." and *De Trinitate*, XIV, i, 1: *PL*, XLII, 1037: "Deus ergo ipse summa sapientia, cultus autem Dei sapientia est hominis."

[27] *Metaph.*, I, i, 981b, 28– 982a, 2; *Eth. Nic.*, VI, v, 1140a, 24 ff.

[28] *De Trinitate*, VII, iii, 4.

[29] Cf. Lactantius, *Instit. Div.*, IV, 3: *PL*, VI, 454. "Idcirco et in sapientia religio, et in religione sapientia est. Ergo non potest segregari; quia sapere nihil aliud est, nisi deum verum iustis ac piis cultibus honorare."

[30] C. N. Cochrane, *Christianity and Classical Culture* (Oxford University Press, 1944), 412.

beatitude is to say that the Trinity is his beatitude and highest good. To distinguish *sapientia* and *scientia* is to make an invidious comparison between wisdom, which is the knowledge and worship of God, and science, which is an inferior knowledge of created things. Technically the distinction flows from the Platonizing dualism of Augustine's epistemology. Emotionally, however, its source is his revolutionary need to confront classical *scientia* with the radically different idea of Christian *sapientia*. To say, finally, that man has an innate notion and love of wisdom is to say that the human soul was created in the image of the Trinity and that its inborn sapiential ideas are activated by the rays of divine illumination. For to remember, know and love God is the triple function of the soul, "and this is wisdom." If, on the contrary, men remember, know, and love themselves and creatural goods, they are fools. Let them, then, simply worship God and hold this piety for wisdom.[31]

Restated, therefore, in its true meaning, Augustine's idea of wisdom has only a verbal similarity to its classical prototypes. Wisdom is transcendent and preëxists the creation of the world. It is identified with God. It is Christ himself, the Word of God, the Second Person of the Trinity and the light of lights "which illumines every man."[32] As Word it is equated with the Logos, the totality of ideas in the intelligible world.[33] By extension it is identified with the Law and the written Revelation of Scripture.[34] As an image of the Trinity in the soul and an innate idea and love of Wisdom, it is immanent in the soul and is thus the source of human knowledge

---

[31] *De Trinitate*, XIV, xii, 15.

[32] *De Trinitate*, VII, iii, 5: *PL*, XLII, 938. "Propterea igitur cum pronuntiatur in Scripturis, aut enarratur aliquid de sapientia, sive dicente ipsa sive cum de illa dicitur, Filius nobis potissimum insinuatur"; *De Beata vita*, 34.

[33] *De Civitate Dei*, XI, x, 3: *Corpus Christianorum*, XLVIII, 332. "Neque enim multae, sed una sapientia est, in qua sunt infiniti quidam eique finiti thensauri rerum intellegibilium, in quibus sunt omnes inuisibiles atque incommutabiles rationes rerum etiam uisibilium et mutabilium, quae per ipsam factae sunt."

[34] Cf. Ecclus. 19:18. "Quia omnis sapientia timor Dei, et in illa timere Deum, Et in omni sapientia disposito legis." and Deut. 4:6.

and wisdom. This is that "certain ineffable and incomprehensible light" by which man participates in Wisdom.[35] For knowledge and love of God is no self-achieved perfection, but a gift of grace. One becomes wise not by any natural light but by an illuminated participation in the divine light. *Omnis sapientia a Domino Deo est.*[36] It is a gift of the Holy Spirit, *desursum descendens,* as St. James said, and an illumination through faith to a knowledge and love of God.[37] Christian wisdom is the only true wisdom.

Wisdom, finally, is a beatifying truth which is man's end. In this life it is the happy effort to know and love God; in the after life it is the tranquil contemplation of God and the enjoyment of divine beatitude.[38] Seven ascending steps lead to it: a fear of God; *pietas,* the worship of God, a submission to the teachings of Scripture and the rejection of the wisdom of the world; *scientia,* now significantly redefined as a knowledge of Scripture whose fruit is a humble love of God and one's neighbor for the sake of God; fortitude, which is the strength to turn away from human, temporal things to "eternal things, that is to say, the immutable and single Trinity"; *consilium,* works of charity to others; and *purgatio cordis,* a cleansing of the heart and soul which leaves only a single devotion to the truth through faith. By these stages man rises to the seventh and last, to Wisdom itself, and becomes wise in the peaceful contemplation and enjoyment of God.[39]

II

In its major lines Augustine's conception of wisdom dominated the Middle Ages until the Aristotelian revival of the late twelfth

[35] *Soliloquiorum,* I, xiii, 23. Cf. *De Trinitate,* VII, iii, 6.

[36] *Enchiridion,* i; Ecclus. 1:1.

[37] *De Natura et gratia,* xvi, 17; James 1:5; 3:5. See also Prov. 2:6; Eccles. 2:26; Sap. 7:7 and 8:21 and Fulbert Cayré, *La Contemplation augustinienne* (Paris, 1927), 53–57.

[38] *Contra Academicos,* I, vii, 23.

[39] *De Doctrina Christiana,* II, vii, 9–11. Cf. *De Sermone Domini in monte,* I, iii, 10 and Isaiah 11:2–3.

century. From the *Sapientia* of the German nun Hrotsvitha to St. Anselm, Abelard, and the prologues of Otto of Freising's *Two Cities*, its principal assertions were faithfully reproduced: the identification of wisdom and Christ; the dualism of divine and human wisdom, "our" wisdom and that of the philosophers; the definition of wisdom as a fundamentally Christian insight, a knowledge of the Christian God and love of Him; the insistence that wisdom is a gift of grace unattainable by the natural man. Only in the thirteenth century was this conception modified in important ways. Under the influence of Aristotle's *Metaphysics* one school of scholastic theology, that associated with the names of Albertus Magnus and Aquinas, replaced Augustine's dualisms by a temporary harmony, rehabilitating a variety of naturally acquired wisdom and crowning it with a wisdom revealed by God. The result was to make metaphysics and natural theology a second respectable variety of wisdom and to emphasize significantly man's natural ability—however small—to acquire wisdom without the aid of grace.

The *Summa theologiae* of Alexander of Hales illustrates this change in progress. There are, he says, two kinds of *scientia*: knowledge of the First Cause and knowledge of the hierarchy of created causes. A science whose object is the First Cause is called *sapientia*; one whose object is only created causes must be called *scientia*. Now there are two sciences whose object is the Cause of causes: theology, the *scientia de Deo, qui est causa causarum*, and metaphysics, or *prima philosophia*.[40] Theology, because it transcends all other sciences, is properly called wisdom. Metaphysics, however, cannot be called *sapientia* with the same legitimacy. It is inferior to theology and its handmaiden; and its end is to know the truth, while the end of theology is to love the good, and this is more admirable. Theology, therefore, is a *sapientia*, but metaphysics is properly a *scientia absoluta*. In slightly different words, theology is *sapientia ut sapientia*; metaphysics is, at best, *sapientia ut scientia*; while any

---

[40] *Sum. Theol.*, Tract. Introduc., Q. I, art. 1, Solutio: *Doctoris irrefragabilis Alexandri de Hales Ordinis minorum Summa Theologica*, B. Klumper, ed. (Quaracchi, 1924–48), I, 2, col. 1.

other science, which is inevitably a knowledge of created causes, is simply *scientia*.[41]

Alexander had studied the *Metaphysics* with care, but his fundamental Augustinianism is clear. He refuses, on the one hand, to call theology a *scientia*, a systematically ordered body of true and certain knowledge derived from the certain but undemonstrable principles of Revelation. And he is equally reluctant, on the other, to call metaphysics a *sapientia*. This would tend to put knowledge of secular truths on a plane with knowledge of the revealed truths of theology. He therefore leaves *sapientia* tied almost exclusively to revealed theology, defining its end as the stimulation of love rather than a knowledge of the truth. Metaphysics he calls an elevated kind of *scientia*. For Hales as for Augustine, wisdom is par excellence a divinely revealed knowledge and love of the Triune God. Yet he could not escape Aristotle completely. Metaphysics is a superior *scientia*, but it is also an inferior *sapientia*, a *sapientia ut scientia*.

Aquinas emphasized the second point and went on further to free metaphysics and legitimize its claims. In an authentic classical revival he reappropriated an antique variety of wisdom and created a temporary balance between it and Augustine's fundamentally Christian wisdom. Like Augustine's his point of departure was a classical definition of wisdom, the Aristotelian. He refers explicitly to his source—the first two chapters of the *Metaphysics*—and reproduces its definitions with precision: wisdom is a knowledge of first

[41] *Sum. Theol.*, I, 2, col. 2. "Theologia igitur, quae perficit animam secundum affectionem, movendo ad bonum per principia timoris et amoris, proprie et principaliter est sapientia. Prima Philosophia, quae est theologia philosophorum, quae est de causa causarum, sed ut perficiens cognitionem secundum viam artis et ratiocinationis, minus proprie dicitur sapientia. Ceterae vero scientiae, quae sunt de causis consequentibus et causatis, non debent dici sapientiae, sed scientiae. Unde secundum hoc dicendum quod doctrina Theologiae est sapientia ut sapientia; Philosophia vero Prima, quae est cognitio primarum causarum, quae sunt bonitas, sapientia, et potentia, est sapientia, sed ut scientia; ceterae vero scientiae, quae considerant passiones de subiecto per suas causas, sunt scientiae ut scientiae."

causes and principles, an *altissimarum causarum cognitio*.[42] It is a science which deals with "divine objects" and a knowledge of "divine things."[43] The wise man considers the "highest cause of the whole universe, which is God."[44]

Like Alexander of Hales Aquinas goes on to say that any science whose object is the First Cause is properly called wisdom. Since the object of both metaphysics and theology is "divine things," the "highest causes," and God, both are properly called wisdom. Unlike Hales he feels no need to qualify this statement excessively, except to say with his usual precision that theology knows the common object *lumine divinae revelationis*, while metaphysics knows it *lumine naturalis rationis*.[45] There exist, therefore, two legitimate varieties of wisdom: metaphysics, an autonomous knowledge of the divine acquired without the aid of grace, and theology, a revealed knowledge of divine things. The two are independent, but—and here Aquinas differs fundamentally from Augustine—not opposed. On the contrary, just as nature is perfected and not destroyed by grace, so also is there no hostility between human and divine wisdom.[46]

Theology, of course, is the nobler science; and although both metaphysics and theology investigate the "supreme cause of the

[42] *Summa contra Gentiles*, I, xciv. "... sapientia in cognitione altissimarum causarum consistit, secundum Philosophum in principio *Metaph*." Cf. *Ibid*., I, i and *Sum. Theol*., Ia, IIae, Q. LVII, art. 2, Resp. For a good, detailed description of Aquinas' idea of wisdom see Sister M. Rose Emmanuella Brennan, *The Intellectual Virtues according to the Philosophy of St. Thomas* (Catholic University of America Press, 1941), 44–52.

[43] *Sum. Theol*., IIa, IIae, Q. XIX, art. 7, Resp. "Cum autem sapientia sit cognitio divinorum." Cf. *Summa contra Gentiles*, IV, xii.

[44] *Sum. Theol*., Ia, Q. I, art. 6, Resp. "Ille igitur qui considerat simpliciter altissimam causam totius universi, quae Deus est, maxime sapiens dicitur."

[45] *Sum. Theol*., Ia, Q. I, art. 1, Resp. ad 2; *In Isaiam prophetam expositio*, III, i.

[46] *In Boet. de Trin*., Q. II, art. 2, Resp ad 1. "... sapientia non dividitur contra scientiam, sicut oppositum contra suum oppositum, sed quia se habet ex additione ad scientiam." Quoted by M. D. Chenu, *La Théologie comme science au XIIIᵉ siècle*, 2nd ed. (Paris, 1943), 107.

whole universe, which is God," the wisdom of the theologian is nobler and more extensive. For Christian theology yields a knowledge of God as First Cause of exemplary precision. It is not content with that knowledge about God which philosophy derives from creatures, but teaches us things about God which can be known to no one but God himself. These He communicates to us by Revelation. *Unde sacra doctrina maxime dicitur sapientia.*[47] By definition such wisdom is profoundly Christian and a gift of the Holy Spirit, *desursum descendens.* It is a kind of inner Revelation, a divine illumination, which raises the mind to a knowledge of those invisible and divine things closed to the light of the natural intellect.[48] It is a revealed knowledge of divine things, a human participation in the Word, which is Wisdom itself and an intellectual participation in the illumination and stability of the Ideas of God.[49]

But metaphysics also has "divine things" and the "highest causes" for its object; and it too, though in a lesser degree, is properly called *sapientia.* In this sense wisdom is a naturally acquired intellectual virtue, a purely speculative *habitus*, by which the speculative intellect perfects itself to a knowledge of the truth. Its object is the end of the universe; but, since the end of an object is also its principle and cause, its end equals Aristotle's first causes. Its content is the knowledge of such causes, that is, a knowledge of God and of the truth, for all causes and all truths reduce themselves to God. Its function is a "perfect and universal" judgment of all lesser sciences.[50] Metaphysics is therefore an autonomous human wisdom, independent of theology and naturally acquired by man without the aid of grace. This is an accurate restatement of Aristotle's idea of wisdom.

The contrast with Augustine is striking. For the first time since

[47] *Sum. Theol.*, Ia, Q. I, art. 6, Resp.

[48] *Sum. Theol.*, Ia, Q. I, art. 6. Resp. ad 2. Cf. *Summa contra Gentiles*, III, cliv, 1.

[49] *Sum. Theol.*, Ia, Q. XLI, art. 3, Resp. ad 4. Cf. *Ibid.*, IIa, IIae, Q. XXIII, art. 2, Resp. ad 1 and Etienne Gilson, *Le Thomisme. Introduction à la philosophie de Saint Thomas d'Aquin*, 5th ed. (Paris, 1947), 484.

[50] *Sum. Theol.*, Ia, IIae, Q. LVII, art. 2, Resp. and Resp. ad 2. Cf. Gilson, *Le Thomisme*, 27.

the end of paganism a virtue which the antique world considered man's noblest embellishment is reattributed to man as his own natural acquisition. With important restrictions, to be sure. Metaphysics remains an inferior type of *sapientia* and it is subordinated to theology as all other sciences are subordinated to it. At times Aquinas even refuses to name it *sapientia* at all. Thus he says that theology properly investigates the First Cause while philosophy only investigates secondary causes; or, again, that the knowledge of invisible things revealed to man by grace is properly called *sapientia* while the same knowledge deduced from creatures is not *sapientia* but *scientia*.[51] The fact remains, however, that Aquinas established a certain equilibrium between Augustine's Christian idea of wisdom and the purely secular wisdom of Aristotle. Augustine refused to recognize a non-Christian wisdom. He established a Christian *sapientia*, while opposed to it, to be used perhaps, but not enjoyed, was classical *scientia*. Aquinas recognizes both a Christian *sapientia* and beside it, inferior but autonomous, a human wisdom more or less identified with Aristotle's metaphysics.

III

The Thomist idea of wisdom remained a recognizable conception throughout the late Middle Ages and the Renaissance, perpetuated, among others, by the fourteenth- and fifteenth-century Paris and Cologne Dominicans, Cardinal Cajetan's Commentary on the *Summa*, and the writings of the sixteenth-century Jesuits. Pierre Charron confirms its influence at the end of the century in his second preface to *De la Sagesse* (1604). The wisdom of theology, he writes, is a knowledge of "divine things," a virtue "infused and a gift of God, *desursum descendens*." It is the first of the seven gifts of the Holy Spirit and is found only among the just and those free of sin. The wisdom of philosophy, on the other hand, is a naturally acquired knowledge of the "first and highest causes of all things," of first principles and of God. It is called metaphysics and is the

---

[51] *Summa contra Gentiles*, II, iv; III, cliv, 2.

first of the intellectual virtues.[52] The object of the two wisdoms is identical; but one reaches its object with the aid of grace, the other by its own unaided efforts.

Aquinas' definition, however, was only one of several even in the thirteenth century. It became more atypical as time went on. Most late medieval thinkers tended to upset his precarious balance of the divergent claims of divine and human wisdom by suppressing the human term of his equation and limiting wisdom to a grace-given knowledge of God. From one point of view this tendency is intelligible as a disintegration of the more balanced, more humane high scholastic doctrine; but from another it is a return to Augustine and a positive reassertion of positions long fundamental to earlier medieval doctrines of wisdom and most characteristic of them. The fundamental medieval idea of wisdom—that wisdom is a Revelational knowledge of the Christian God—was never more strongly or eloquently stated than at the moment it had begun to be replaced by more novel conceptions.

Nicholas of Cusa's *De sapientia* (1450), the most important discussion of wisdom in the late Middle Ages, is such a statement. Its aim, like that of Cusanus' philosophy as a whole, is to defend faith, intuition, and the mystic's vision by narrowing the operating realm of natural reason. The two fundamental doctrines which axe the Cusan system were designed to achieve this aim. *Docta ignorantia* defeats the "proud spirit of reason";[53] the coincidence of contraries is a frontal attack on scholastic rationalism and the sect of

---

[52] *De la Sagesse*, Amaury Duval, ed. (Paris, 1820–24), I, xxxvii–xxxviii.

[53] *De visione Dei*, 9: *Haec accvrata recognitio trivm volvminvm opervm clariss. p. Nicolai Cvsae card.*, Jacques Lefèvre d'Etaples, ed. (Paris, Badius Ascensius, 1514), I, 219v. This edition is noted henceforth as Paris. Cf. J. Uebinger, "Der Begriff docta ignorantia in seiner geschichtlichen Entwicklung," *Archiv für Geschichte der Philosophie*, VIII (1894), 10–25; E. Vansteenberghe, *Autour de la docte ignorance. Une controverse sur la théologie mystique au XVe siècle* (Munster, 1914); and L. Baur, *Cusanus-Texte*, III. *Marginalien, 1. Nicolaus Cusanus und Ps. Dionysius im Lichte der Zitate und Randbemerkungen des Cusanus* (Heidelberg, 1941), 84. For a more detailed discussion of the meaning Cusanus gives *sapientia* see Eugene F. Rice, Jr., "Nicholas of Cusa's Idea of Wisdom," *Traditio*, XIII (1957), 345–368.

Aristotelians.[54] One consequence of defeating reason was skepticism (*nihil perfecte homo noscere poterit*, as Cusanus himself puts it).[55] A second was a corresponding emphasis on the *intellectus* and the fusion of faith and reason in intellectual cognition (*nisi credideritis, non intelligetis*).[56] A third was to open the now humbled soul to divine illumination. In this perspective Cusanus' thought is valuably representative, both as a reaction against that kind of rationalism of which Aquinas had already become a symbol and as a typically late medieval combination of skepticism in philosophy and mysticism in religion.

Cusanus' idea of wisdom is similarly rooted in characteristic forms of contemporary thought. It is partly based on a nominalist epistemology. Its formulas derive from the mystics, Eckhart, Lull, the Brethren of the Common Life, and, through their predecessors from the Pseudo-Dionysius to the theologians of the School of Chartres, from the Neo-Platonic tradition of the declining Empire. Its fundamental assertions are Augustinian: wisdom is a knowledge of divine things; divine things are to be understood in a Christian sense; wisdom is not naturally acquired, it is a gift of grace. Cusanus, indeed, pushes this most common medieval conception of wisdom to its furthest consequences. The result is appropriately paradoxical: a work unusually representative precisely because its originality consists in stating traditional ideas with provocative extremism.

[54] *Apologia Doctae ignorantiae: Nicolai de Cusa Opera Omnia iussu et auctoritate Academiae Litterarum Heidelbergensis fidem edita*, E. Hoffman, R. Klibansky, L. Baur, *et al.*, eds. (Leipzig, 1932 sq.), II, 6. This edition is noted henceforth as Heidelberg. Cf. Ernst Hoffman, "Die Vorgeschichte der cusanischen coincidentia oppositorum," prefacing Karl Fleischmann's translation *Uber den Beryll* (Leipzig, 1938) and Paul Wilpert, "Das Problem der coincidentia oppositorum in der Philosophie des Nikolaus von Cues," *Humanismus, Mystik und Kunst*, J. Koch, ed., 39–55.

[55] *Apologia Doctae ignorantiae:* Heidelberg, II, 3. See also *De Docta ignorantia*, I, 17: Heidelberg, I, 35 and R. Stadelmann, *Vom Geist des ausgehenden Mittelalters. Studien zur Geschichte der Weltanschauung von Nicolaus Cusanus bis Sebastian Frank* (Halle, 1929), 44–65.

[56] *De Docta ignorantia*, III, 11: Heidelberg, I, 151–152. The phrase is a mistranslation of Isaiah 7:9. It goes back to the Septuagint and is often quoted by Augustine in this form.

The core of the *De sapientia* is the identification of wisdom with Christ. Since Paul named Christ "the power of God and the wisdom of God" in his *First Epistle to the Corinthians*, and Augustine elaborated this suggestion into coherent doctrine in the *De Trinitate*, this identification had been a Christian commonplace. The fourteenth and fifteenth centuries embroidered on the idea with metaphysical subtlety and pictorial explicitness. A woodcut illustrating the 1482 edition of Suso's *Orologium sapientiae* shows Christ as *die ewig Weyszhait*; while the English morality play *Wisdom, Who is Christ* (about 1460) stages the same majestic figure, a ball of gold with a cross in his left hand, a scepter in his right, with a golden wig on his head, and clothed in "purpull clothe of golde."[57] Cusanus' wisdom is more abstract but equally regal. *Sapientia* is eternal, preceding all birth and creation, simple, indivisible, and powerful. It is the *principium* of all things and embraces all things. It is, therefore, "God, one simple, eternal, universal principle."[58] More precisely, it is God's Word, His Son, the Second Person of the Trinity, or, in Cusanus' Augustinian terminology, absolute *aequalitas*, the formal principle of being, a close approximation of the Thomist *ipsum esse subsistens*.[59] Wisdom is thus "the equality itself of Being, the word or reason of things. It is an infinite intellectual form, for the form gives formal being to the thing that is formed. Therefore an infinite form is the actuality of all formable forms and the most precise equality of them all."[60] Such a form is

[57] *The Macro Plays*, F. J. Furnivall and A. W. Pollard, eds., *Early English Text Society*, Extra Ser. XCI (London, 1904), 35. The Morality of Wisdom has been often studied. See J. J. Molloy, O. P., *A Theological Interpretation of the Moral Play, Wisdom, Who Is Christ* (Catholic University of America Press, 1952) and the works there cited. For the illustration see *Des Mystikers Heinrich Seuse O. Pr. Deutsche Schriften*, Nikolaus Heller, ed. (Regensburg, 1926), 142.

[58] *De pace fidei*, 5: *Nicolai de Cusa De pace fidei*, R. Klibansky and H. Bascour, eds. (London, 1956), 14.

[59] *De sapientia*, I: Heidelberg, V, 19; *Cribratio Alchorani*, II, 3: Paris, I, 134v. For a detailed analysis of Cusanus' doctrine of the Trinity and its sources see the important recent monograph of R. Haubst, *Das Bild des Einen und Dreieinen Gottes in der Welt nach Nicholaus von Kues* (Trier, 1952).

[60] *De sapientia*, 20.

the treasury of being out of which flow all existing things and a treasury of wisdom filled eternally with the Ideas of these things.[61] As Christ or the Word of God, Wisdom is thus the formal principle of creation. It is in this sense too that we recognize *sapientia* as our *principium, per quod, in quo et ex quo sumus et movemur*, as our beginning, middle, and end, and as the *exemplar tantorum varietatum rerum universarum*.[62] Wisdom is thus Christ in His most subtle metaphysical ramifications: as logos, infinite form, the Form of forms, the Quiddity of quiddities, the principle of all that is.

If Christ is Wisdom, man's search for it is clearly only a special case of his relation to and search for God. Cusanus called this search a *venatio sapientiae*. He found a characteristically ambiguous statement of its conditions in an arbitrarily constructed and paradoxical Biblical text: *sapientia foris clamat in plateis, et est clamor eius, quoniam ipsa habitat in altissimis*.[63] Wisdom cries aloud in the streets and its cry is that it dwells in the highest places. Cusanus has based an elaborate argument on this text. His exegesis of *in altissimis*, for example, establishes wisdom's transcendence and spells out the most important consequences of this. "That is highest which cannot be higher. Only infinity is so high. Of wisdom, therefore, which all men by nature desire to know and seek with such mental application, one can know only that it is higher than all knowledge and thus unknowable, unutterable in any words, unintelligible to any intellect, unmeasurable by any measure, unlimitable by any limit, unterminable by any term, unproportionable by any proportion, incomparable by any comparison, unfigurable by any figuration, unformable by any formation, unmovable by any motion, unimaginable by any imagination, insensible to any sense, unattractable by any attraction, untasteable by any taste, inaudible to any ear, invisible to any eye, unapprehendable by any apprehension, unaffirmable in any affirmation, undeniable by any negation, indubitable by any

[61] *De possest*: Paris, I, 182v; *De docta ignorantia*, II, 9, p. 95.

[62] *De sapientia*, 13, 17 and 32.

[63] *De sapientia*, 5; Prov. 1:20. "Sapientia foris praedicat; in plateis dat vocem suam."; Ecclus. 24:7. "Ego in altissimis habitavi, Et thronus meus in columna nubis." Cf. *De apice theoriae:* Paris, I, 219v.

doubt, and no opinion can be held about it. And since it is inexpressible in words, one can imagine an infinite number of such expressions, for no conception can conceive the wisdom through which, in which and of which all things are."[64]

And yet wisdom cries out its transcendence from any public place: *foris clamat in plateis*. Its point of departure is the simplest object of sense experience, and its message is more accessible to the simple than to the learned of this world. In the *De sapientia* it is a *pauper quidem idiota*, full of innocent simplicity and learned ignorance, who tells an arrogant Renaissance orator what wisdom really is, quoting Pauline texts, classic for the Christian idea of wisdom, which give added dimensions to the hint from Proverbs: "For the wisdom of this world is foolishness with God" and "Knowledge puffeth up."[65] The philosophers, indeed, have perished in their own vanity; but the humble and ignorant, knowing that wisdom is a gift of grace, have been granted it. For God, although He is a *Deus absconditus*, above all rational and intellectual activity, wants to be found, "because it is his will to reveal Himself and manifest Himself to those who seek Him."[66] By the Incarnation of His Word and by divine illumination He opens Himself to men living virtuously and humbly in a simplicity enforced by poverty and manual labor.[67] Christ illumines them and enables them to participate in His Wisdom through faith. "See how many mysteries are in the words of Christ, voices in which lies hidden eternal Wisdom itself. But if they are to be heard, they must be approached with faith and reverence; and to this end we are illuminated and assume His

[64] *De sapientia*, 9–10. Cf. *De possest:* Paris, I, 183v.

[65] *De sapientia*, 3; I Cor. 3:19; and I Cor. 8:1. Maurice de Gandillac, *La Philosophie de Nicolas de Cues* (Paris, 1941), 57–73 gives a detailed analysis of the meaning and sources of the Cusan *idiota*.

[66] *De quaerendo Deum: Nicolaus von Cues. Texte seiner philosophischen Schriften nach der Ausgabe von Paris 1514, sowie nach der Drucklegung von Basel 1565*, Alfred Petzelt, ed. (Stuttgart, 1949), I, 217.

[67] *De possest:* Paris, I, 178r. "Est enim deus occultus et absconditus ab oculis omnium sapientum; sed reuelat se paruulis seu humilibus quibus dat gratiam. Est vnus ostensor magister scilicet Ihesus Christus."

plenitude."[68] The Spirit of Christ, which is the spirit of wisdom, pours down and reforms man in its image, forging an amorous nexus between itself and the spirit of the intellect in which the intellect finds its happiness.[69]

Wisdom, in short, is in the area of grace rather than in that of nature. It cannot be naturally acquired. It is a gift of the Holy Spirit *desursum descendens*. It must be requested as a gift from the Father of Lights and can be got in no way except *dono gratiae* or *attractione Patris*. Wisdom, the Second Person of the Trinity and the Word of God, gives man wisdom.[70]

The paradox of a virtue which is at once unattainably transcendent (because it is the Second Person of the Trinity) and attainable to man (because human wisdom is a participation in divine wisdom[71] and a gift of God to an intellect naturally capable of receiving it)[72] tempts Cusanus to define wisdom as the unattainable attainment of the unattainable and the joyful comprehension of the incomprehensible.[73] These problematical formulas suggest that wisdom is knowledge of Christ radically limited by the abyss which separates man, who is finite, from an infinite God. Cusanus makes the idea more precise by restating it metaphysically. Returning to his conception of divine Wisdom as an infinite form or the quiddity of quiddities, he defines

---

[68] E. Hoffmann and R. Klibansky, *Cusanus-Texte*, I. *Predigten*, 1. *"Dies Santificatus" vom Jahre 1439* (Heidelberg, 1929), 38. Cf. Josef Koch, *Cusanus-Texte*, I. *Predigten*, 2./5. *Vier Predigten im Geiste Eckharts* (Heidelberg, 1937), 124.

[69] *De venatione sapientiae*, 25: Paris, I, 211r.

[70] *De dato Patris luminum*, 1: Petzelt, 239–242; *De quaerendo Deum*: Petzelt, 218. "Sed illi, qui dixerunt non posse attingere sapientiam et vitam intellectualem perennem, nisi daretur dono gratiae, ac quod tanta esset bonitas Dei cunctipotentis, quod exaudiret invocantes nomen suum, salvi facti sunt."; *De pace fidei*, 12: Klibansky, 35. "Omnis autem sapientia in omnibus sapientibus ab illa est quae est per se sapientia, quoniam illa Deus."

[71] Koch, *Vier Predigten im Geiste Eckharts*, 80. "Et nota quod quamdiu aliquis sapiens potuit esse sapientior non fuit Sapientia recepta, sed participatio eius. Sapientia autem absoluta, quae est ars omnipotentiae, non fuit neque in angelis neque hominibus neque prophetis, uti est, recepta."

[72] *De sapientia*, 13, 16, and 17.

[73] *De sapientia*, 13, line 5; 8, line 23– 9, line 2.

human wisdom as a conjectural intellectual image of the infinite form which is the Word of God. Finite man is wise to the extent that he can know and love an infinite form.

The difficulty is that a finite mind must necessarily remain ignorant of an infinite form. This is why wisdom is unattainable. The search for truth proceeds by comparison. We know an object, not in itself, but as an image which can be compared *per similitudinem* to the object. The difference between image and object implied by the very action of comparison can be diminished but, *aeternaliter*, never wholly eliminated because no man's intellect is "so joined to the exemplar of all things, as the image to the Truth, that it could not be more nearly joined and more actually united to it; and, therefore, it does not understand so much that it could not understand yet more, had it access to the exemplar of all things from which every thing actually existent derives its actuality."[74] The form of forms, in which every specific form participates, is infinite; and the infinite, which can only be measured by itself, can never be reached by the categories of likeness or measurement.[75] Finite understanding, therefore, can never reach the essence or quiddity of a thing.[76] We can know, for example, the form of man as individuated in each man; we can, to a degree, know the form of man as a species; but "that unindividuated humanity which is the exemplar and idea of the individuated, and, as it were, its form and truth" can not be known because it is the Infinite Form itself, because it is an absolute specifically identified with God.[77] Truth is one, an indivisible entity. Truth, in the last analysis, is God; and our thought is an image of God.[78] Our finite mind stands to it in the same relation as possibility

---

[74] *De visione Dei*, 20: Paris, I, 110r. Cf. *De docta ignorantia*, I, 11, p. 22.

[75] *De docta ignorantia*, I, 1, pp. 5–6.

[76] *De docta ignorantia*, I, 3, p. 9. "Quidditas ergo rerum, quae est entium veritas, in sua puritate inattingibilis est et per omnes philosophos investigata, sed per neminem, uti est, reperta."

[77] *De visione Dei*, 9: Paris, I, 103r. Cf. *De mente*, 2: Heidelberg, V, 54.

[78] *De mente*, 5: Heidelberg, V, 65. "Habet [mens] ex eo, quia est imago exemplaris omnium: Deus enim est omnium exemplar. . . . Unde mens est viva descriptio aeternae et infinitae sapientiae."

to necessity or, in the Cardinal's favorite image, as the polygon to the circle: it ceaselessly approaches it but never reaches it.

In relation to this absolute truth, which is unattainable, human knowledge is a series of conjectural images or similitudes. It is these intellectual images which define the content of human wisdom. They are mathematical symbols of the infinite, and through them the intellect achieves a partial comprehension of the *Forma formarum* which itself remains incomprehensible in its plenitude. A characteristic symbol or image of wisdom is the infinite straight line, the *actus infinitus* and form of all possible figures. For God too is an absolute Rectitude; and as the universal Exemplar He has the same relation to all created things as the infinite line—if such a line were possible—has to all figures. Just as the infinite line necessarily envelops all figurable figures because it engenders them and because at infinity they all resolve themselves into the simplicity of an infinite line, so does the absolute Rectitude, since the infinite Form is the immediate root of all forms, envelop all things that can be formed and their species.[79] God and an infinite line have this in common: both are the exemplar, model, precision, truth, measure, the justice, goodness, and perfection of all that exists or can exist.[80]

An infinite line is therefore a relative and conjectural intellectual image of the infinite Form which is the Word of God. It is more. Since every formable form can be reduced to it, it is the only adequate intellectual image of the infinite Form possible in this life. The Word of God is divine Wisdom. This image of it forms the content of human wisdom. The Word of God is incomprehensible. This image is the human comprehension of the incomprehensible. Human wisdom is the partial comprehension by an illuminated intellect of the infinite Form which is an incomprehensible God.

But the sweetest flower of partial comprehension is still to illuminate even more clearly than before the final incomprehensibility of the divine object. Cusanus points his conclusion in a beautiful passage: "This knowledge of its incomprehensibility is the most joyful and most desirable comprehension, not as it relates to the

---

[79] *De sapientia,* 38.
[80] *De sapientia,* 36.

comprehendor, but to the loveliest treasure of his life. For if any man should love anything because it were lovable, he would be glad that in the lovable there should be found infinite and inexpressible causes of love. And this is the lover's most joyful comprehension, when he comprehends the incomprehensible loveliness of the thing beloved; for he would not rejoice to love any second loved object, that were comprehensible, as much as when it appears that the loveliness of the thing beloved is utterly unmeasurable, undetermined, and wholly incomprehensible. This is the most joyful comprehension of the incomprehensible and lovable learned ignorance: to know partially and yet to have no perfect knowledge."[81]

IV

Renaissance thinkers prized wisdom as highly and speculated on its character as indefatigably as their medieval and classical predecessors. Many of them defended varieties of wisdom best understood as medieval survivals. This is the case with the numerous repetitions of the conceptions of Aquinas, Alexander of Hales, and Bonaventura, vigorously perpetuated by the monastic orders and the theological faculties of continental universities. It is the case with the popular *De vera sapientia* of the Pseudo-Petrarch, most of which is an exact reproduction of Cusa's *De sapientia* and an effective channel of the Cardinal's influence in the later fifteenth and sixteenth centuries.[82] It is substantially the case with the Florentine Neo-Platonists and with certain northern European humanists like John Colet and Jacques Lefèvre d'Etaples. Augustine, finally, dominated not only vast segments of medieval thought but important areas of Renaissance thought as well. Most spectacularly, his idea of wisdom was given new vigor by the Reformation and practically institutionalized in its theology.

But alongside these largely medieval varieties of wisdom, there were others of greater originality. They too took their point of departure from traditional antique definitions and sources. But these sources were reread with a new sympathy, understanding, and per-

---

[81] *De sapientia,* 12–13.
[82] See below, Ch. II, note 1.

spective; and new sources were discovered. Furthermore, certain definitions—particularly the notion that wisdom was a knowledge of human as well as divine things and the idea of wisdom as an active moral virtue—known to the Middle Ages but largely neglected, were found to coincide remarkably with contemporary ideals and needs. The Renaissance revived them—as it revived dormant philosophical systems like Epicureanism and Skepticism—gave them a new emphasis and significance, and made them peculiarly its own. Neither these nor other classical definitions were perpetuated in words alone. All gradually developed new meanings, and these meanings were far closer to the original than those of the Middle Ages.

It is this integral reappropriation of the antique—a reintegration of antique word and antique meaning paralleling that reintegration of classical motif and classical form which, according to "Panofsky's Law," is a fundamental criterion of the Renaissance in art—that is the essential characteristic of Renaissance wisdom and defines its innovation and break with medieval thought. The process is humanistic in its reverence for the classics, its interest in human things, its active worldly moralism. It is a process of secularization as well. Whatever their definitions, innovating varieties of wisdom in the sixteenth century are autonomous. Wisdom is acquired, that is, by man's own unaided efforts, and describes a natural human perfection. It is in the area of nature, not in that of redemption; and has, consequently, no necessary relation to Christianity. This is at once a return to the central characteristic of all classical definitions of wisdom and a rejection of the Christian assumptions which had transformed the significance of all medieval restatements of those definitions. The secularization of the idea of wisdom is, in this sense, a significant part of the effort of Renaissance thought to free philosophy and science from their traditional status of handmaidens to theology. Religion itself remained untouched; but several areas of human knowledge, of which ethics was the most important, achieved a new and preponderant importance. As a tribute to their splendor and their classical sources the sixteenth century freed them from theology, usurped its medieval name, and called them wisdom.

Renaissance humanism was not mistaken, therefore, when it defined its effort and its final success as a return to a *prisca sapientia*, when, after a thousand years of "Gothic barbarism" and "darkness," it not only repeated the antique definitions of wisdom—these the Middle Ages had had as well—but also reappropriated many of their original, pristine meanings.

Chapter 2

Active and Contemplative Ideals of Wisdom in Italian Humanism

Italian humanists of the later fourteenth and fifteenth centuries initiate the Renaissance effort to recapture the *prisca sapientia* of the ancients by debating the relative merits of the active and contemplative lives and asking whether wisdom is a moral or an intellectual virtue.

The Middle Ages, preferring the contemplative life, had tended to assume that wisdom was a contemplative virtue. The Italian Quattrocento challenged this assumption. Aquinas normally confined wisdom to a knowledge of immaterial being and the contemplation, "vibrant with joy and delight" of God; and in the *Divine Comedy* only Beatrice, who leads Dante to the ultimate happiness of contemplating God, can be fittingly associated with wisdom. Florentine humanists imagine the possibility of a wisdom whose meaning is ethical rather than metaphysical and active rather than contemplative. They give the word lay and civic meanings which suggest the world as well as the cloister and university. In the minds of some humanists—and over the now conscious opposition of others—wisdom becomes worldly in precise ways: it is civic, not solitary; it includes human things among its objects; it is more preoccupied with virtuous action than with knowledge of the truth. The modest beginnings of this transformation are already visible in the works of Petrarch.

I

Petrarch[1] was a literary moralist sensitive to both Augustine and Cicero. Most of his works are informal, common-sense essays designed to foster an active piety and virtue. They contain little

[1] Petrarch's most important discussion of the idea of wisdom is the dialogue "De sapientia," *De remediis utriusque fortunae*, I, 12. The section "De

speculative philosophy, metaphysics, or systematic theology. His aim was rather the eloquent propagation of a wisdom doubly rooted in a knowledge and worship of the true God and the ideas and examples of the greatest pagan ancients. The nature of this wisdom and how it is got are distilled in two Petrarchan sentences: *sapientia est pietas* and *nihil altius ascendat quam humilitas operosa.* The first sentence is a humanist's repetition of the Augustinian equation of wisdom and piety. *Humilitas operosa* is the humble beginning of wisdom's transformation from an intellectual to a moral virtue, from a type of knowledge—in this case a knowledge of Christian doctrine—to an ethical category.

Identifying wisdom and piety, Petrarch locates wisdom's beginning in a fear of God and defines piety as the knowledge and worship of Him.[2] Wisdom's first characteristic, therefore, is religious truth: it is made up of truths about God compatible with Christian Revelation. Its second characteristic is love of God; for since the true wisdom of God is Christ and true philosophy is love of wisdom, we will philosophize correctly only by loving and worshiping His

sapientia," *Rerum memorandarum libri,* III, 31–99 also has a certain interest. The *De vera sapientia,* first published in the Netherlands about 1473 and later included in all editions of the *Opera omnia* is a forgery, possibly by Francesco Filelfo. Its chief sources are Nicholas of Cusa's *De sapientia,* Book I and Petrarch's own dialogue on wisdom in the *De remediis.* See R. Klibansky, "De dialogis Petrarcae addictis De vera sapientia," in Nicholas of Cusa, *Opera omnia* (Heidelberg ed.), V (Leipzig, 1937), xxi–xxiv and the literature there cited. Giuseppe Saitta, *Il Pensiero Italiano nell'Umanesimo e nel Rinascimento* (Bologna, 1949), I, 88–91 is an interesting analysis of Petrarch's idea of wisdom, weakened by the acceptance of the *De vera sapientia* as an authentic work.

[2] *Le Familiari,* Vittorio Rossi, ed. (Florence, 1933–42), X, 5, 8: II, 312. "Et quamvis veram sapientiam unam esse non sit dubium, Deum nosse et colere, propter quod scriptum est: 'pietas est sapientia'"; *De remediis utriusque fortunae* (Leyden, 1585), I, 13, pp. 52–53. "Pietas est sapientia, et per alium. Initium sapientiae est timor domini.... Quid sit autem pietas ostendit [Hermes Trismegistus as quoted by Lactantius, *Divin. Instit.,* II, xvi: *PL,* VI, 335–336. Cf. *Corpus Hermeticum,* IX, 4; XVI, 10.] alio loco his verbis: Pietas enim scientia est dei." Cf. *De remediis,* I, xlvi, pp. 191–192 and *De sui ipsius et multorum ignorantia,* L. M. Capelli, ed. (Paris, 1906), 30. Petrarch's source for the phrase *pietas est sapientia* is Augustine, who quotes Job 28:28 in this form several times. See above, Ch. I, note 26.

wisdom.[3] The true philosopher is thus an *amator Dei* and the true
wise man, described in a phrase which points the way to Erasmus,
is a "philosopher of Christ."[4]

It can come as no surprise, then, when Petrarch calls wisdom a
"divine gift" and quotes Ecclesiasticus 1:1, *Omnis sapientia a
Domino Deo est*, as his authority for its source.[5] Yet it would be
a mistake to think that the possession of wisdom is inseparable from
grace. On the contrary—and this assertion will distinguish Petrarch
and his humanist successors from the radical dualisms and the exclusively Scriptural emphasis of the Reformation—wisdom has a
variety of sources, both pagan and Christian, extending from
Socrates and Cicero to Solomon and the parables of Christ. It is true
that all wisdom is from God and that only cleansed and pious souls
can know and love it.[6] It is true that no man can become wise,
virtuous, or good outside the doctrine of Christ and without His
help; for Christ, not Minerva, is the God of wisdom and we drink
wisdom not from the "fabulous spring of Pegasus in the folds of
Mount Parnassus" but from that true and unique spring which is
in heaven.[7] Yet it is true also that much was achieved by the pagan
ancients. Of course, they did not know the true God perfectly. This
comes from grace alone and not from any human effort. But we must
praise them as ardent investigators of truth who rose, as Paul says,
from a knowledge of the visible world to a knowledge of the one
invisible God.[8] Did not Cicero describe "one single God as the
governor and maker of all things, not in a merely philosophical but

[3] *Fam.*, VI, 2, 3–4: II, 55–56. "... denique sic philosophemur, ut, quod
philosophie nomen importat, sapientiam amemus. Vera quidem Dei sapientia
Cristus est; ut vere philosophemur, Ille nobis in primis amandus atque colen-
dus est. Sic simus omnia, quod ante omnia cristiani simus."

[4] *Invective contra medicum*, Pier Giorgio Ricci, ed. (Rome, 1950), 56, 65.
Cf. Augustine, *De civitate Dei*, VIII, 1.

[5] *Invective contra medicum*, 31; "De sapientia," *De remediis*, I, 12, p. 47.
Noted henceforth as *De sap*. Cf. Prov. 2:6.

[6] *De remediis*, I, xlvi, pp. 191–192.

[7] *De ignorantia*, 69; *Contra medicum*, 92. Cf. Boccaccio, *Genealogie deorum
gentilium libri*, Vincenzo Romano, ed. (Bari, 1951), I, 72–73 and Salutati,
De laboribus Herculis, B. L. Ullman, ed. (Zürich, 1951), II, 424.

[8] *Contra medicum*, 71. Cf. Rom. 1:20.

almost in a Catholic manner of phrasing it?" Sometimes, in fact, "you would think you were hearing not a pagan philosopher but an Apostle."[9] And do not the sayings and exemplary deeds of the greatest ancients instruct in wisdom? Petrarch insists they do. He calls this the "common wisdom of men"; and he has assembled specimens of it in the section of the *Rerum memorandarum libri* called *De sapientia*, a treasury of worldly wisdom, wise sayings, and deeds of Roman emperors, Athenian statesmen, antique philosophers both Greek and Roman, the seven sages of early Greece, Cato the Censor, and Virgil, whose poetry, he says, "hides secrets of great wisdom."[10]

Clearly, wisdom has both pagan and Christian sources, sources which only the liberally educated man can master, and combines the essential facts known to ignorant faith with those truths—if not essential at least useful—gathered from the antique poets and philosophers. Wisdom, that is, is not only piety, it is a learned piety, a *docta pietas*. He knows, Petrarch tells Boccaccio in a famous letter, that many ignorant, uncultivated men have achieved a noble sanctity. But nobler, more glorious is the learned road to wisdom. For study of the classics incites a man to virtue and diminishes the fear of death; and so "ignorance, however devout, is by no means to be put on a plane with the enlightened devoutness of one familiar with literature."[11] The great pagans were skilled and learned in the wisdom of the world, but ignorant of Christ. Theirs was a *literata ignorantia*, an interpretation of the idea of learned ignorance quite different from Nicholas of Cusa's.[12] Certain Christians, on the other hand—Petrarch would have been familiar with Jacopone da Todi and the spiritual Franciscans—obstinately pride themselves on a faith whose purity is guaranteed by ignorance. Echoing a phrase of St.

---

[9] *De ignorantia*, 45, 48. Hans Nachod, tr.

[10] *Rerum memorandarum libri*, Giuseppe Billanovich, ed. (Florence, 1943), III, 31–99, pp. 124–189.

[11] *Rerum senilium*, I, iv: *Opera quae extant omnia* (Basel, 1554), 823. See Giuseppe Toffanin, *Storia dell'umanesimo*, 2nd ed. (Bologna, 1950), II, 116–124.

[12] *De ignorantia*, 29.

Jerome's, he calls this attitude *devota rusticitas*.[13] *Docta pietas* is the happy mean between these two reprehensible extremes, a harmonious body of "true opinions" on the nature of God derived from both Scripture and the classics.

The significance of such wisdom, however, either as an intellectual virtue or a treasury of individual truths, should not be overestimated; but must be seen in terms of man's ultimate ignorance. A wise man never says that he is wise. On the contrary, to think oneself wise is the first step to foolishness, and the next is to proclaim it.[14] "A generous soul will realize how meager a portion of knowledge is that which is allotted to all men combined, if we compare it to human ignorance and to divine wisdom."[15] The wise man is fully conscious of this ignorance. The peak of his knowledge is the knowledge of what he lacks. "It is the mark of a wise man to know and acknowledge his imperfection."[16] Petrarch even notes with approval some who have said that a really wise man has never existed, and finally only rejects this judgment because it would probably induce desperation and discourage men's zeal for wisdom. Thus, he remarks that certain Greeks and Romans, the seven sages, Laelius, and Cato, seemed to their successors unworthy of the title of wise men. Socrates was called the only wise man by the oracle of Apollo, but perhaps, he conjectures, "the false God used this false testimonial only to prick the one man nearest to wisdom into folly and pride."[17]

Nicholas of Cusa, after Petrarch, insisted on the ignorance of man, but his motive was to strengthen man's dependence on grace and prepare him for a mystical intuition of the divine. Petrarch's conclusion from the same premise is different: the rarity of true knowledge, the difficulty of gaining true opinions, of wisdom, that is, as *docta pietas*, must force man towards a more laborious, but more

[13] *Rerum senilium*, I, iv: *Opera omnia*, 823. Cf. Jerome, *Epistola LIII*, 3: *PL*, XXII, 542 who speaks of *sancta rusticitas*.

[14] *De sap.*, 47.

[15] *De ignorantia*, 87.

[16] *De sap.*, 47.

[17] *De sap.*, 49. Cf. *Contra medicum*, 49.

human, goal, wisdom as *humilitas operosa*. *Ubi fuerit superbia,* Petrarch read in Proverbs, *ibi erit et contumelia, ubi autem est humilitas, ibi et sapientia.*[18] And Plato said that he is blessed who has been able to reach wisdom and "true opinions" even in his old age;[19] for its attainment is not the short work of several years, as is perfection in other arts, but the prize of a lifetime of constant and prolonged effort. The path to this intellectual blessedness, and its equivalent for the vast multitude who will never achieve it, is a humble and minute self-examination, a catalogue of all aberrations from virtue, all evil deeds, all things which should be blushed at, wept over, and expiated by penance.[20] Boast of nothing, lay aside all pride and false opinions, recognize and avoid foolishness. Above all, recognize that wisdom is an active virtue, a *humilitas operosa*. "It is one thing to speak wisely, quite another to live wisely; it is one thing to call oneself wise, another to be a really wise man."[21]

An active humility is thus the specific attitude to life of the wise man. It is an attitude of athletic, Christian moralism. Piety remains the wise man's greatest good, but less because it is a knowledge of God, which is difficult to attain, and at the best uncertain, than because God sets the pious man squarely on the path to virtue. Similarly, because it is the most important function of the study of antique literature to incite to virtue, his learning serves the same end. Humility is his consciousness of the gap between the few true opinions he has achieved and the wisdom of God. It both justifies a placid skepticism—for "ignorance" is precisely the lever which shifts the central meaning of *sapientia* from knowledge to virtue— and urges him on to a constant activity in self-improvement and good works. All elements of Petrarchan wisdom focus on an incipient moralism, and it is fitting that he should open his "De sapientia" with an identification which echoes and grows stronger

---

[18] Prov. 11:2.

[19] *De sap.*, 47.

[20] *De sap.*, 48. Cf. the Pseudo-Vergilian poem *Vir bonus, Appendix Vergiliana, sive Carmina minora Vergilio adtribvta*, R. Ellis, ed. (Oxford, 1907).

[21] *De sap.*, 49.

in humanist literature until the end of the sixteenth century: the pursuit of wisdom is inseparable from virtue.[22]

II

Coluccio Salutati (1331–1406),[23] Chancellor of Florence and the greatest of Petrarch's early humanist successors, reinforces this ethical emphasis in his discussions of wisdom in the *De nobilitate legum et medicinae* and in his letters. He goes further, and says that just as action is better than speculation so is wisdom unthinkable without prudence. The only reason he does not say that prudence is nobler than wisdom is that he is prepared to take a further step and, by defining wisdom as moral philosophy, identify the two.

Salutati derives his active, ethical conception of wisdom from a consistently developed doctrine of the supremacy of the will over the intellect. He argues that the will rules the intellect because it is active and the intellect is passive. The intellect is acted upon by the external world, naturally moved—*necessitate naturali* said Duns Scotus—by external objects. It receives passively from without the species which activate it and constitute its knowledge; and it cannot move itself to action unless the will commands it, nor persist in action unless the will helps it. The will, on the other hand, is self-sufficient, free, unmoved by anything but itself. The will orders and the intellect obeys.[24]

Salutati concludes that the will is nobler than the intellect and that love, which is the act of the will, is nobler and more perfect than contemplation or vision, the act of the intellect. He would have agreed with the consequences the aging Petrarch drew from the same conclusion:

---

[22] *De sap.*, 46.

[23] A useful survey of the literature on Salutati is given by Eugenio Garin, *Prosatori latini del Quattrocento* (Milan and Naples, 1952), 5–6.

[24] *De nobilitate legum et medicinae*, Eugenio Garin, ed. (Florence, 1947), 184; Francesco Novati, *Epistolario di Coluccio Salutati* (Rome, 1891–1905), III, 445–446.

It is safer to strive for a good and pious will than for a capable and clear intellect. The object of the will, as it pleases the wise, is to be good; that of the intellect is truth. It is better to will the good than to know the truth. The first is never without merit; the latter can often be polluted with crime and then admits no excuse. Therefore, those are far wrong who consume their time in learning to know virtue instead of acquiring it, and, in a still higher degree, those whose time is spent in learning to know God instead of loving Him. In this life it is impossible to know God in his fulness; piously and ardently to love Him is possible.[25]

This emphasis on the will and love is a traditional characteristic of those medieval thinkers who kept their Augustinian fervor undampened by Aristotle's intellectualism. For Anselm, Bernard, the twelfth-century Victorines, Bonaventura, and Scotus it was a position which, they felt, guaranteed the possibility of enthusiasm and kept high the temperature of piety. They deduced from it important satisfactions for a religious sensibility which saw in all autonomous human and social claims a derogation of the divine majesty. Particularly they used it to discredit the arid overreaching of human reason. Salutati undeniably shares something of this sensibility and intention. He makes no case for the power of human reason; but, like Petrarch, concludes in a certain skepticism. He writes much on the primacy of grace; and his Augustinian conception of free will is not softened by liberal evasions. But from the same voluntarism, from the same emphasis on love, he draws potentially more secular conclusions. For, as the will is above the intellect, so is the good above the true and the active life above the speculative life. It "manifestly follows that the active life, in so far as it is distinguished from the speculative life, is to be preferred in all ways to speculation, both on earth and in heaven."[26] The practical result of this on earth is to condemn solitary contemplation—did not God

[25] Petrarch, *De ignorantia*, 70. Hans Nachod, tr. Cf. Novati, III, 446–447 and *De nobilitate legum*, 190.

[26] *De nobilitate legum*, 190–192. Cf. Salutati, *De laboribus Herculis*, II, 487–488 and Novati, III, 305–307.

Himself say, in Genesis 2:18, *Non est bonum esse hominem solum?*
—as well as withdrawal from the world and any intellectualism
divorced from life and virtue. Wise men should actively occupy
themselves with the affairs of the republic. Man is a political animal
whose primordial duties are to his family, friends, and country.
Civil duties do not corrupt, they perfect men.[27]

This bias in favor of active, civil life which Salutati has deduced
from rather theoretical propositions on the superiority of the will to
the intellect has important consequences for his conception of
wisdom. For one thing, it means that Salutati is suspicious and
critical of all purely intellectual definitions of wisdom. The doctor
against whom he wrote the *De nobilitate legum et medicinae*, start-
ing from the proposition that metaphysics is the only free science,
and that therefore, as Aristotle says, the speculative always precedes
the practical, maintained that wisdom was a speculative virtue, the
perfection of the highest part of the soul, the intellect, and related
to prudence as master to servant.[28] Salutati answered that wisdom
is not merely speculative. Without prudence—right reason in practical matters—there is no wisdom and no wise man. Would you call
a man wise, he asks, who knew the sky, stars, separate substances,
and the truths of all things except human actions if he were not
prudent, even if he had attained some knowledge of the divine
essence? Is the man who knows as much as the human intellect can
about celestial and divine things wise if he cannot support himself
or aid and advise his family, friends, relatives, and country?[29] No.
To limit wisdom to a knowledge of divine things is culpably partial;
and Salutati maintains this position whether divine things are understood as natural theology, separate substances, or the causes of Aristotle's metaphysics. Leave it to doctors, who are physicists not
philosophers, to find, if they can, "the principles and causes of

[27] Novati, II, 454–455; III, 520. Cf. Alfred von Martin, *Coluccio Salutati
und das humanistische Lebensideal* (Leipzig and Berlin, 1916), 124 and
Eugenio Garin, *L'Umanesimo italiano. Filosofia e vita civile nel Rinascimento* (Bari, 1952), 39.

[28] *De nobilitate legum,* 176.

[29] *De nobilitate legum,* 178, 180. Cf. Novati, III, 348

things."[30] He himself will always maintain, like Petrarch, that prudence perfects wisdom and that wisdom must be inseparable from prudence, for without it wisdom is empty and imperfect.[31]

Salutati's authority for this conclusion is Cicero's definition of wisdom in the *Tusculan Disputations: sapientiam esse rerum divinarum et humanarum scientiam.*[32] Understood literally, this must mean that wisdom is an encyclopedic knowledge of all things divine and human. But Salutati was less attracted by the encyclopedic implications of Cicero's definition than by his inclusion of human things among the objects of wisdom. He read the same intention into Augustine's explanation of Cicero's text. "The study of wisdom," Augustine said in the *City of God*, "is either concerning action or contemplation, and thence assumes two several names, active and contemplative, the active consisting in the practice of morality in one's life, and the contemplative in penetrating into the abstruse causes of nature, and the nature of divinity; Socrates is said to excell in the active, Pythagoras in the contemplative."[33] Salutati remarks that a wisdom which thus combines action and contemplation, human things and divine things is a *summa consummataque sapientia*. But such wisdom—and this is the second important consequence which he draws from his conviction that the active life, which controls human things, is to be preferred to the speculative life, which contemplates divine things—is easier to imagine than find; and so in practice it is better to limit ourselves to human things. "To tell the truth," he says in a striking passage, "I will boldly affirm and openly confess that I will willingly and happily give up to you and to those who lift their speculation to the sky all other truths, if only the truth and reason of things human are left

[30] Novati, III, 588.

[31] *De nobilitate legum*, 178.

[32] Novati, III, 458. "nonne legisti apud Ciceronem nostrum sapientiam esse rerum divinarum et humanarum scientiam, que cuiusque rei causa sit? ex quo, sicut subdit, efficitur, ut divina imitetur, humana omnia inferiora virtute ducat." Cf. Novati, III, 604; IV, 165 and Cicero, *Tusc. Disp.*, IV, xxvi, 57 and *De Off.*, II, ii, 5.

[33] *De civitate Dei*, VIII, 4.

to me."[34] Solitary speculation, the lonely search for truth, and the unshared joy of its discovery and possession, these are lesser goods. It is nobler to be always active, to be useful to oneself, to one's family, relatives, and friends, and to help one's country by example and useful works.[35] A wisdom based on purposes like these will inevitably find its object more in human things than in divine.

This is an important change from the normal medieval emphasis on divine things as the proper object of wisdom. It reflects too the shift from metaphysical and scientific to ethical interests which is so characteristic of humanism. In the Middle Ages the term "human things" meant all things composed of the four elements, all links below the angels in the great chain of being; Salutati limits it to man and his individual, family, and social activities. He specifically excludes physics, imitating Socrates who superseded the causal investigations of the early "physicists" with a "new type of speculation and the study of a true and moral philosophy which is called wisdom."[36] This new wisdom does not investigate the principles and nature of things but confines itself to human actions, man's soul and its potentialities for good and evil, the rules for a life of probity and virtue. Physicians—Salutati's stock figure for the scientist—investigate motion, vacuums, the eternity of species, time, the generation and corruption of things, the eternity of the world.[37] True philosophers deal with morals. "With this true and moral wisdom, which the Latins call *sapientia*, it is right, honest, and most useful to occupy oneself. Here we are not always dealing with knowledge *quia* as the physicists are, but we often use knowledge *propter quid*," knowledge, that is deduced from absolute principles rather than got by generalizations from particulars.[38]

Wisdom, clearly, is little else than moral philosophy. It is active, focused on men and their interrelations in the family and state.

[34] *De nobilitate legum*, 180; Novati, III, 604. Cf. Cicero, *De Oratore*, I, xv, 68–69.

[35] *De nobilitate legum*, 180.

[36] Novati, III, 587.

[37] *Ibid.*, 588–589.

[38] *Ibid.*, 589, lines 19–23.

It is not a speculative science. Its three parts are ethics, politics, and economics, the divisions of Aristotle's practical philosophy.[39] For Petrarch wisdom was piety; for Salutati it is virtue.

How is this virtue acquired? Salutati is a surprisingly rigorous Augustinian when he answers this question. He echoes—and sharpens—a passage in the *De libero arbitrio* where Augustine discusses the relation of virtue and free will, defining virtue as a *habitus*, "by which man lives righteously and avoids evil and which God alone controls."[40] He quotes I Corinthians 3:7, "So then neither is he that planteth any thing, neither he that watereth; but God that giveth the increase."[41] He interprets both texts to mean that the virtues are not acquired from works or experience, "as the philosophers hold," but from God alone; that we must attribute nothing to man, but all things to God who works invisibly through His creatures; that men must become God's instruments and fit themselves to receive His grace. For what we do is not our own; and what we think we do, in reality He does through us—*quicquid sumus Dei gratia sumus*.[42] Just as our hands obey our wills, although they don't know it, so we obey God when we do anything, although we may not know that God wills this and accomplishes it through us. God is the author of all goods and the first cause of all acts, a first cause whose influence is far greater than any secondary causes and which tends to destroy their autonomy. Man would do nothing good unless the first cause opportunely moved him to it. "Thus all things which God performs through us as though we were his hands, should properly be called works of God and not our own. They can be called ours not *proprietate nature*, but only *participatione gratie*."[43] We can elect a good or bad deed, a good or bad life; but we choose the good with the help of grace and the evil from the

[39] *Ibid.*, 587–588, 604.
[40] *Ibid.*, II, 184–185, 319; III, 414–415, 560; IV, 46. Cf. Augustine, *De libero arbitrio*, II, xix, 51.
[41] *Ibid.*, II, 308, 408, 446.
[42] *Ibid.*, II, 184, 424; III, 85, 94–95.
[43] *Ibid.*, III, 115.

malice and corruption of our own nature: "For the good we do God is responsible; the evil comes from ourselves."[44]

Thus our wisdom comes from God, the "Father of lights," and our foolishness from ourselves. For is it not written that "to one is given by the Spirit the word of wisdom; to another the word of knowledge by the same Spirit"?[45] What can this mean but that the natural man's wisdom is in truth a lack of wisdom and a blind ignorance? And that the only real wisdom is necessarily Christian, far superior to the natural foolishness of the pagans?[46] From one point of view this is a return to the Socratic theme of ignorance of Petrarch's *De sapientia*. Salutati puts it epigrammatically: "Our knowledge is no more than rational doubt";[47] and like Petrarch he repeats the doctrine that the conceit of knowledge is the greatest ignorance. He who thinks himself wise is foolish; the wise man is precisely he who knows how much he doesn't know.[48] But in another perspective Salutati's meaning is more pessimistic than Petrarch's. Petrarch had had a capacious faith in man's ability to be good. Salutati lacked this faith. He went farther than Petrarch in identifying wisdom with moral philosophy, but he found man particularly insufficient precisely in the moral field. He concluded that wisdom was a largely moral virtue given to man by God.

Salutati's conclusion reflects the transitional character of his humanism. His views on how wisdom is acquired are profoundly unclassical. Yet his wisdom has as its primary object man and human things; it is an active virtue, inseparable from prudence and almost indistinguishable from practical philosophy; it makes some use of an antique definition of wisdom—Cicero's—and recovers something of its antique meaning. Moreover, it is a learned virtue as Petrarch's was a learned piety, for neither the active commitment to civic life

[44] *Ibid.*, II, 117, 475–476. Cf. *De laboribus Herculis*, II, 487 and Luigi Gasperetti, "Il 'de fato, fortuna et casu' di Coluccio Salutati," *La Rinascita*, IV (1941), 570 ff.

[45] *Ibid.*, II, 479. Cf. I Cor. 12:8.

[46] *De laboribus Herculis*, I, 78.

[47] Novati, III, 603. "scire nostrum nichil aliud est quam rationabiliter dubitare."

[48] *Ibid.*, II, 382.

nor the necessary dependence of wisdom on grace obviates the necessity of learning. The active life may be better than the speculative; but before we act we must know how to act, we must find out with certainty what must be done and what must not. This is *doctrina* or learning. It is got by literary study and consists of the ethical teachings of the ancients and the lessons of history, perfected, of course, by a knowledge of Christian doctrine.[49] In this sense *sapientia* is a perfection of *scientia* as well as of *prudentia*, and its opposite is not only idle contemplation but ignorance also.[50] At this point, finally, the meaning of wisdom actually merges with that of *humanitas*, for it too consists, in Salutati's definition, of learning, *doctrina*, and virtue, *scientia moralis*. *Sapientia*, like humanism itself, is an *eruditio moralis*.[51]

III

Neither Salutati's strong tendency to put the object of wisdom in human things and identify wisdom and moral philosophy nor his even stronger insistence that moral virtue is a divine gift were developed in any consistent way by Italian *quattrocento* humanism. The first theme, at least in the form Salutati gave it, was taken up again only by Erasmus and other sixteenth-century humanists; the second was little emphasized until the emergence of Florentine Neo-Platonism and until that powerful Augustinian and Pauline revival which marked the turn of the century gave it prominence in the thought of men like Savonarola, Lefèvre d'Etaples, John Colet, and the young Luther. The immediate Italian successors of Salutati abandoned his voluntarism in favor of a more Aristotelian preoccupation with the intellect and minimized the importance he gave to grace in the acquisition of wisdom. At the same time, they took up and continued to develop what were becoming by then traditional humanist ideas: Petrarch's concern with the coexistence of wisdom and virtue and Salutati's effort to tie wisdom more closely to the

[49] *Ibid.*, III, 605.

[50] One of the meanings Salutati gives for the battle between Hercules and the Hydra is the triumph of wisdom over ignorance. *De laboribus Herculis*, I, 193.

[51] Novati, III, 517, 536.

active life. As a result, although their definitions of wisdom are more speculative than Salutati's, their conception of man, only one of whose virtues is wisdom, is far more worldly.

The writer who did more than any other to express this more secular ideal of human life was Leonardo Bruni, Salutati's successor as Chancellor and the most important humanist in Florence. Bruni's novelty was to rethink the moral ideas of Aristotle and Cicero, grasp firmly their fundamental civic and political implications, and use his new understanding to phrase an ideal of man and human conduct which would satisfy the aspirations and justify the ambitions of the burghers of the independent city-state of Florence.[52] These were new men, self-consciously separate from the clergy and the older aristocracy, rich, patriotic, active in the administration of their own businesses and of the city. They wanted a theoretical, moral justification of their achievements, their wealth, their commitment to the active life, of the kind of men they were. Bruni gave them this in a history of their own city whose theme was the relation of civic virtue to liberty from foreign domination without and tyranny within;[53] by an attack on late medieval asceticism, Franciscan ideals of poverty, and the Stoic ideal of the wise man, that "harsh, inhuman" personage who scorned all goods but virtue;[54] and, finally, by recreating Aristotle's idea of wisdom in Aristotle's own civic context of devotion to the state and honest respect for wealth and worldly goods.

For Bruni, as for Aristotle, wisdom was the noblest of five intellectual virtues: *sapientia, scientia, prudentia, intelligentia,* and *ars.*[55]

[52] Hans Baron, "The Historical Background of the Florentine Renaissance," *History,* N.S. XXII (1937–38), 315–327. The pages which follow owe much to this article and to Hans Baron's other stimulating work on Bruni.

[53] B. L. Ullman, "Leonardo Bruni and Humanist Historiography," *Medievalia et Humanistica,* Fasc. IV (1946), 59–60.

[54] Hans Baron, "Franciscan Poverty and Civic Wealth as Factors in the Rise of Humanistic Thought," *Speculum,* XIII (1938), *passim.*

[55] Hans Baron, *Leonardo Bruni Aretino humanistisch-philosophische Schriften* (Berlin and Leipzig, 1928), 29; *Leonardi Bruni Epistolarum Libri VIII,* L. Mehus, ed. (Florence, 1741), II, 140. Cf. Salutati, *De laboribus Herculis,* II, 502 and Aristotle, *Eth. Nic.,* VI, iii, 1139b, 15.

He defined *intelligentia* as knowledge of the principles and highest causes of things; while *scientia* is knowledge deduced from these certain but undemonstrable principles. *Sapientia* is a composite of these two virtues. It knows and judges both principles and the conclusions which flow from them. "It is plain then," as Aristotle said, "that wisdom is the union of scientific knowledge and intuition, and has for its objects those things which are most precious in their nature."[56] Bruni concluded, like Salutati, and with less than perfect logic, that it is rightly defined as the knowledge of divine and human things. Prudence, in contrast, deals not with things which are eternally the same, but with mutable human things in which there is always the possibility of deliberation and choice. It is right reason in action and the ruler of the moral virtues.[57]

This difference between wisdom and prudence is based on a division of the rational soul into two parts, a *pars consultativa* and a *pars scientifica*. With one we deliberate about the mutable, with the other we know the immutable and true. From this same duality of the soul flow the distinctions between the moral virtues, which are consultative, and the intellectual virtues, which are scientific; between the active and contemplative lives; and between the two parts of philosophy, one dealing with knowledge, the other with action.[58] Wisdom is an intellectual virtue, it is linked with the contemplative life, its object is knowledge of the truth.[59] Prudence, on the other hand, is wholly concerned with action. Contemplative wisdom is rarer and nobler than prudence, for it more closely

---

[56] *Eth. Nic.*, VI, vii, 1141b, 3–4.

[57] Baron, *Bruni Schriften*, 39. "*Scientia* vero contra de his est rebus, quae semper eodem modo sunt et aliter esse non possunt; principia tamen non tractat, sed ab illis iam cognitis discurrit. *Intelligentia* vero principiorum est et circa illa versatur. At *sapientia* utramque complectitur; nam et de principiis et de his, quae a principiis manant, iudicat et discernit. Itaque recte diffinita est rerum divinarum humanarumque cognitio. O praeclaram supellectilem, inquit, et quasi divinam quamdam intelligentiae silvam!" For *prudentia* see *Ibid.*, 38.

[58] *Ibid.*, 38, 121. Cf. *Eth. Nic.*, VI, i, 1139a, 4 ff.

[59] *Ibid.*, 72–73.

resembles the divine life; but an active prudence is more useful to the community.[60]

Paradoxically, Petrarch's depreciation of reason and his corresponding emphasis on the will, the faculty of virtue and action, led to the ideal life described in the *De vita solitaria*, a life of studious leisure, isolated from the entanglements of family and politics; while Bruni united an insistent intellectualism with a utilitarian program of civic action and a system of education designed to train citizens rather than scholars. There is a real exaltation of theoretical knowledge in Bruni.[61] He admires contemplative wisdom, insists on its purely speculative character, and underlines its superiority to action. But he tempers his intellectualist enthusiasm by a warm defense of active life. Soaked in the Ciceronian and Aristotelian idea that the individual personality develops all its potentialities and achieves its end only by participation in the life of the *polis* or *respublica*, his image of the philosopher is not a man isolated in contemplation, but a man whose family, economic, and political activity completes and perfects his intellectual work. He found this ideal balance of speculation and action in the lives of Cicero and Dante, both of whom combined wisdom and learning with family obligations, military service, and civic responsibility.[62] In the same way as they, mature men must combine action and contemplation, wisdom and prudence.

A glorification of active civic life is a striking characteristic of Florentine humanism in the first half of the fifteenth century. Vespasiano da Bisticci, exalting the civic end of man, said that "every citizen is obligated, after God, to his country."[63] Alberti attacked the opinion of Anaxagoras that man is born to contemplate the sky, the stars, the sun, and all other divine works. He is not born to spend his life in melancholy solitude: "Man was born to be

---

[60] *Ibid.*, 39; Mehus, *Epistolarum Libri*, II, 137.

[61] Saitta, *Il Pensiero italiano nell'Umanesimo e nel Rinascimento*, I, 171.

[62] Baron, *Bruni Schriften*, 53, 114, 145. Cf. Hans Baron, "Cicero and the Roman Civic Spirit in the Middle Ages and the Early Renaissance," *Bulletin of the John Rylands Library*, XXII (1938), 90–91.

[63] Vespasiano da Bisticci, *Tratato contro a la ingratitudine . . . a Luca de gl'Albizi*, Magliab. VIII, 1442, 241r. Quoted by Eugenio Garin, *Testi inediti e rari di Cristoforo Landino e Francesco Filelfo* (Florence, 1949), 10.

useful to man."[64] Bruni's position is the same. Civic life is the end of man on earth. Like Salutati he preferred the study of man to the study of nature, maintaining that it was more useful to live well than to know the causes of frost, snow, and the colors of the rainbow. He deplored theory without practice and disliked learned men who were of no use to the community. He compared intellectuals devoted exclusively to science and philosophy to men who pay much attention to other people's business and none to their own.[65] He even said once that the glory of science, literature, and eloquence was inferior to military glory because it was less useful to the state.[66] The proper work of man, in short, is rational activity; and his proper life the active not the contemplative. "For he does not contemplate in so far as he is a man, but in so far as he is something divine and separate. As a man he exercises justice, temperance, fortitude, and other moral virtues. Consequently, that is the proper life of man which acts through the moral virtues."[67]

Man, it is clear, is a weak animal whose human nature, condemning a static and egoistic devotion to contemplation, gains strength and perfection through active association with his fellow citizens: *numquam privatum esse sapientem*.[68] Therefore, knowledge of first principles and zeal in the investigation of truth must be balanced by a powerful civic concern. Wisdom is nobler than prudence, the contemplative life is more divine than the active; but the man who has fully developed his human potentialities will be both prudent and wise, active and contemplative. This notion of the harmonious flowering of the whole man is Bruni's ideal—and Florence's. Gianozzo Manetti expressed it well when King Alfonso of Naples asked him what the proper duty of man was. He

[64] *I Primi Tre Libri della Famiglia*, Francesco Carlo Pellegrini, ed. (Florence, 1911), 233; *Opere Volgare di Leon Batt. Alberti* (Florence, 1845), III, 92.

[65] Baron, *Bruni Schriften*, 21.

[66] Hans Baron, "La Rinascita dell'ethica statale romana nell'Umanesimo," *Civiltà Moderna* (1935), 16.

[67] Mehus, *Epistolarum Libri*, II, 135–136.

[68] Baron, *Bruni Schriften*, 73. Cf. Cicero, *De Repub.*, II, xxv, 46.

answered: *agere et intelligere*.[69] Alberti called man a mortal but happy god because he combined rational understanding with the capacity for virtuous action, alluding thus to the wonderful lines in Cicero's *De Finibus* where he says that, "just as the horse is born to run, the ox to plow, the dog to scent a trail, so is man, as Aristotle says, born to two things, to know and to act, and in this he is almost a mortal god."[70] The same ideal appears in Alamanno Rinuccini's funeral oration for Matteo Palmieri, author of the famous *Vita civile* in which Bruni's civic humanism was vulgarized for those citizens who knew no Latin: "There are, as the philosophers tell us, two kinds of happiness and two modes of living, one based on common civic action, the other far from all action, intent only on the search for a knowledge of the highest things. The most prudent man will follow a certain mean between them."[71]

Such a mean is a combination of wisdom and prudence, and from it comes a happiness based on a possession of the goods common to both active and contemplative lives. These goods were traditionally classified as goods of the soul, the body and fortune. Goods of the soul are wisdom—the highest—fortitude, justice, and the other moral and intellectual virtues. Bodily goods are health, strength and beauty. External goods are wealth, power, and social position. In the same way as human nature would be crippled in its development if man's wisdom were to find no useful prolongation in action, so human happiness is incomplete unless man has all three categories of good. Wisdom alone is not enough for happiness; and virtue is not either, despite the Stoics. The wise and virtuous man who is exiled, childless, and poor is certainly not happy. Indeed, he cannot even be wise or virtuous without external goods like wealth. For wealth is an instrument of virtue, and without it it is almost impossible to be liberal, strong, and just in reparation. Wisdom too is not self-sufficient, but usually conditioned by prior happiness

[69] Vespasiano da Bisticci, *Vite*, II, 157. Cf. Eugenio Garin, *Filosofi italiani del Quattrocento* (Florence, 1942), 242.

[70] *Della Famiglia*, 235; Cicero, *De Fin.*, II, xiii, 40.

[71] Ferdinando Fossi, *Monumenta ad Alamanni Rinuccini vitam contexendam* (Florence, 1791), 133. Quoted by Garin, *Filosofi italiani*, 254.

in active life, a healthy body, and material security.[72] We must conclude that the happy, mature man combines contemplation and action, political and literary activity, wisdom and prudence; and enjoys all the goods of mind, body, and fortune.

Here is an ethic distinct from the chivalric code of the nobility and the monastic virtues of the clergy which the ruling class of republican Florence could make their own. It justified their wealth and their preoccupating activity in the world. It encouraged and approved the independent intellectual activity of the laity. It developed a new conception of the wise man and of wisdom suitable to their needs and aspirations. The quest for wisdom no longer defines a separate spiritual estate. It has become the citizen's noblest ideal and, combined with an active virtue and the goods of body and fortune, his highest happiness.

IV

The civic enthusiasm of Bruni, Palmieri, Manetti, and Alberti is only one facet of Italian humanism in the fifteenth century; and it would be misleading to suppose that ideas of wisdom which got their special flavor from this civic emphasis on active life were necessarily typical either of Italy or of the century as a whole. They appear, indeed, to have been limited both in time and place: to Florence, with the occasional exception of the Venetian Republic, and to the first three-quarters of the century. Outside of Florence the ideals of humanism and the burgher class were less closely allied, and speculation on the meaning of wisdom tended to reflect, not the novel interests of the *bourgeoisie*, but the traditional attitudes of princely or ecclesiastical governments or the more personal, often pessimistic sentiments of individual humanists.[73] The important consequence was a tendency to renew—or simply perpetuate—the traditional emphasis on contemplative and religious elements in the idea of wisdom, an attitude as typical of the period as the more original position of Bruni.

[72] Mehus, *Epistolarum Libri*, II, 10–13; Baron, *Bruni Schriften*, 25–26, 135.
[73] Charles E. Trinkaus, Jr., *Adversity's Nobleman. The Italian Humanists on Happiness* (New York, 1940), 108–109.

The character of this more traditional conception of wisdom is adequately suggested in the works of Francesco Filelfo (1389–1481), long a brilliant ornament of the Milanese court, and Giovanni Pontano (1426–1503), the learned Secretary of State of Ferdinand I of Aragon, King of Naples.

Despite a largely justified claim to be the only man of his age who had mastered the whole literature of the ancients in both Greek and Latin, Filelfo's doctrine of wisdom is hardly more than a recapitulation of Petrarch's rereading of Augustine. He begins by defining wisdom as the knowledge of divine things. As opposed to *scientia*, which looks down on temporal, mobile things, it contemplates the eternal and immutable.[74] As opposed to prudence, which deals with inferior human things, it investigates the truth of divine and celestial things.[75] "Since among those things which are both eternal and immutable none is greater, none more excellent, none nobler, none better than God, all our contemplation must be accounted worship of God. For by this one splendid, happy virtue and by this way alone, not only do we know what is true and pure, but we also arrive at the most brilliant light of divine truth itself." God Himself is the highest wisdom; human wisdom is piety, as holy Job said: *Ecce pietas est sapientia*; and piety is the worship of God, what the Greeks called εὐσέβειαν.[76] As the highest contemplative virtue, wisdom's proper task is to contemplate the divine nature and essence and to know spiritual and invisible things: good and bad angels, souls, and God. This is the real and true philosophy. If the

---

[74] *De Morali Disciplina Libri Qvinqve* (Venice, 1552), 26.

[75] *Epistolae* (Venice, Bernardinus de Choris de Cremona, 1489), a, iii, r. "Quod enim animal in terris eam considerat ueritatem: quae in celo est? Haec sola sapientia est: quae et inquirit et nouit. Prudentia enim sapientiam ita ut ars naturam imitata ueritatem quidem inquirit: sed non rerum superiorum atque diuinarum: sed inferiorum et humanarum." Cf. *Ibid.*, g, iv. v. "Nam alii prudentiam summum bonum esse dixerunt: eandem hi quidem prudentiam appellantes: quam sapientiam: quae tota in ueri inuestigatione cognitioneque consistit."

[76] *De Morali Disciplina*, 26; *Conviviorvm Francisci Philelphi Libri II* (Cologne, Joannes Gymnicus, 1537), 117, 138.

gentiles had found it, they would not have remained mere lovers of wisdom, but would have become themselves wise men.[77]

Yet even now when all true philosophers are Christians, it is not easy for man to become wise. Unaided by God, he is in the position of the pagans: not wise, but a lover of wisdom. Filelfo lists the traditional ways man can know things far above him like the divine essence and the divine persons: *cognitio naturae*, the way of Plato and the other gentile philosophers; *cognitio fidei*, the way of Christian philosophers while they are in this world; and, finally, *cognitio gloriae*, the immediate knowledge of those wise men and saints who look on the divine essence face to face in heaven.[78] Like Salutati he quotes I Corinthians 12:8, a favorite text of all for whom the word of wisdom was a gift of the Spirit.[79] He differs here from Bruni, who had said little about how to acquire wisdom except that the happiness it brought was open to any well-endowed man provided only his search was sufficiently assiduous, his life long, and his health good.[80] By identifying wisdom and Christian piety, Filelfo by-passes Bruni's incipient secularism and reaffirms a traditional partial dependence of wisdom on grace.

So pious a wisdom is inevitably the noblest of the virtues.[81] Filelfo calls it "a kind of queen or empress," ruling prudence and the other virtues as the soul rules the body.[82] Being wholly of the mind,

[77] *Epistolae*, f, v, r. "Intellectu autem ad scientiae cognitionem peruenimus: et quod est sapientiae proprium diuinam essentiam naturamque contemplamur." Cf. *De Morali Disciplina*, 28.

[78] *Conviviorvm Libri*, 154; *Epistolae*, m, v, v.

[79] *De Morali Disciplina*, 26; *Conviviorvm Libri*, 92. But cf. *Epistolae*, g, iv, r. "Neque prudentes nascimur nec sapientes. Alterum doctrina gignit: alterum longissimi usus temporis et multarum uariarumque rerum praebet experientia."

[80] Mehus, *Epistolarum Libri*, II, 137.

[81] *Epistolae*, g, i, r. "Nam uera et incommutabilis uirtus sapientia est: quae nihil fictum: nihil simulatum admittit: sed ad ueritatem caelestium rerum tota deumque refert. Omnis autem scientia hac inferior: et scientiae partes: quas actiuas et morales dicimus: ita uirtutem sapiunt: si sapientiae se coniunxerint. Nam scientia omnis huiusmodi quae sapientiam non habet et manca est et debilis nullorumque neruorum."

[82] *Epistolae*, a, v, v.

it is the virtue of the contemplative life, noblest of all the possible modes of living. In it lie man's highest happiness and his highest pleasure. Characteristically praising Anaxagoras because he said that man is born to contemplate the sky and the whole order of the world, Filelfo puts man's highest happiness in knowledge of the truth. His highest pleasure is contemplation of the divine essence, which delights not only the soul but the body as well.[83] But he never says—no more than did Bruni—that wisdom is a good which excludes all others or makes them unnecessary, nor that it alone can make anyone happy. For man is made up of both soul and body, not of a soul only or a body only. To be happy, therefore, he needs not only wisdom, the chief good of the soul, but also virtue, the good of the active life, and pleasure, which is a good of both the soul and the body. Filelfo's ideal is Pythagoras, who pursued a contemplative wisdom all of his life. But he recognizes that wisdom must be complemented by virtue; and he does not spurn those legitimate pleasures of the body which complement the wonderful pleasure to be got from the exercise of honorable actions and the contemplation of divine things.[84]

In a way this is a Petrarchan position; and, indeed, Filelfo is very close to Petrarch when he says that in his opinion man must cultivate not only wisdom but virtue also. For this is the central teaching of that *christiana philosophia* by which we both know the true and do the good.[85] On the other hand, Filelfo also seems to have been influenced by the civic humanism of Bruni and his circle. Contemplation, he says, is nobler than action in the same degree as divine things are to be preferred to human; nevertheless "contemplative study, which consists in a perception of the truth, should not be so praised as to cast a slight on action." True men, unlike women and children, should never abdicate from what is properly called action: an active life of virtue.[86] For theoretical knowledge is absurd

[83] *De Morali Disciplina*, 37; *Conviviorvm Libri*, 162.
[84] *Epistolae*, g, iv, v; *De Morali Disciplina*, 37–38.
[85] *De Morali Disciplina*, 38.
[86] *Epistolae*, o, iv, v.

if it is not used and so find its end in active life.[87] This is the sense of Filelfo's allegorical explanation of the *Aeneid*. Vergil's theme is the relation of the active and contemplative lives; his message that the *summum bonum* is a union of wisdom and virtue. Aeneas, who combines action and contemplation, wisdom and prudence, symbolizes this union. The wise man in short, must be prudent, for no man is really wise unless he is virtuous also; the good man must be wise, for no one can be virtuous who has not first known the truth.[88]

If Filelfo differs from Bruni because he renews the traditional equation of wisdom and piety, Giovanni Pontano differs from him because he is less careful to insist that a contemplative wisdom must find its end and perfection in action. Divergent sources are not responsible for this difference. Aristotle is the inspiration of both men, particularly those passages in the sixth book of the *Ethics* where he defines and distinguishes between *sapientia, scientia, prudentia, intelligentia*, and *ars* and says that "the wise man must not only know what follows from first principles, but must also possess truth about the first principles. Therefore wisdom must be intuitive reason combined with scientific knowledge—scientific knowledge of the highest objects which has received as it were its proper completion."[89] In his *De Prudentia* (1498–99) Pontano defines wisdom in the same way and, like Bruni, carefully reproduces the Aristotelian distinctions between wisdom and the other intellectual virtues.[90]

---

[87] *Conviviorvm Libri*, 84–85.

[88] *Epistolae*, a, iii, r; f, v, v; g, i, r.

[89] *Eth. Nic.*, VI, vii, 1141a, 16.

[90] *Opera omnia* (Florence, 1520), II, 61r ff.; Erasmo Percopo, *Vita di Giovanni Pontano* (Naples, 1938), 261. Cf. Cristoforo Landino, *De anima*, A. Paoli and G. Gentile, eds., *Annali delle Università Toscane*, N.S. II, fasc. 3 (1917), 41. "A speculativa tres virtutes nanciscimur; si enim principia ipsa animadvertimus, ea elucet, quam vel intellectum vel intelligentiam nominant; si vero quae a principiis manant, conclusiones investigamus, ea exoritur, quae vero vocabulo scientia appellatur, quae per demonstrationem fit, cum a principiis in conclusiones et a causa in effectum ratiocinando deducimur; quod si et principia simul et quae a principiis sunt, connectamus, efficitur sapientia. In mente vero activa, quae curam capit rerum agendarum, prudentia eminet. In opere postremo efficiendo ars versatur."

The most important of these distinctions is that between wisdom and prudence. The function of prudence, says Pontano, is to direct human actions by deciding according to right reason what is to be followed and what avoided. The prudent man deliberates well about what is good and expedient for himself and what is conducive to living well. He is skilled in domestic management, business, and civil government and constantly occupied in active life.[91] Wisdom, on the other hand, investigates the nature of heavenly and divine things; the wise man contemplates the principles and causes of the highest things.[92] The two virtues differ as the human differs from the divine, the active from the contemplative, the man of experience from the philosopher or seer.

It need not follow, of course—certainly it did not follow for Bruni—that wisdom and prudence are opposed. Nor does Pontano, at least in the opening pages of the *De Prudentia*, draw such a conclusion. He points out that man is by nature a social and political animal unable to live for himself alone; that he is born to know the causes of things and to act virtuously; that a perfect life combines the two possible kinds of life, the active and the contemplative; that ideal happiness unites the pleasures of honorable actions with those of intellectual contemplation.[93] This echoes the ideals of Bruni and Salutati's conviction that the man who cannot actively benefit himself, his family, and his country does not deserve to be called wise, however much he knows about celestial and divine things. Yet Pontano also concludes that prudent men cannot be wise and that wise men are necessarily imprudent. He suggests, that is, that wisdom and prudence are not only different, but mutually exclusive.

The prudent man is skilled in action. He is the *experiens vir*, industrious, practical, committed to civic and business life. He is

[91] *Opera*, II, 61v–62r, 65v.

[92] *Ibid.*, 65r. ". . . sapientia tamen, et illorum quae coeli, ac Dei sunt, rerumque naturae perspectionem sequitur, nedum humanarum siue rerum siue opinionum perscrutationem." *Ibid.*, 66r. "Cum sapientia ea solum curet sequaturque, quorum certa sit cognitio, ac scientia, quaeque natura ipsa sint praestantissima, atque ut maximi pretij."

[93] *Ibid.*, 5v, 8v–9r, 29v. Cf. Saitta, *Il Pensiero italiano nell'Umanesimo e nel Rinascimento*, I, 656–657.

admirable of his kind, but he cannot pretend to investigate the principles and causes of things. Conversely—and this is the point Pontano emphasizes again and again—the wise man lacks prudence almost by definition.[94] He is so preoccupied with high intellectual matters that when the time comes for action he is usually ridiculously unprepared and inept. Aristotle had already observed that "Anaxagoras, Thales, and men of that stamp, people call wise, but not prudent because they see them ignorant of what concerns themselves; and they say that what they know is quite out of the common run certainly, and wonderful, and hard, and very fine no doubt, but still useless because they do not seek after what is good for them as men."[95] As a modern example of the wise man Pontano cites Theodore of Gaza whom he venerated as a young man for his consummate knowledge of the nature of things, but who was almost unfit for civic action and the duties of civil life. Wisdom, clearly, is purely speculative, exclusively concerned with the contemplation of celestial things, and necessarily isolates a man from active, civic life.

By opposing wisdom so sharply to prudence, Pontano re-emphasizes its traditionally contemplative character. He reinforces this by rejecting the one nonspeculative meaning Aristotle had given wisdom. In the arts, said Aristotle, we ascribe wisdom to those who "carry their arts to the highest accuracy. Phidias, for instance, we call a wise or cunning sculptor . . . meaning in this instance, nothing else by wisdom than an excellence of art."[96] By extension wisdom came to mean excellence in any craft or profession, a meaning clearly defined by Aquinas: "For since it is part of a wise man to order and to judge, and since lesser matters can be judged in the light of some higher cause, he is said to be wise in any genus who considers the highest cause in that genus. Thus in the realm of building, he who plans the form of the house is called wise and architect, in relation to the subordinate laborers who trim the wood and make ready the stones. . . . Again, in the order of all human

---

[94] *Ibid.*, 68v–69r.
[95] *Eth. Nic.*, VI, vii, 1141b, 5.
[96] *Eth. Nic.*, VI, vii, 1141a, 10.

life, the prudent man is called wise, inasmuch as he directs his acts to a fitting end: thus it is said, *Wisdom is prudence to a man.* (Prov. 10:23)"[97] Pontano notes the currency of this definition in his own day. By using *sapientia* in this loose way, he says, the best lawyers are often called wise; while the vulgar call any man wise who manages public and private business well. He remembers how, as a boy, he used to hear it said that Cosimo de Medici and Francesco Foscari, Doge of Venice, were *sapientes*, "because both administered public affairs well and very prudently."[98] But Pontano rejects such usage because it blurs his rigid separation of wisdom and prudence. Prudence, he insists again, is concerned only with action and choice; wisdom only with knowledge. Foscari, therefore, or a ruler like Frederigo, Duke of Urbino, is not a wise man, but a prudent commander and governor. Similarly, Gentile da Fabriano, Giotto, and Van Eyck painted marvelously; but they are not to be called wise men for this. It is more appropriate in Latin to call such excellence in the arts and professions *peritia* rather than *sapientia*. And so we say of Bartolus and Baldus, of Niccolo Picinini and Francesco Sforza, Valla and Donatello that they were skilled in civil law, in the art of war, in oratory and sculpture rather than that they were wise men.[99] The wise man, conversely, knows the true but cannot do the useful.

Pontano has clearly abandoned Bruni's effort to tie a speculative wisdom indissolubly to civic action. Their definitions of wisdom and their sources are identical; but Bruni arranged, even twisted, his sources to point up the necessary interdependence of wisdom and prudence, while Pontano arranged them so that they are in fact mutually exclusive. Bruni insisted that Aristotle's speculative wisdom be perfected by an active life. Pontano tended to draw no civic conclusions from it and fragmented Bruni's generous ideal of man by exalting the noble, solitary *sapiens* above the prudent *experiens vir.* The result is a wisdom more rigorously contemplative, a wise man more single-minded, but more lonely, in his pursuit of truth.

---

[97] *Sum. Theol.*, Ia, Q. I, art. 6, Resp.
[98] *Opera*, II, 66r.
[99] *Ibid.*, 66r–67r.

Filelfo's revival of the traditional association of wisdom with Christian piety and Pontano's emphasis on its purely intellectual and contemplative nature suggest the changed direction of Italian humanist speculation on wisdom in the later fifteenth century. The full extent of that change is mapped in the intellectual interests of the Florentine Neo-Platonists.

Chapter 3

The Wisdom of Renaissance Platonism

Ficino and Pico della Mirandola restated the contemplative ideal in a perspective and vocabulary derived from a new and direct contact with the pagan mysticism of Plotinus and Proclus. They found the pattern of life they wished to imitate in Proclus' tribute to Plotinus: "His soul, which he had always kept pure, took flight towards the divine principle, prayed to it and adored it. He had always endeavored to raise himself above the stormy waves of this brutal life which is nourished on flesh and blood. It is thus that this divine man, whose thoughts were always turned to the Supreme God and the unseen world, merited the privilege of beholding several times the immediate presence of the Godhead, who has neither sensible nor intelligible form, since he is exalted above intelligence and being itself."[1]

This is the beatific vision, the end of knowledge and the highest wisdom. It is a form of pure contemplation and it can be attained only with God's help. Both assertions distinguish Florentine Neo-Platonism from earlier civic humanism. Just as Florence's taste in art shifted in the course of the fifteenth century from the monumentality and simplicity of Masaccio, Brunelleschi, and Donatello to the agitated refinement of Botticelli and Benedetto da Maiano, so Pico and Ficino blunt the civic ideals of Bruni by a renewed defense of the contemplative life. And where Bruni and his contemporaries had suggested that wisdom was a naturally acquired perfection, Pico and Ficino stress the active part of God in human knowledge and the importance of divine illumination.

[1] W. R. Inge, *Mysticism in Religion* (University of Chicago Press, 1948), 108.

This emphasis on the incomparable superiority of the contemplative life and on the active role of God in human knowledge is common to the medieval idea of wisdom and to that of ancient Neo-Platonism. This is a source of ambiguity. Looked at from one angle, Pico's and Ficino's definitions of wisdom repeat the medieval one: wisdom is a revealed knowledge of divine things. Looked at from another, they simply define pure contemplation in the classical Neo-Platonic sense. This was surely deliberate in thinkers so consciously bent on harmonizing with Christianity a "Platonism" derived more from Plotinus, Augustine, and the Pseudo-Dionysius than from Plato. Ficino wrote commentaries on the *Dialogues* of Plato; but he also wrote one on the *Epistle to the Romans*. He described God and the beatific vision in the philosophical vocabulary of Plotinus; but his God was the Christian God who worked in the human mind through an illumination assimilated to the grace of traditional theology. Ficino's and Pico's idea of wisdom is the restatement of a medieval commonplace in the framework of first-hand knowledge of antique Neo-Platonism.

I

In a very free epitome of the Pseudo-Platonic dialogue *Theages* Ficino repeats the traditional Aristotelian distinction between absolute and conditional wisdom. Absolute wisdom is the knowledge of those things of which real knowledge is possible, that is, of those things which are always the same, the *summa rerum principia*, the *aeternae rerum omnium rationes*. Put more generally, it is a knowledge of divine things.[2] Leo Hebraeus, court physician to

[2] *Marsilii Ficini, Philosophi, Platonici, Medici atque Theologi omnium praestantissimi, Operum.* . . . (Basel, 1576), II, 1131. "Prima partitione Sapientia duplex dicitur. Vna absoluta, conditionalis altera. Absoluta, quae simpliciter absque additione aliqua sapientia nominatur. Conditionalis, quae non simpliciter sapientia, sed sapientia quaedam dicta est. Illa sic definitur. Cognitio earum rerum de quibus haberi scientia potest. Habetur autem scientia de ijs quae semper eadem, et eodem modo sunt, huiusmodi sunt summa rerum principia, et aeternae rerum omnium rationes, haec autem diuina dicuntur, quo fit ut sapientia sit diuinarum rerum scientia, quae quidem absoluta sapientia est." Cf. Boethius, *Inst. Arith.*, I, i. "Est enim sapientia earum rerum que vere sunt cognitio et integra comprehensio."

the Spanish Viceroy of Naples, Don Gonsalvo de Cordoba, has amplified this definition in his popular *Dialoghi d'Amore* (1502): "Wisdom is a faculty concerned alike with the principles and the conclusions touching all that exists; it alone attains to the highest knowledge of spiritual things, which the Greeks call θεολογία, i.e. Science of the Divine, and which is also called First Philosophy, as being the crown of all the sciences. And therein it is that our intellect acts according to its ultimate and most perfect nature."[3]

Conditional wisdom does not have this universality. It describes a limited perfection, the mastery of a particular art or science. The man who best assures the success of the desired end of any art or science is wise in respect to that art or science. Thus Ficino speaks, as had Aristotle and Aquinas, of the wisdom of a ship's pilot, or of military wisdom, or, highest of all, of civil or political wisdom.[4] But like Pontano, Ficino and other Renaissance Platonists neglected and belittled this prosaic and conditional wisdom. In this they were only following the "divine" Plato himself, who remarked in the *Theatetus* that the "wisdom of politicians or the wisdom of the arts" is coarse and vulgar in comparison with knowledge of the Good. Professional wisdom, he argued, is chained to the world, while the mind of the philosopher, "disdaining the littlenesses and nothingnesses of human things, is 'flying all abroad' as Pindar says, measuring earth and heaven and the things which are under and on the earth and above the heaven, interrogating the whole nature of each and all in their entirety, but not condescending to anything which is within reach."[5] Ficino had an equally ineffable idea of the philosopher; and he and his successors were as reluctant to admit that the mastery of a profession or craft constituted more than the

[3] Leone Ebreo, *The Philosophy of Love* (*Dialoghi d'Amore*), F. Friede-berg-Seeley and Jean H. Barnes, trs. (London, 1937), 37.

[4] Ficino, *Opera*, II, 1131. "Conditionalis [sapientia] vero omnibus artibus et facultatibus est communis. Nam summitas cuiusque artis sapientia quaedam vocatur, ut sapientia gubernatoria, sapientia aurigaria, sapientia militaris. Ex omnibus autem quae cum additione sapientiae nuncupantur praecipua est, quae caeteris ut ministris utitur, cuiusmodi ciuilis sapientia est." Cf. *Opera*, I, 608.

[5] *Theatetus*, 173 E.

merest introduction to wisdom as they were to say that experience
is a significant source of wisdom. Most Renaissance men, indeed,
knew very well that wisdom was much more esoteric and mysterious
than that. They knew that wise men were very few in number and
that true wisdom was as rare as it was noble. They generally concluded by saying with Ficino: *Profanis sapientia non conceditur.*[6]

What Ficino called absolute wisdom, therefore, is the only real
and true wisdom because it alone is exclusively concerned with
divine things. *Sapientia est divinarum rerum scientia.*[7] But what
does Ficino mean by "divine things"? To describe them he uses
traditional phrases drawn indiscriminately from Plato, Aristotle,
the Neo-Platonists, Augustine, and the Scholastics. With Aristotle
he calls them the highest principles of things, the highest causes
and the eternal reasons of all things; with Plato, intelligibles and
Ideas.[8] Like Plotinus and the "Platonists" he locates divine things
in the *prima mens* or says that they are ideas subsisting in that fountain of intelligibility which is the divine light.[9] When he equates
them with the Ideas in the mind of God, *exemplaria rerum omnium
in ipso Deo*, he is following a tradition which goes back to Middle
Platonism and the Fathers of the Church.[10] With the Scholastics,
finally, he talks—like Cusa did—of intelligible forms, substances
separate from matter, *species primae, primae naturae*, divine
essences, and angelic intellects.[11]

But of these several terms which make the meaning of divine
things more concrete, the one that Ficino and his fellow Platonists
use most often is Ideas. This is one sense, at least, in which their
doctrine of wisdom is Platonic, however different their understanding of Ideas may be from Plato's. Already in Petrarch's time it was
fashionable to talk about the Ideas. Both he and Salutati said that

[6] Ficino, *Opera*, I, 787.
[7] *Ibid.*, II, 1131.
[8] *Ibid.*, I, 437; II, 1137.
[9] *Ibid.*, I, 612–613. Cf. Pico della Mirandola, *De hominis dignitate. Hepta-
plus. De ente et uno e scritti vari*, Eugenio Garin, ed. (Florence, 1942), 465–
466.
[10] *Opera*, I, 436.
[11] *Opera*, II, 1018, 1145, 1369–1370, 1411.

Plato meant by Ideas the forms and reasons of things, the exemplars of things in the mind of God.[12] Early in the next century Francesco Filelfo defined an idea as a substance separate from matter existing in the intellect and imagination of God, a *principalis quaedam ratio rerum*—immutable, eternal, uncreated—according to which all mutable things were created.[13] Ficino's conception is not significantly different. Ideas are the thoughts of God, universals existing in the divine intellect, archetypes of the substantial and accidental forms contained in created things. Each idea, he says poetically, is a particular aspect of the divine essence, a particular color in the fullness of the divine light.[14]

Florentine Neo-Platonism took the further traditional step of identifying the Ideas with the intellect, Word, or Wisdom of God. In his *Commentary on a Love Song by Girolamo Benivieni* Pico della Mirandola explores some of the implications of this identification. Following Plotinus he says that God produced *ab aeterno* a perfect creature, the *prima mente*, whom Platonists and early philosophers like Hermes Trismegistus and Zoroaster call "now son of God, now Wisdom, now Mind, now divine reason, and sometimes Word."[15] And he assimilates this Wisdom, this son of God, to Christ, the true son and Word of God, and to *chochmah*, the second sephiroth of the Cabalists.[16] In each case the divine intellect or

---

[12] Petrarch, *De vita solitaria*, Antonio Altamura, ed. (Naples, 1943), 41 and Novati, *Epistolario di Coluccio Salutati*, III, 561, 593–594.

[13] Eugenio Garin, *Filosofi italiani del Quattrocento* (Florence, 1942), 152.

[14] Paul Oskar Kristeller, *The Philosophy of Marsilio Ficino*, Virginia Conant, tr. (Columbia University Press, 1943), 246; Marian Heitzman, "L'agostinismo avicennizzante e il punto di partenza della filosofia di M. Ficino," *Giornale critico della filosofia italiana*, sec. ser., III (1935), 299. Cf. Ficino, *Opera*, II, 1145.

[15] Pico della Mirandola, *De hominis dignitate . . . e scritti vari*, 466.

[16] Pico, *De hominis dignitate*, 549–550. In his *De verbo mirifico* Reuchlin makes the same identifications: Joseph L. Blau, *The Christian Interpretation of the Cabala in the Renaissance* (New York, 1944), ch. IV. Cf. Giordano Bruno, *Opera Latina*, F. Fiorentino, ed. (Naples, 1876), I–I, 13. "In primo gradu a Cabalistis appellatur et notatur mens divina per *sephirot cochma*, in secundo ab Orphicis theologis nominatur Pallas seu Minerva, in tertio communiter nomine Sophiae inscribitur."

wisdom contains the ideas or forms by which God created all things. Just as the architect has in his mind a figure of the building he undertakes, which, as his model, he tries to imitate exactly, so God has in His divine mind the Ideas and exemplars of all things, the Ideas of the sun and moon, men, all animals, plants and stones, the elements, and all things generally. This mind—and here is the identification on which Christian Platonism is based—is the intelligible world, where all things exist, not in a material or sensible manner of being, but in a truer, nobler, more beautiful way, the ideal or intelligible.[17] Conversely, the intelligible world is the Word of God adorned with Ideas. It is a world of ideal beauty symbolized by Saturn, god of contemplation, and the celestial Venus. Zoroaster called it Paradise and urged us to "Seek, seek Paradise."[18]

Generally speaking, then, wisdom is a knowledge of divine things; but since divine things are normally identified with the Ideas in the mind of God, it is more accurate to say that wisdom is a knowledge of them: *Mentis diuinae idearumque cognitio sapientia dicitur.*[19] In different words, the wisdom of men is the image of divine wisdom. As God's wisdom is a treasure house of Ideas, man's wisdom is made up of the images of those ideas; and by becoming wise the human soul becomes similar to God, *qui sapientia ipsa est*, and in this similitude Plato puts the highest stage of blessedness.[20] When divine wisdom is symbolized by Saturn, who here represents the intelligible world, man's wisdom is a speculative virtue, a *contemplatio diuinorum*, in contrast, says Ficino, to *scientia* which is the knowledge of natural things and prudence which is an active

[17] Pico, *De hominis dignitate*, 468.

[18] *Ibid.*, 475, 498, 502.

[19] In this particular form the sentence is found among the *Sententiae Pvlcherrimae, ex Marsilii Ficini . . . Operibus Collectae* at the end of *Opera*, I. Cf. the words of Filelfo (Garin, *Filosofi italiani*, 154): ". . . [Plato] affirmabat tantam vim inesse in iis ideis ut nemo sapiens esse possit qui eas minus animo percepisset intellexissetque. . . . Solum igitur eum sapientem et dicendum arbitrabatur et iudicandum, qui ideam veritatemque calleret."

[20] Ficino, *Opera*, I, 608, 613.

preoccupation with public and private business.[21] When divine
wisdom is symbolized by the celestial Venus, who represents "the
intelligible beauty which is in the Ideas," human wisdom is, in
Pico's words, a kind of celestial love: *desiderio intellettuale di ideale
bellezza*.[22] Wisdom is a good which embraces all others, the only
good per se as foolishness is the only evil per se. It is a good which
all men should earnestly seek by piety and philosophy.[23]

They must seek it in the right place. Not on earth, but in heaven;
for wisdom is divine, not human; wholly spiritual and intellectual,
not sensible or corporeal. Its end is true knowledge, not sensual
delight: *Circa veritatem vero sapientia, circa id quod delectat
voluptas*, says Ficino in his *Commentary on the Philebus*.[24] The
effort to reach it, therefore, must always consist, as Plato said, in
turning from terrestial to celestial things, from the mobile to the
immobile, from sensible to intelligible.[25] Already Petrarch had seen
this as the kernel of Plato's message: "For what does the doctrine
of the heavenly Plato show," he asks, "but that the soul must separate
itself from the passions of the flesh and tread down its imaginings
before it can rise pure and free to the contemplation of the mystery
of the Divine; for otherwise the thought of its mortality will make
it cling to those seducing charms."[26] More accurately Platonic, Ficino
says the same thing: in order to rise up to wisdom the intellect
must purge itself of false opinions and the perturbations of the
passions. It must turn from the forms of sensible things to the intellectual forms innate in it; and rise through them to intelligible
forms, that is, to the Ideas. It will then pass from the Ideas to the

[21] *Opera*, I, 657. "In eo genere [the speculative virtues] sunt sapientia,
contemplatio diuinorum, scientia, quae est cognitio naturalium, prudentia, hoc
est, notitia rerum priuatim et publice recte administrandarum, ars denique
quae est recta efficiendorum operum regula."

[22] Pico, *De hominis dignitate*, 498, 500.

[23] Ficino, *Opera*, I, 608.

[24] *Opera*, II, 1214.

[25] *Opera*, II, 1408. Cf. *Opera*, II, 1411.

[26] *Secret or The Soul's Conflict with Passion*, William H. Draper, tr.
(London, 1911), 77.

divine mind itself and to the supreme Good which is the light and beginning of the Ideas.[27]

The soul cannot make this ascent unaided. For both Pico and Ficino, Ideas are partial aspects of the divine substance. They are divine things "above nature" which man cannot know without the help of God. Their perception is not an independent act of thought, but an active influence of God on the mind. For the mind cannot lift itself up to a sight of the divine substance and the Ideas which are its colors and embellishments "by an increase of its natural force and light only, for such an action differs more than 'by genus' from the natural action of the mind, but a new force is needed and a new light descending from a higher cause. They call it the light of grace and glory, and illuminated by it and kindled even more the mind assumes divine substance . . . like a flame."[28] Ungrateful men assert they see true things by their own natural light, whereas they really see them in the common and divine light.[29]

It is true that germs or forms of all universal concepts, the so-called *formulae*, are naturally innate in the soul. But it is not true that these seeds can blossom naturally and of themselves into a knowledge of the ideas in the mind of God. The passage of the *formulae* from potency to act, and so the passage of the mind from the shadows of the sensible world to a perception of the bright reality of the Ideas, is not the work of the mind itself, but of God. It is God's light shining in the sanctuary of the mind which animates the rudimentary forms innate there. In the act of thinking God is the primal and common cause; the *formulae* are the proper and second cause; the sensible image is the original incitement to thought; and the mind takes the place of matter.[30]

Ficino elaborates this conception by comparing God and the sun, the intellect and the eye. As the eye sees the movement of a colorful

[27] Ficino, *Opera*, II, 1411.

[28] *Opera*, I, 411–412. Quoted by Kristeller, *Ficino*, 246. Cf. Ficino, *Opera*, II, 1836.

[29] *Opera*, I, 269. Cf. Giuseppe Anichini, *L'Umanesimo e il problema della salvezza in Marsilio Ficino* (Milan, 1937), 59–60.

[30] *Opera*, I, 671–672. Cf. Kristeller, *Ficino*, 248–249 and Walter Dress, *Die Mystik des Marsilio Ficino* (Berlin and Leipzig, 1929), 66–67.

object only when it is revealed by the sun's light, so the intellect knows the truth of intelligible things only when they are illuminated by the light of God.[31] Ficino found this image in the Sixth Book of the *Republic*, but the meaning he gives it derives from Augustine rather than Plato. Plato, he explains in his *Commentary on the Symposium,*

says that the light of the mind for understanding everything is the same God Himself by whom everything was created, and he compares God and the sun with each other in that God stands in the same relation to Minds as the sun to eyes. The sun generates eyes and it bestows upon them the power to see. This power would be in vain, and would be overwhelmed by eternal darkness if the light of the sun were not present, imprinted with the colors and shapes of bodies. . . . In the same way, God creates the soul and to it gives mind, the power of understanding. The mind would be empty and dark if it did not have the light of God, in which to see the principles of everything; whence, through the light of God, it understands, and it knows. . . . Thus, we understand everything through the light of God, but the pure light itself and its source, we cannot see in this life. Clearly the whole richness of the soul consists in this, that in its inner recesses glows that eternal light of God, filled with the concepts and Ideas of all things. To this light the soul can turn whenever it wishes through purity of life and the greatest steadfastness of purpose, and once it is turned, it shines with the light of the Ideas.[32]

It is because a knowledge of Ideas is the result of divine illumination that wisdom is said to come from God. Not only do the sacred texts of Jews and Christians say that only God can teach wisdom, and that it can only be got by faith, hope, and charity; but Plato also tells how he daily asked God for wisdom.[33] This is the divine

[31] *Opera*, I, 267.

[32] Sears R. Jayne, *Marsilio Ficino's Commentary on Plato's Symposium. The Text and a Translation, with an Introduction*, University of Missouri Studies, XIX (1944), 206–207. Cf. P. O. Kristeller, *Supplementum Ficinianum* (Florence, 1937), I, 64–65; Augustine, *Solil.*, I, 6 and Aquinas, *Sum. Theol.*, Ia., IIae, Q. 109, art. 1, obj. 2.

[33] Ficino, *Opera*, I, 842.

meaning hidden in the Orphic fable of the birth of Minerva from the head of Zeus. Explained by Ficino and his followers, who were themselves following Boccaccio, the myth meant that all wisdom has its origin in God and is mysteriously infused in us by God. Wisdom is not produced by us, but springs from the head of Jove, free from all earthly blemish.[34] At this crucial point Ficino joins Nicholas of Cusa and the Christian mystics: wisdom is a gift of the Holy Spirit, a supranatural infusion of divine light. "For who properly adores wisdom," he asks, "unless he does so wisely? But he alone adores wisely who asks Wisdom for wisdom."[35]

If the mind is flooded with divine light in answer to this prayer, the highest human wisdom is a blinding intellectual vision of Wisdom and a mystical union with It. Caught up by God and formed by Him, the intellect which contemplates divine things is then renewed and transformed into the same shape with God and becomes one spirit with Him. This union Ficino calls the *summum contemplationis fastigium*, an intellectual vision shared by very few individuals and then only for a brief moment.[36] Plato too had described this last and consummate wisdom as a "beatific vision" and a "divine contemplation"; and Pico della Mirandola explains it more fully when he says that "with this sight Moses saw, Paul saw, and many other of the elect saw the face of the Lord; and this is the sight our theologians call intellectual cognition, intuitive knowledge; with this sight, St. John the Evangelist says the just will see high God, and this is the whole of our reward."[37] So bright is wisdom that those who have been ravished to a vision of that intellectual beauty are blinded with too much brilliance, like blind Tiresias who once dared look on Pallas nude, look, that is, on "that ideal beauty from which comes all pure wisdom not veiled or hid in matter."[38] Such a vision is a kind of ecstasy. It has been described

---

[34] Cf. Giovanni Boccaccio, *Genealogie deorum gentilium libri*, Vincenzo Romano, ed. (Bari, 1951), I, 72–73 and Bruno, *Opera latina*, I–I, 10–11.

[35] *Opera*, I, 780.

[36] Kristeller, *Ficino*, 246.

[37] Pico, *De hominis dignitate*, 498.

[38] Pico, *De hominis dignitate*, 529.

beautifully in Spenser's celebration of Sapience in *An Hymne on Heavenly Beautie.* He is describing the emotion of those whom Sapience has allowed to see her lovely face,

> Whereof such wondrous pleasures they conceave,
> And sweete contentment, that it doth bereave
> Their soule of sense, through infinite delight,
> And them transport from flesh into the spright.
> In which they see such admirable things,
> As carries them into an extasy,
> And heare such heavenly notes and carolings
> Of Gods high praise, that filles the brasen sky;
> And feele such joy and pleasure inwardly,
> That maketh them all worldly cares forget,
> And onely thinke on that before them set.[39]

II

So ineffable a wisdom did not lend itself to civic propaganda. It demanded a contemplative life. In his *Camaldulensian Disputations*, Cristoforo Landino, a third important member of the Platonic Academy, showed why this must be so.

Landino taught humanities at the Studio from 1458 on and took an active part in the intellectual life of Florence almost a generation after the older *Florentina libertas* had given way to the *Pax Medicea* and when, in intellectual life, the Aristotelianism of Argyropulos and Bruni was beginning to face the competition of Ficino's Neo-Platonism.[40] The first book of the *Camaldulensian Disputations*, in which he discusses the general problem of the relation of wisdom to active and contemplative lives (and which depends closely, sometimes verbatim, on Ficino), is a fascinating record of some of the tensions and competing ideas which accompanied those changes. In it he subtly plays off the older activist ideals of Bruni, Manetti, and Palmieri against the contemplative ideals of the Medicean circle. Ironically, Landino gives the defense of civic wisdom to the young

[39] *An Hymne on Heavenly Beautie*, lines 56–66.
[40] Eugenio Garin, *Testi inediti e rari di C. Landino e F. Filelfo* (Florence, 1949), 5.

Lorenzo the Magnificent, while the new exaltation of contemplation is championed by the most articulate and civic-minded of the older burgher aristocracy, Alberti.

There are two modes of living suitable to man, Alberti begins, the active and the contemplative, based on two essential activities proper to man, to act rationally and to contemplate the truth. The active life is an opportunity for the exercise of moral virtue; the contemplative for speculation on the immortal and divine. In the first, man lives uprightly and virtuously in society, caring for parents, children, and friends and cultivating the just and right. In the other, inflamed by an ardent love of celestial things, he rises by means of the intellectual virtues from sensible to divine things and finally to a sight of the divine essence itself, which nourishes his soul on nectar and ambrosia.[41] Both these modes of living are good and natural to man. The active life is to be in no way condemned; but, "since our mind, by which alone we are men, is perfected not by mortal action but by immortal knowledge . . . who does not see that speculation is much superior to action?"[42]

Lorenzo replies by attacking what he calls the *sapiens ociosus* and magnificently defending the active life. The contemplative wise man, shut up alone in his library in the difficult quest for knowledge of divine things and the secrets of nature, associating with no one, engaged in no responsible public or private business, forgetful of the world and of his own body, is only half a man. No one wants such a person as his fellow citizen: he is like a lazy drone feeding off honey not his own. The really wise man is not solitary and egoistic but puts his learning at the service of the state, like Camillus, Cato, and the Scipios in antiquity, or, in contemporary times, like Federigo da Montefeltro, Duke of Urbino, a man both wise, learned, cultivated in letters, and a great soldier and statesman. Turning to myth, Lorenzo points out that "Hercules was a wise man. Yet he was not wise for himself alone, but benefited almost all men by his

[41] *Disputationes Camaldulenses* (Venice, ca. 1500 [Proctor, 5716]), a, v, r–vi, v.
[42] *Ibid.*, b, ii, v.

wisdom." His was no *ociosa sapientia*; he killed monsters, over-
turned tyrants, freed individuals and whole peoples.[43] Christian
authority, finally, is persuasive in the same sense. Paul didn't with-
draw from the world to meditate in a monastic cell and so neglect
the salvation of others. And he did not do this for a combination
of Christian and classical reasons which buttress every *quattrocento*
defense of action: "Did not God tell man to love his neighbor as
himself; but what is nearer you than the state itself? . . . For all who
have ever been philosophers say that we are born to communal,
social life and they call no one man who is not a citizen, and no
one citizen who neglects the care of the city in which he was born."[44]

Alberti's (one should say rather the Pseudo-Alberti's) reply to this
speech sums up a view of the relation of wisdom and action which
is as characteristic of later fifteenth-century Florence as Bruni's was
of an earlier time. Naturally, he first questions Lorenzo's emphasis
on the composite nature of man. Literally man is made up of both
a soul and a body; but it is his mind which is the noblest thing in
him, which separates him from beasts and makes him a man. Since
its function is speculation rather than action, it is clear that contemplation and the investigation of truth are the divinest things a
man can do and far above action. The true wise man, therefore, is
like Paolo Toscanelli, who, though a citizen, chose to flee the tumult,
care, and struggle of civic life and devote himself entirely to the
search for truth.[45] It is truth, after all, not action which is significant.
Take Cicero: his active life benefited one city for a limited time; but
his writings on how to live well and blessedly have benefited all
ages. For actions die with the men who made them, but thought,
triumphing over the centuries, endures forever. The man who acts
judiciously is, of course, admirable; but the man who has been able,
as Virgil says, to know the causes of things is a god among men.
Let the wise man give himself to the active life insofar as his human
nature, family affection, and love of country demand. But let him

[43] *Ibid.*, b, iv, r–v, r.
[44] *Ibid.*, b, v, v–vi, r.
[45] *Ibid.*, b, vi, r–vi, v.

remember that he was born to contemplate celestial things and seek his highest good in knowledge of truth.[46]

This is admirably put. The real Alberti, however, had said that "man was born to be useful to man."

III

Through Ficino's translations of the *Dialogues* and his commentaries on them, through his original works and those of Pico, Landino, and other members of the Florentine Academy, the authority of the Platonic tradition was immeasurably enhanced and the doctrines of the "Platonici" penetrated many of the most characteristic productions of the sixteenth-century Renaissance. Among these doctrines was the "Platonic" idea of wisdom. The less original sixteenth-century Platonists accepted uncritically the formulas of the Medicean circle. Others, by coming to understand more clearly what Plato's own conception of wisdom had been, made important changes in them.

It is important to fix precisely what these changes were. Later Platonists did not normally disagree with the Florentines in their definition of wisdom. Like their predecessors they defined it as the knowledge of immutable, invisible, intelligible, and divine things. Nor did most of them try to associate wisdom more closely with the active life, despite increasingly aggressive attacks on them by its defenders. They were careful to say, with Petrarch, that wisdom is inseparable from virtue; but they boast of the solitary, esoteric character of the wise man. The crucial point of innovation lies elsewhere, in their insistence on man's natural capacity to become wise. Their wisdom is an easy comprehension of the comprehensible and reason's unaided attainment of its own particular end and good. Wisdom thus becomes a natural virtue, naturally acquired. When they speak of divine things, they mean God and the Ideas like Ficino did; but when they open the realm of the invisible and divine to the unaided penetration of a potent natural reason they have passed beyond him. To measure this distance is to measure

[46] *Ibid.*, c, ii, r–c, ii, v.

an important element in the Renaissance secularization of the idea of wisdom and an important further stage in the accurate re-appropriation of classical Platonism.

Cardinal Jacopo Sadoleto's *De philosophia*, written in 1533 and published in 1538, admirably mirrors this change.[47] The book is made up of two dialogues written in as pure and elegant a Ciceronian style as the sixteenth century achieved. The first dialogue is called "Phaedrus"; the second, "Hortensius seu de laudibus philosophiae." The scene is at Rome during the pontificate of Leo X, and the interlocutors are Sadoleto himself and Tommaso Fedro Inghirami. Inghirami (called Phaedrus to commemorate his virtuosity in an impromptu performance of Seneca's tragedy) was Vatican librarian in the last years of Julius II, Secretary to the College of Cardinals and the Lateran Council (he was painted by Raphael about 1512 in the scarlet garment of this office), the most fashionable preacher in Rome, and a luminary at the court of Leo X.[48] He died in 1516. Sadoleto outlived his friend by thirty years and made an exemplary literary and ecclesiastical career: canon of S. Lorenzo in Damaso, Bishop of Carpentras, Cardinal, a member of Paul III's reform commission, and a leader, with Contarini, Giberti, and Pole, of that reformist and conciliatory party in the Curia which was ulti-

---

[47] *Iacobi Sadoleti de laudibus Philosophiae Libri duo* (Lyons, Seb. Gryphius, 1538). My references to this, as to Sadoleto's other works, is to the eighteenth-century Verona edition: *Jacobi Sadoleti Cardinalis et Episcopi Carpentoractensis viri disertissimi, Opera quae exant omnia*, 4 v. (Verona, 1737–1738). Useful bibliographies will be found in S. Ritter, *Un umanista teologo, Jacopo Salodeto (1477–1547)* (Rome, 1912); Sadoleto, *Elogio della Sapienza (De laudibus philosophiae)*, Antonio Altamura and Guiseppe Toffanin, eds. and trs. (Naples, 1950); and in the *Dictionnaire des lettres françaises. Le seizième siècle* (Paris, 1951). Sadoleto's unedited manuscript works are described by Alessandro Ferrajoli, "Il ruolo della Corte di Leone X. Prelati domestici. Iacopo Sadoleto," *Archivio della R. Società Romana di Storia Patria*, XXXVIII (1915), 256–281.

[48] For further biographical details see Sadoleto, *Elogio della Sapienza (De laudibus philosophiae)*, 11, note 1; Philip Hendy, *The Isabella Stewart Gardner Museum. Catalogue of the Exhibited Paintings and Drawings* (Boston, 1931), 284–287; and A. Joly, *Etude sur J. Sadolet, 1477–1547* (Caen, 1857), 87.

mately swamped by the triumph of Caraffa and the beginnings of the Counter Reformation.

The debate between these two men, so different in temperament and opinion, is of extraordinary interest. Two points of particular importance emerge. The first is made by Sadoleto when he insists that wisdom, Platonically defined, is naturally acquired. The second is Inghirami's redefinition of wisdom as a self-interested method of worldly success. The two dialogues, in other words, are a sixteenth-century reworking of the *Protagoras*; and they mark both the appearance of a Platonic idea of wisdom somewhat closer to Plato's than Ficino's had been and a further stage in the great controversy on the relative merits of action and contemplation: a continued defense of contemplative wisdom, but now against arguments of an unusual audacity.

Sadoleto and Inghirami agree that wisdom is magnificent and desirable, the divinest of things; that there is nothing in heaven or earth more beautiful; that its very name enflames man's desire to know it; that to be called wise is the greatest distinction a man can have. Here agreement ends. Sadoleto's wisdom is firmly contemplative, a typical conception of *sapientia* as a knowledge of divine and immutable things; Inghirami's is secular, skeptical, naturalistic even, based on experience, self-interest, and public opinion, a utilitarian wisdom plunged in active civic life and designed to insure the acquisition of wealth, glory, and political authority.

Utilitarian wisdom alone, Inghirami maintains, is a true and solid wisdom. Philosophy arrogantly claims a monopoly for teaching wisdom, but its wisdom has no body or soul; it is merely a vain and empty image, a pale echo of the works and advantages of real wisdom. Real wisdom must be tangibly useful to living men and to oneself.[49] It is an active virtue dynamically centered in self-interest. Nothing is more absurd than to pretend that the wise man neglects the fine cultivation of his own interests. On the contrary, he refers all things to himself on a simple, egoistic priority, rightly feeling that no one can more worthily enjoy life's advantages and honors

---

[49] *De philosophia: Opera*, III, 137, col. 2–138, col. 1.

than he. He takes as his motto a phrase of Pacuvius: The wise man unable to benefit himself has no wisdom whatever.[50] To act wisely, therefore, is to act with prudence, courage, diligence, and honor to further fittingly and usefully one's own glory.[51]

The end of wisdom is glory and success, and its rule is the judgment of the masses. The definition of success is created by public opinion, and the wise man identifies his own aims and desires with those of his contemporaries. As he conforms to the common will and tastes of the multitude in his dress, diet, in the architecture of his house and in all the externals of his style of life, so also he conforms his public acts and his inner ends and ambitions to the same standard. Wisdom is the art of acquiring those things which are most esteemed and most sought after by the men with whom one spends one's life.[52] Its content is the sum of those goods most prized by the generality of men. It is the best part of widom to pursue, and the victorious competitive struggle to possess, certain honors whose brilliance, beauty, and dignity attract men's souls. "Such is the art, such is the science of living which I call wisdom; a kind of civil and popular philosophy inciting men to actions splendid and glorious in the sight of the multitude and making them great, powerful, noble and, in short, the first of all men."[53]

The goods which normally define success and form the content of wisdom are good health, glory, and *jocunditas*, the fulfilling enjoyment of what one desires most.[54] And what most men, and therefore the wise man too, desire most is riches, power, and *imperium*. With a high heart, a penetrating intelligence, and foresight, sagacious and active, the wise man benefits all men by his virtue and seeks for himself the greatest things: wealth, empire, power, and

[50] *Ibid.*, 149, col. 2. "... non enim obliviscitur sui sapientia, nec suorum penitus commodorum curam abiicit, sed refert ad se omnia sapiens, consulitque sibi potissimum, nec putat digniorem esse quemquam, qui commodis vitae honoribusque fruatur: habetque illud in ore, opinor, Pacuvii, Sapientem qui sibi prodesse nequeat, nequidquam sapere."

[51] *Ibid.*, 157, col. 2.

[52] *Ibid.*, 147, col. 1–col. 2.

[53] *Ibid.*, 149, col. 2.

[54] *Ibid.*, 147, col. 1.

glory.[55] All of these goods are enveloped in the supreme objective good of *auctoritas* and the supreme subjective good of *existimatio*. To command is to enjoy like a god the homage of the crowd and the grandeur of personal power. From such possession will flow ineluctably the satisfaction of every desire—wealth, pleasure, and each particular and coveted embellishment of leisure.[56]

Governance, therefore, and its complement of honors and power, is the end of wisdom. The wise man cuts deeply into life. He refuses isolated contemplation, the discovery of useless things, sophistical arguments and the empty play of words. He molds his life in the society and assemblies of men without dissipating his force and dignity in the solitude and inertia of philosophy.[57] The so-called seven wise men of ancient Greece were really fools. They spent their lives contemplating celestial things and investigating their secret causes. But this was a vain activity. The knowledge to be derived from physics or astronomy is radically uncertain; even if it were certain it is quite useless to men; and, finally, only men who are failures in active life devote themselves in any case to such ridiculous pursuits. Lycurgus, on the other hand, was a wise man because, during an active, useful life, he founded the legislative structure of Sparta, governed men, and taught them to support fatigue and danger, and in so doing won power and glory for himself. Similarly, Pericles was really wise because he governed the Republic and was for forty years the leading man in Greece; and Romulus, because he founded Rome and laid the basis of her future greatness, is justly said to be endowed "with a particular and almost divine wisdom." But Caesar is the finished model of the wise man. Adroit, brilliantly intelligent, full of prudent foresight, benefiting others by his talents but never neglecting the gratification of a personal and immense ambition, he personifies a wisdom whose end is the magnificence of empire.[58]

Wisdom is obviously not an intellectual virtue, nor any form of

---

[55] *Ibid.*, 149, col. 2. Cf. *Ibid.*, 165, col. 1.
[56] *Ibid.*, 172, col. 1–col. 2.
[57] *Ibid.*, 137, col. 2.
[58] *Ibid.*, 138, col. 2; 149, col. 1–col. 2; 151, col. 1–col. 2.

speculative or contemplative knowledge. It is an art and method of worldly success, the art of acquiring *auctoritas* and its attendant benefits. A desire for it is naturally innate in every man.[59] There is no one who does not wish to be wise, who does not consider it the divinest of things. Popular opinion is its source and popular opinion determines its end in accordance with the success images of each age and moment. As a method of success it is essentially dynamic, a watchful calculation and adaptability to changing circumstance. For the precepts of wisdom are not eternal, but change with time and fortune, "whose privilege it is to dominate the affairs of men." Times change, popular opinion changes. New styles appear and men want new things. Wisdom changes concomitantly. It is buried in time. The first duty of the wise man is to know the time and moment, to change with it, to conform his opinion and action to what this new time demands. Wisdom has a glorious and difficult role: to readapt its forms in order to profit from every event and change.[60] The philosopher, perhaps, stoically maintains a fixed line of conduct and opinion. The wise man never does.

Philosophy, in fact, has nothing whatever in common with wisdom. Its squalid pursuit corrupts the naturally upright soul and turns it away from matters of real seriousness.[61] Philosophy promises wisdom, but falsely; for none of its three branches—physics, ethics, or logic—contains any real and solid wisdom. Examine ethics, says Phaedrus. No one will discover the natural virtues or be incited to them by reading philosophy. The philosophical definition of courage, for example, does not incite a man to do a brave deed; rather heroic action springs, not from philosophy, but from an innate greatness of soul and a natural constancy.[62] Justice, like wisdom, has no natural permanence of definition. To find it one must not read

[59] *Ibid.*, 139, col. 2.

[60] *Ibid.*, 148, col. 1. "... sic sapientiae consilia non perpetuo una sunt, sed ad tempus se accommodant, et ad fortunam, cujus praecipuum est, in humanis rebus posse dominari."

[61] *Ibid.*, 135, col. 1.

[62] *Ibid.*, 159, col. 1.

philosophy but study the laws of one's own country and the customs of one's ancestors.[63] Virtue itself is a natural *habitus*, a strength and vigor for the life of action; and its objects are identical with those of wisdom: empire, power, glory, and wealth.[64]

Inghirami has concluded that the old "philosophical" and intellectual wisdom is incompatible with a new society's legitimate demands and patterns of success. He resolves this incompatibility—very differently from Bruni—by redefining wisdom as the precise method of attaining such success and becoming a rich, powerful, and famous man. Such wisdom remains inseparable from virtue; but Phaedrus redefines virtue itself—further evidence of the changing meaning of the word *virtù*—as the pursuit of wealth and power.

This is a radical and important reassessment, but as atypical of normal Renaissance conceptions as the audacities of the second book of Valla's *De Voluptate* (with which it has a good deal in common) or of Machiavelli's *Prince*. Inghirami's notion of wisdom was no doubt common in practice; and it is, as such, a vivid insight into realities often masked by idealistic platitudes. But it was never a respectable theory in its original form. Leonardo da Vinci's refutation is characteristic of contemporary opinion. "I know," he says, "that many men will say that [the older wisdom] is useless. They are like the men of whom Demetrius said that he did not prize the wind which produced the words in their mouths more highly than the wind which issued from their lower parts; men who desire only corporeal riches and pleasure and entirely lack any desire for true wisdom, which is the food and only secure wealth of the soul. Because they prize the soul no more than the body, they prize the riches of the soul no more than those of the body. And often when I see one of them take up a work of real wisdom, I expect him to

---

[63] *Ibid.*, 163, col. 2. "... nihil habet [justitia] omnino cum natura commercii, sed opinionibus totum et consensione plurium in unum coetum coeuntium conficitur."

[64] *Ibid.*, 165, col. 2. Virtue is a "vis et efficientia quaedam in animo cujusque, qui quidem ad res gerendas natus, vigorque et diligentia naturalis." Cf. *Ibid.*, 166. col. 2.

stick it to his nose like a monkey or ask me if it is something to eat." [65]

IV

Sadoleto's rebuttal is less picturesque. He bases his first traditional distinctions between *sapientia, scientia,* and *prudentia* on Aristotle's physical duality of a human, sublunar world, the realm of generation, flux, and mutability, and a divine heaven, the realm of immutability and changeless perfection. *Sapientia* is a contemplation of divine and immutable things. [66] Its object, and Sadoleto emphasizes this with esoteric complacence, is high among the most elevated things, far above a possible contamination by any vulgar comprehension. The Greeks called wise only those chosen few who devoted themselves solely to intellectual pursuits and tried to discover things "hidden in nature." [67] Such men frequently lacked prudence. But they were wise because they contemplated the stars and every immutable, sublime, and admirable thing.

Prudence and *scientia,* on the other hand, deal with the mutable human things of the sublunar world. The role of *scientia* is to know them; that of *prudentia* to govern them. Prudence is the active, managerial virtue, characteristic of men who distinguish themselves in public life. It is reason governing and ruling human things, things mobile and variable which have no necessary or certain innate cause and the knowledge of which is opinion rather than truth. The seven wise men, contemplators of celestial things, were truly called

[65] *Proemi,* 5: *Tutti Gli Scritti. Scritti Letterari,* Augusto Marinoni, ed. (Milan, 1952), 146.

[66] *De philosophia,* 202, col. 1–col. 2. "Alteram vero partem divinarum rerum immutabilium, quarum perpetuus semper et eniusmodi esset status, sapientiae voluerunt esse subjectam, ut in iis cernendis contemplandisque dumtaxat, nullo alio munere, districta sapientia teneretur."

[67] *Ibid.,* 203, col. 2. "Sapientiam vero, cujus est nomen positum in altissimis rebus, quarum rerum cognitio a vulgo est longe semota, cujusmodi caeli illa, et caelestium rerum indagatio est, illis attribuerunt, qui in sola mentis atque animi exercitatione versati, res in natura abditas, ad quas populus ne aspirat quidem, investigare sunt conati."

wise, but Pericles, as Aristotle said in the *Ethics*, is the model of the prudent man.[68]

Scientia, which like prudence has its origin in *sapientia*, is the knowledge of the same opaque, human things which prudence rules. There are two kinds of knowledge: a knowledge of the fixed and constant, which is knowledge of the truth; and knowledge of the mutable, which is opinion. The one is partial and particular; the other certain and universal. *Scientia*, that knowledge given by the individual arts and sciences, is such particular knowledge of the accidents of individual things subject to change and generation. It knows the mobile particular; *sapientia* knows the motionless universal.[69]

Sapientia, *scientia*, and *prudentia* thus define the content of the three great divisions of philosophy: metaphysics, natural and moral philosophy. Insofar as philosophy takes as its object "things which are sublime and constant in their eternal immutability," it is rightly called wisdom because it is the source of prudence and every science. When, on the contrary, it turns toward things subject to change and generation, it is called natural science, or what the Greeks called physics. And when it begins to direct human actions, to rule and instruct men, it is called prudence.[70] The three terms correspond to what the humanists liked to called *philosophia triformis*: *sapientia*, metaphysics, the knowledge of divine things; *scientia*, or physics, a knowledge of the individual human things below the moon; and *prudentia*, or moral philosophy, the guide and governor of human conduct.

[68] *Ibid.*, 202, col. 1–203, col. 1. Cf. *Ibid.*, 234, col. 1–col. 2 and Cicero, *Tusc. Disp.*, V, iv, 10–11.

[69] *De philosophia*, 222, col. 2–223, col. 1.

[70] *Ibid.*, 232, col. 2. "Quae quatenus in summis et sempiterna immutabilitate constantibus versatur rebus, jure ac merito dicta est sapientia: fontes enim in illis sunt et scientiae omnis, et prudentiae. Qua vero ad mutantia genitabiliaque confertur, scientia naturalis, eadem Graece Physice est appellata. Moralis autem, quum humanis dirigendis actionibus adhibetur. Qua trimembri divisione in Philosophia exposita atque monstrata, praeclare illa definitur rerum esse scientia, et divinarum simul, et humanarum."

The natural man can acquire a knowledge of divine things by his own, unaided efforts. By nature he desires wisdom; by nature he burns for the good.[71] Furthermore, the idea and content of that sapiential good is naturally known to him. The ideas of what the wise man is and of what wisdom itself is are innate, engraved by nature in the human soul.[72] Natural man, therefore, has both a precise knowledge of his highest intellectual good and a desire to possess it. He also has, again naturally, the instrument and power necessary to possess it: a powerful natural reason. Man knows that wisdom is a knowledge of divine things, he desires this knowledge, and by the power of his unaided reason he is sure to acquire it.[73]

It is the natural end of man's reason to know the same "divine things" which define the content of wisdom. The human soul, reflecting in this the three types of living beings in the world— plants, animals, and men—is tripartite: vegetative, sensitive, and rational. The vegetative soul, the body's form, nourishes man and controls his physical growth; the sensitive soul, like the soul of animals, abstracts sense images and stores them in the memory and has a certain power of judgment; the reason, which defines man and makes him what he is, carefully examines sense experience, but then gradually elevates itself above all sensible things to a contemplation of what is necessarily immortal and divine.[74] Since men have three faculties of the soul, three different manners of being, there are three corresponding goods proper to each faculty. The end and good of the vegetative soul is utilitarian—life and good health; that of the sensitive soul is *voluptas* or pleasure; and that of the "heavenly and divine reason" is knowledge and truth.[75]

---

[71] *Ibid.*, 137, col. 1. "Quod enim sapientia nec in caelo, nec in terra quidquam est praestantius, idcirco ipso nomine commoti, accenduntur ad cupiditatem aliquam cognoscendi"; *Ibid.*, 208, col. 2. "Incredibile autem est, quantopere nos et amore boni natura ardeamus et aspectu delectemur."

[72] *Ibid.*, 199, col. 2. "... illa sapientiae notitia ... quam in animis nostris natura ipsa descripsit"; *Ibid.*, 190, col. 1. "... notionem sapientis, quam in animis nostris natura inseruit."

[73] Cf. Toffanin, *Elogio della Sapienza*, xxviii.

[74] *De philosophia*, 212, col. 2–213, col. 1.

[75] *Ibid.*, 216, col. 2–217, col. 1. Cf. *Ibid.*, 221, col. 2.

Truth must be sought where it in fact shines brightest: in divine and eternal things.[76] Reason should take for its object only the perpetual and immortal because, even if there exists some image of immortality in things which are born and die, still it is toward the more excellent, constant part of nature, that glistening realm above the moon, that it should turn to search for truth. It is reason's function, when it is considered in itself, to contemplate what is always the same; to know things which are true, stable, and constant, divine qualities never found in fleeting and mortal things.[77] Since, therefore, both the content of wisdom and human reason's natural end and good are alike defined as a knowledge of divine things, they are the same. Wisdom is reason's end and final cause.

Wisdom and rational exercise merge in a knowledge of the truth; and truth is a knowledge of the one Good and all the goods which flow from it, a knowledge, that is, of God and the ideas of created things.[78] God is truth (although He cannot, of course, be limited by any human conception of truth or knowledge); and He is the cause of truth in every created thing. A knowledge of the divine essence, therefore, because without it man can have no knowledge of truth, order, or beauty, is the summit and condition of wisdom. Happily this knowledge is not difficult to acquire: and we should be grateful to God that our reason can "so easily" embrace what we so ardently desire and what is so fundamentally necessary to us.[79] There is a sublime and easy passage from an admiration of the movement, form, and beauty of the celestial bodies, from an astonished knowledge of their perpetual order and regularity, to a presumption that the world "has a supreme author and master by whose commandment and will all things were moved and ordered." Not content merely to suspect this, the earliest philosophers solidified and

---

[76] *Ibid.*, 213, col. 1–col. 2.

[77] *Ibid.*, 214, col. 1. Cf. *Ibid.*, 225, col. 2. "Quum igitur peculiare officium rationis sit, indagare veritatem, in divinis autem et sempiternis maxime exsistat veritas, divinorum indagatio in primis rationi est proposita."

[78] *Ibid.*, 223, col. 1.

[79] *Ibid.*, 227, col. 2; 229, col. 2.

4+

clarified their insight by abstract speculation. Leaving sense experience and the flux of human things, they began to consider movement in itself, time in itself, infinity, and the diversity of forms and natures which structure the created world. From an investigation of movement and causal sequences, knowing that all things have a cause and that all movement seeks what it does not have in itself and desires to attain it, they understood that the author and master of the universe was necessarily one, eternal, all powerful, and immutable.[80]

This easily and naturally acquired knowledge of God conditions man's ascent to lesser truths, to divine things below the absolute divinity of God. Whatever truths, whatever intelligibility—the capacity of being adequately known—shines in human things, comes from Him. The divine essence is the source of both the being of a thing and of its intelligible essence or nature, which is its truth.[81] Similarly, God is the cause of truth in the human soul because he has formed and illuminated it with the intelligible light of natural reason. Truth flows out from the divine essence as a kind of formal and intelligible light. In man this formal light is the soul, the body's form, and reason, the soul's highest faculty.[82] In external objects it is the essence or form of each object. The divine essence, because it has created both the intelligibility of things and the capacity of the human mind to grasp that intelligibility, guarantees the adequate correspondence of mental image and external form which is truth.[83] In this sense, truth in man and in the things he knows is a variety of divine illumination. But, because intelligibility in man is identified with his natural reason and intelligibility in things with their

[80] *Ibid.*, 227, col. 1–col. 2. Cf. *De liberis recte instituendis: Opera*, III, 120, col. 1–col. 2.

[81] *De philosophia*, 229, col. 2–230, col. 1.

[82] *Ibid.*, 229, col. 2. God is the cause of truth "nostra autem in anima, quatenus eam lumine illo intelligibili, et ex sese, et ex rerum essentiis ab eodem ipso manantibus, informat, atque illustrat . . ."; *De liberis recte instituendis*, 96, col. 2. ". . . hoc lumen [veritas], quod est sua cuique ratio, certissimis scientiis ac doctrinis illuminata, et sibi ipsa in omni consilio actioneque praegrediens, neque alieno indigens ductu philosophia ipsa continet."

[83] *Ibid.*, 224, col. 2. Cf. *Ibid.*, 223, col. 2.

forms, it remains an illumination in the area of nature, and not in that of grace. It defines the natural man and assures his capacity for truth; it is not designed to repair his incapacity.

To illustrate this point Sadoleto uses the same Platonic comparison Ficino had used to illustrate its opposite. As the sun illuminates external objects and enables the eye to see them, so does the divine essence, by endowing them with form, illuminate internally these same objects and enable human reason to know them. When it is dark the eye cannot see. Similarly, the *ratio* can find no truth in the opaque mutability of human things, but only in the divine essence itself and in things, or that part of things, brightened to intelligibility by the formal light of the divine essence: intelligible forms where truth and beauty shine.[84] Truth is thus both a physical condition and a mental image. In man it is reason, a divine light implanted in the human soul at the moment of creation. In things, it is the nature or form of each thing. Truth, finally, is the knowledge our reason has of intelligibles, a perfect fusion, guaranteed by their mutual and similar relation to the divine essence, of the intelligible light of reason and the intelligibility of things.[85]

Clearly, the power of reason is such that, unaided, it can adequately reach its sapiental end, grasping thus its highest and particular good. Sadoleto indulges in no Cusan or Ficinian separation of *ratio* and *intellectus* and its corollary debasement of reason.

---

[84] *Ibid.*, 228, col. 1–229, col. 1.

[85] The contrasting positions of Sadoleto and Ficino on this point are exactly paralleled by an objection and reply in the *Summa Theologiae* of Aquinas. Ia, IIae, Q. 109, art. 1, obj. 2, after quoting the same comparison from Augustine, *Solil.*, I, 6, goes on: "Now the bodily senses, however pure, cannot see any visible thing without the sun's light. Therefore the human mind, however perfect, cannot, by reasoning, know any truth without divine light; and this pertains to the aid of grace." Aquinas replies: "The material sun sheds its light outside us, but the intelligible Sun, Who is God, shines within us. Hence the natural light bestowed upon the soul is God's illumination, whereby we are illumined to see what pertains to natural knowledge; and for this there is required no further illumination, but only for such things as surpass natural knowledge."

His work is a tribute to the natural man and the reason which defines him. Reason is a divine and admirable gift.[86] It is clear-sighted; and, because it participates in the clarity of light, it sees all things clearly and completely.[87] Led by it, man seeks those things which are the chief goods of the gods themselves: a knowledge of divine things, glory, and dignity—a human expansion which in a way transforms him from a man into a god.[88] Reason, indeed, is universally competent. Sadoleto finds its potency symbolized by Hippias, who proclaimed to all Greece assembled at the Olympic games that he had mastered universal knowledge, every science, and every liberal art, and that he had made the ring on his finger and his own shoes and cloak. By this he proved that no art can escape the intelligence and penetration of the human mind.[89]

Nothing proves more persuasively the ability of natural reason to achieve wisdom by its own efforts than the sapiential triumphs of the antique philosophers. Although they lived before the time of Christ (and Sadoleto nowhere suggests that the ancients were divinely illumined), they reached the *summam vim et gloriam perfectae sapientiae*.[90] Socrates, Anaxagoras, Empedocles, Democritus, Pythagoras, Varro, Nigidius, Plato, Aristotle, Theophrastus, and Cicero were in every respect complete and perfect men. Nothing concerning the nature of things or the knowledge of any art or science escaped them.[91] Cicero especially, although Sadoleto piously regrets that he died before he could hear the good news of Christ, crowned his prudence and eloquence with perfect wisdom.[92] Few men, of course, can attain the perfect and "absolute"—the word is Sadoleto's—wisdom achieved by the ancients. But some men demonstrably have —and by their own efforts and a proper use of their natural reasons. Wisdom is the good and end of the *ratio*: and it is the *ratio* which

[86] *De philosophia*, 206, col. 2.
[87] *De lib. rec. instit.*, 73, col. 1–col. 2.
[88] *De philosophia*, 207, col. 1.
[89] *De lib. rec. instit.*, 121, col. 2.
[90] *Ibid.*
[91] *De philosophia*, 185, col. 1. Cf. *De lib. rec. instit.*, 121, col. 2–122, col. 1.
[92] *De lib. rec. instit.*, 108, col. 1.

grasps it.[93] Human reason is fully competent to know a wisdom which is its own end and good.

Sadoleto concludes that wisdom is, first, natural knowledge of the divine things of metaphysics, forms, species, and the *naturae rerum omnium*; and, second, knowledge of God. In Him the seeker of wisdom reaches the divine itself and the truth itself. A knowledge of God is the perfection of wisdom in another sense. A man already wise in the knowledge of divine things seeks always to perfect his wisdom by a knowledge of their causes. He finds this cause in God, the efficient and final cause of all things. To define wisdom, therefore, as a knowledge of God and intelligible forms is to say that *sapientia* is the knowledge of divine things and their causes.

v

Sadoleto broke with the tradition of Florentine Neo-Platonism by emphasizing that wisdom is a human virtue naturally acquired. This is an important change. Its significance is reinforced by the identical conclusion of another "Platonic" discussion of wisdom exactly contemporary with Sadoleto's: Sir Thomas Elyot's *Of The knowledg which maketh a wise man. A disputacion Platonike* (1533).[94]

Wisdom, for Elyot, is knowledge of invisible, intelligible, and divine things. Elyot speaks of them variously: as species and forms; as numbers; as rules or principles; as divine Ideas which are

[93] *De philosophia*, 207, col. 1.

[94] Standard on Elyot's life and works is Henry Herbert Stephen Croft's introduction to his edition of *The Boke named the Governour* (London, 1880). For later literature see the *Cambridge Bibliography of English Literature*. The dialogue has been edited by Kurt Schroeder as an appendix to his *Platonismus in der Englischen Renaissance vor und bei Thomas Eliot, Palaestra*, LXXXIII (Berlin, 1920). My references are to this edition. Elyot's only other work, aside from the *Governour*, to deal with the idea of wisdom is the *Bankette of Sapience* (London, Thomas Berthelet, 1534). It is a collection of moral sentences from the Fathers, Scripture, and the ancient philosophers. The section entitled "Sapience" (fol. 41r–v), for example, is made up of quotations from Euripides, Cicero, Seneca, and the wisdom books of the Old Testament.

exemplary causes of all human things. He describes them as immutable, steadfast, fixed, or eternal. He opposes them to the corporeal and sensible. It is, he emphasizes, the pressing function of the understanding to escape from the control of body and senses and to pierce through the flux of sense experience to the immutable and intelligible forms behind contingent objects, to things which bear in themselves their own causes, necessity, and divinity. This is the knowledge that makes a wise man.

Such knowledge is acquired by natural reason. It "belongethe to understandynge," that is to say, the way to know intelligible things "is called raison, and the knowlage therof is named understanding."[95] The understanding is the third principal part of the soul. Far above the vegetative and sensitive parts, it is the soul's intellectual part, "whiche is of all the other mooste noble, as whereby man is mooste lyke unto god, and is preferred before all other creatures."[96] Its naturally given end is sapiential knowledge: intelligibles and "the begynnynge or originall causes of thynges";[97] and it has an autonomous power sufficient to attain this end. Rudiments of wisdom are innate in the soul; they are activated and perfected by the soul's understanding of itself and of numbers. A capacity for wisdom defines the natural man; and its fulfillment is his perfection and end, a perfection attainable by reason without the aid of grace. Wisdom, in short, is a knowledge soon and easily learned: "In good faythe sooner thanne Primero or Greeke: Suche is the straunge propertie of that excellent cunnynge, that it is sooner lerned, than taught, and better by a mannes rayson than by an instructour."[98] Elyot rejects any excessively Revelational doctrine which makes im-

---

[95] Schroeder, 49*, 38*.

[96] *Governour*, II, 371.

[97] *Governour*, II, 374–375. "It [the *intellectus*] is the principall parte of the soule whiche is occupied about the begynnynge or originall causes of thynges that may falle in to mannes knowlege, and his office is, before that any thynge is attempted, to thinke, consydre, and prepence, and, after often tossyng it up and downe in the mynde, than to exercise that powar, the propertie whereof is to espie, seke for, enserche, and finde out."

[98] Schroeder, 7*. Cf. Fritz Caspari, *Humanism and the Social Order in Tudor England* (University of Chicago Press, 1954), 95–96.

possible a passage from sensible to intelligible without the aid of grace. The ascent to the invisible is guaranteed by, and made the perfection of, a potent natural reason.

But this ascent is not unconditional. Understanding, which is the natural knowledge of intelligibles and the content of wisdom, is not perpetual and in all ways immutable in the human soul as it is in God; "but durynge the tyme that hit is conserved by contemplacyon of the divine maiestie, hit is perfecte and make the mannes soule lyke unto god. And whanne hit is ioygned unto corporaile affectes, hit is made thanne unperfecte, and the fourme of the soule, is in a parte decayed frome the ryght symilytude of god. But if the soule beinge dedycate to vices, be ones fallen frome the possession of rayson, thanne understandynge is vanysshed awaye, and the soule remaynethe with the bodye transfourmed, as we spake of before."[99] In the state of innocence the soul had entire dominion over the body, and man was fully a man. Now, however, it often happens that the body's appetites and desires overpower the reason and suppress the natural virtues and affections of the soul. Man is then little better than a beast, and understanding vanishes in a swamp of sensuality.[100] The condition of understanding, and of wisdom, therefore, is the cardinal rule of Stoic ethics: the soul's preëminence over the passions, reason's holding the senses of the body "under due rule and obedience."[101]

Reason enforces its dominion over the senses and is capable of wisdom as long as it is conserved by contemplating the divine majesty. The contemplation of God is both the means for securing that dominion and the final perfection of wisdom. "To knowe the good lorde is perfecte Justice, And to knowe thy Justyce and vertue is the very roote of Immortalitie: And therein is the knowlege, that

---

[99] *Ibid.*, 47*.

[100] *Ibid.*, 30*. Cf. *Ibid.*, 92*. If the senses are allowed "to delyte in thynges whiche be corruptible, they wyll than conspire and rebelle agayne understandynge, and drive him from the soule, and than shulde man be transformed frome the image of god untyl a brute beest, beinge governed and ruled onely by sensis."

[101] *Ibid.*, 31*. Cf. *Ibid.*, 92*.

is very wysedome."[102] Wisdom culminates in a knowledge of God, the supreme Intelligibility, the source of all intelligible, invisible things. To contemplate His majesty is to contemplate His goodness and providence. Such contemplation is a form of knowledge, and like the soul's self-knowledge and the reason's knowledge of numbers and lesser intelligibles, it is purely natural. It too "belongethe to understandynge,"[103] and is open to the natural reason. The perfection of wisdom is a natural theology.

This final wisdom is based on a knowledge of God's existence, which is self-evident "sens that the order of al thyng that is visible, declareth that there must nedes be one principall cause and beginnynge, whiche we call god. And also that order can not be withoute providence and one perpetuall governance."[104] When he beholds the goodness of God, man recognizes that it is the source of virtue; when he considers His providence he realizes that nothing is made without cause, but that "all thynges be made for a pourpose, profitable, and also necessary, and so the respecte therof al thynges be good."[105] These insights are first principles of wisdom. As corollaries one learns that virtue is good because its source is goodness, that vice is bad because it opposes the good, and that the universe is axed on an order which "like a streyghte lyne issueth oute of provydence, and passethe directely throughe all thynges that be created. And therin be degrees, wherin those thynges beinge sette, one hathe preemynence over a nother in goodnes."[106] Man himself—a final corollary—is preëminent over all other things in the world.

Wisdom for Elyot is a naturally acquired intellectual virtue: reason's knowledge of divine things—the soul and the formal seeds innate in it, forms and numbers, God. A capacity for wisdom distinguishes man from the brute beast, but he is only fully a man when the soul controls all the bestial qualities of his nature. The wise man was always one "in whom the soule had intiere and ful

[102] *Ibid.*, 7*. Cf. *Sap.* 15:3. "Nosse enim te, consummata justitia est: et scire justitiam, et virtutem tuam, radix est immortalitatis."

[103] *Ibid.*, 49*.   [104] *Ibid.*, 42*.
[105] *Ibid.*, 48*.   [106] *Ibid.*, 49*.

auctorite over the sensis, and alway kept the affectis in due rule and obedience, followyng only the counsayle of Understanding, and by that governaunce was moste like unto god."[107] A natural knowledge of the goodness and justice of God reveals to him the source and sanction of the human virtues which are their mundane participations. The natural knowledge of His majesty and providence yields the vision of a line of Order in which man has the "highe place" of one created in the divine image.[108] Wisdom, therefore, is a natural knowledge of divine and immutable things, from the intelligibles of metaphysics to the "things invisible" of natural theology. It is potential in the soul's knowledge of the ideas innate in it; partially perfected in the knowledge, symbolized by mathematics, of universal forms; and in act, and fully perfected, in the contemplation of the divine majesty.

VI

"Wisdom," wrote Josse Clichtove, a pupil of Jacques Lefèvre d'Etaples, "is the knowledge of divine things. If it ascends from the human disciplines to celestial things, it is metaphysics; but if it descends from the most holy and divinely revealed Scriptures, it is theology."[109] Lefèvre d'Etaples himself amplifies Clichtove's definition of wisdom as metaphysical knowledge. It is, he says, a knowledge of first principles and first causes and of the highest and most honorable essences in nature. "The wise man is a metaphysician, an elect, supreme, divine and supramundane philosopher."[110]

[107] *Ibid.*, 95*.
[108] *Ibid.*, 96*.

[109] Josse Clichtove, *In artium divisionem* (Paris, Henricus Stephanus, 1505), C, i. r. Cf. *Ibid.*, B, vii, r. "Metaphysica est ars supernaturalis quod ex inferiorum scientiarum adminiculis ad celestium contemplationem subvehit. Theologia vero: que sublimiore modo ex sacris eloquiis ad divinorum cognitionem assurgit."

[110] Lefèvre d'Etaples, *Introductio in metaphysicorum libros Aristotelis* (Paris, 1493), a, IV, v. "Sapientia est que maxime scibilia primas causas et prima principia contemplatur. Prime cause et prima principia: supreme illa entia et honorabilissima in natura. Sapientia metaphysica. Sapiens est qui hanc possidet sapientiam. Sapiens metaphysicus, primus, supremus, divinus supramundanusque philosophus."

4*

Substantially this is the Thomist view. When, therefore, Elyot and Sadoleto define wisdom as naturally acquired knowledge of divine things and their causes, they are restating an identification of *sapientia* and metaphysics which can be found without interruption from Aquinas to Charron. They are aware, too, that wisdom was often defined as revealed theological knowledge, and that its origin is God. Elyot says that one should pray to Him as follows: "Gyue to me, good lorde, sapience that sytteth by thy throne."[111] Sadoleto, in his *Commentary on Paul's Epistle to the Romans*, says that Scripture is the sole source of true wisdom. Only God can raise up the simple, humble, and pure in heart to the secrets of his own wisdom. Compared to this, all human wisdom is empty and vain.[112]

Yet Elyot and Sadoleto have not really restated the Thomist position. Aquinas, and following him Lefèvre d'Etaples and Clichtove, gives impartial attention to a naturally known metaphysical wisdom and a divinely revealed theological wisdom. When it is derived by an upward progress from sense experience, wisdom is called metaphysics and lies within the sphere of natural reason. When it proceeds downward from the principles of Revelation, it is called theology and lies in the area of faith and illumination. Wisdom is thus two essential and complementary aspects of one and the same

[111] *Governour*, II, 359. Cf. *Sap.* 9:4. "Da mihi sedium tuarum assistricem sapientiam, et noli me reprobare a pueris tuis."

[112] Sadoleto, *In Epist. Pauli ad Rom.: Opera*, IV, 3, col. 1. Cf. *Ibid.*, 2, col. 2. "Nostra vero haec, quae sola veram in se continet sapientiae facultatem, sacrarum rerum, litterarumque cognitio, tametsi ea summis, atque altissimis divinorum consiliorum mysteriis referta est, nullis tamen ingeniis, nisi credulis, atque simplicibus percipiendam se praebet, genereque novo instituendi, et docendi prius persuasos vult esse sectatores sui, quam aliquid illis ipsa persuadeat, prius ut credant, quam doceantur: prius ut ament, quam noverint plane, quid illud sit, quod ante omnia illis est amandum." Cf. also *Ibid.*, 135, col. 2–136, col. 1. "Namque et ego fidei vim tacitus mecum contemplans, plus etiam sapientiae in ea quam credulitatis, videor agnoscere, quamquam inest quidem utrumque, sed istud magis. Nam et confidere Deo, magis quam mundo, verioris sapientiae est et sempiterna appetere, potiusquam mortalia, animi multo praestantioris." For the closely related problem of the relation of faith and reason see the texts assembled and discussed by S. Ritter, *Un Umanista teologo*, 34 ff.

thing: a knowledge of divine things. This balance is abandoned by Elyot and Sadoleto in favor of natural reason, as Nicholas of Cusa had abandoned it in favor of Revelation and the Florentine Neo-Platonists in favor of a mystical intuition of the divine. They all tend to regard the Thomist equilibrium, not as a coherent whole, but as a choice between two different possibilities, natural or revealed wisdom. Cusanus restricted wisdom to a revealed knowledge of the divine; Elyot and Sadoleto choose to restrict it to a natural knowledge of the divine.

This restriction is purely *de facto*. Neither Sadoleto nor Elyot ever explicitly rejects the theological term of the Thomist equation. Occasionally they do mention it; but where Nicholas of Cusa wrote of nothing else, they note it casually, in other contexts and in works not devoted to a coherent investigation of the meaning of wisdom. The *Disputacion Platonike* and the *De laudibus philosophiae* have no mention of the theological definition. Change is indicated, not by polemic, but by the simple fact that Cusanus devoted an entire book to a definition of wisdom which Sadoleto and Elyot discuss in a paragraph; and, conversely, that Elyot and Sadoleto write books in praise of a wisdom which Cusanus—Luther will do the same— abruptly dismissed as false.

It is just this emphasis on wisdom as metaphysical knowledge naturally acquired, on the one hand, and the *de facto* absence of wisdom as revealed theological knowledge, on the other, which indicates a certain secularization of the idea of wisdom. Wisdom remains—what it had been for so many of the ancients—a knowledge of divine things only, things which, as Charron was ironically to remark, "have never yet been seen," so perfect that human nature is incapable of them except in his imagination. It remains a contemplative rather than an active virtue. Sadoleto denies each of Inghirami's activist, utilitarian affirmations: the wise man is above the crowd and cares nothing for public opinion; his aim is truth, not political or financial success; he is motivated not by self-interest but by ideas of disinterested scholarship, educational service, and contemplation; he does not question that truth can be found; and the wisdom he seeks is both eternal, above time and fortune, and intellectual rather than prudential. For all this, however, it is not a perfection whose possession is contingent on divine illumination. The wisdom of Sadoleto and Elyot is the culminating virtue of the natural man. This is a "Platonism" still far from Plato; but its rational emphasis is rather closer to the assumptions of classical Greek thought than the Neo-Platonism of Ficino.

Chapter 4

The Wisdom of Prometheus

Renaissance intellectuals were catholic in their efforts to recapture the several varieties of ancient wisdom. "Platonists" like Cardinal Sadoleto and Sir Thomas Elyot reproduced approximations of Plato's idea of wisdom. Following the scholastics, Bruni, Pontano, and Pomponazzi repeated Aristotle's definition. Other humanists— also returning to what they called *prisca sapientia*—revived a third variety of ancient wisdom: that encyclopedic wisdom invented by the Stoics and described by Cicero as the knowledge of all things divine and human and their causes.

Sapientia est rerum divinarum et humanarum scientia. The sentence can be found in Salutati and Bruni, in Reuchlin's *Breviloquus vocabularius* and in Elyot's *Governour,* in Erasmus, Cardanus, Pontus de Tyard, and Bodin, in every country of Europe and in virtually any year between the end of the fourteenth century and 1600. The definition was clearly a popular one.

This popularity contrasts remarkably with the neglect of the Stoic definition in the Middle Ages. Medieval thinkers took their cue here from Augustine, who had made it plain in the *Contra Academicos* that human things were not among the proper objects of wisdom. He quoted the Stoic definition; but he parried the difficulties its acceptance would inevitably have raised by distinguishing between *scientia,* the knowledge of things human, and *sapientia,* the knowledge of things divine. For the notion that knowledge of the human had a properly sapiential character was not obviously in harmony with the conviction that the Second Person of the Trinity, knowledge of whom came exclusively from Revelation, was the fundamental object of wisdom. Nor was it likely to appeal to his successors or to an age which tended to insist on the fragility, transitoriness, and corruption of the human. It is the more striking, therefore, to see fifteenth- and sixteenth-century humanists go behind Augustine to the Stoic definition he had split and restore its human term. This is a humanistic conclusion in precisely definable ways: first, as a reintegration of an antique definition and its antique meaning; second, as a literal humanization of the object of wisdom, one connected, no doubt, with that somewhat more secular view of human life and human nature suggested by the notion of the dignity of man.

Characteristically, Renaissance humanists found in Prometheus the adequate symbol of this all-embracing wisdom and of the adventurous effort to possess it. "We should actively rejoice," wrote the French humanist Robert Gaguin in 1496, "at the felicity of this age in which, although many other things have perished, many men of genius are nevertheless incited, like Prometheus, to seize the splendid torch of wisdom from the heavens."[1] Guillaume Budé has developed the Promethean image further. Prometheus, he says, represents the human mind "cultivated by the study of an encyclopedic philosophy" and adorned once more with what he calls *prisca sapientia*. "I think that Prometheus is the philosophic intellect which, having successfully mastered natural science, astronomy, and the other parts of philosophy, rises confidently, helped by human conjecture, to an intelligence of divine things. He represents what man is: he frees man, that is, for a full use of the natural reason proper to him so that he may prudently know all things divine and human."[2]

Two examples—Conrad Celtis and Carolus Bovillus, early sixteenth-century contemporaries, one French, the other German—will make clear the character of this Promethean wisdom.

---

[1] *Epistole et Orationes*, Louis Thuasne, ed. (Paris, 1904), II, 26.

[2] *De Stvdio literarvm recte et commode institvendo* (Paris, Badius Ascensius, 1532), XX, v; XVII, v. Cf. *Ibid.*, XV, r–v. "Nam qui rerum humanarum diuinarumque scientia, dicendi facultate coniuncta, praediti sunt, sic praestare videntur ipsi inter mortales, vt aurum inter metalla praestat." For additional details on the myth of Prometheus in Renaissance philosophy see Ernst Cassirer, *Individuum und Kosmos in der Philosophie der Renaissance* (Leipzig, 1927), 101–102.

I

Just as Erasmus revived a primitive philosophy of Christ, or Botticelli recreated the *Calumny* of Apelles, and Machiavelli read Livy
for lessons to profit his own age, so the turbulent and amorous
Conrad Celtis[3] urged the return to a *prisca et vera philosophia* and
a *prisca sapientia* which he defined as the knowledge of all things
divine and human and their causes.[4] The Ciceronian definition of
wisdom was common coin in Celtis' circle. Hartmann Schedel, for
example, the Nürnberg humanist and Celtis' friend, has left a
description of frescoes in the library of the Premonstratensian
monastery in Brandenburg in which Cicero is pictured over the following inscription: "Philosophy investigates the reasons of all things
divine and human."[5] Celtis himself echoes the words of the *De
Officiis*, investing them with much of their old ethical and scientific
significance.[6] Once more *sapientia* includes a "love of astronomical
and physical investigations" paralleling Cicero's praise of those

[3] Despite a rich subsequent literature, Friedrich von Bezold, "Konrad
Celtis, 'der deutsche Erzhumanist,' " *Aus Mittelalter und Renaissance* (Munich
and Berlin, 1918), 82–152 (first published in 1883) remains the best single
study. See also two books by Gustav Bauch, *Die Anfänge des Humanismus in
Ingolstadt* (Munich and Leipzig, 1901) and *Die Reception des Humanismus
in Wien* (Breslau, 1903). A useful book with a good bibliography is Leonard
Forster, *Selections from Conrad Celtis, 1459–1508* (Cambridge University
Press, 1948). The most recent and best treatment of Celtis' philosophy is
Lewis W. Spitz, "The Philosophy of Conrad Celtis, German Arch-Humanist,"
Studies in the Renaissance, I (1954), 22–37.

[4] Hans Rupprich, *Der Briefwechsel des Konrad Celtis* (Munich, 1934), ep.
179, lines 70–71, 137. Cf. Cicero, *De Off.*, II, ii, 5; *Tusc. Disp.*, IV, xxvi, 57;
Sextus, *Adversus Physicos*, I, 13; and Seneca *Ep. Moral.*, LXXXIX, 4.

[5] Julius von Schlosser, "Giustos Fresken in Padua und die Vorläufer der
Stanza della Segnatura," *Jahrbuch der Kunst-historischen Sammlungen des
allerhöchsten Kaiserhauses*, XVII (1896), 96.

[6] *Conradus Celtis Proctucius: Quattuor Libri Amorum secundum quattuor
latera Germaniae*, Felicitas Pindter, ed. (Leipzig, 1934), IV, 4, lines 19–22.
"Invenies paucos, quos φρόνησις alma tenebit
    Et quos naturae sollicitaret opus,
Divinas atque humanas qui pectore causas
    Versarent, raro sidere proveniunt."

"who devoted themselves to the contemplation of nature."[7] Occasionally, and here he follows Petrarch as well as the ancients, Celtis emphasizes its ethical character and locates the source of wisdom in the moral maxims of antiquity, in the *honestae artes* or the *bonarum artes disciplinae*, "especially those which incite to living well and blessedly."[8] Or again, he uses a Neo-Platonic vocabulary to describe wisdom as the contemplation of God or Love. But embracing all these partial definitions is a wisdom conceived with the Stoics as the encyclopedic knowledge of all things, divine and human, and their causes.

Celtis justifies his reappropriation of the antique definition historically, on the basis of a necessary intellectual and sapiential *translatio* from Rome to Germany. The motif was popular in a Germany intellectually backward but still the seat of empire. Otto of Freising had introduced it in the twelfth century. Wisdom (*sapientia*), he said, originated in Babylonia and was then passed, concomitantly with empire, to Egypt, Greece, Rome, and finally to the Christian West. The careful student of history thus observes "that all human power and knowledge (*scientia*) had its origin in the East, but is coming to an end in the West, that thereby the transition and decay of all things human may be displayed."[9] Celtis, with suitable alterations, renews this theme. Wisdom was discovered by the Chaldeans and Egyptians, written down by the Greeks, and appropriated by the Romans, who "after taking over the empire of the Greeks, assimilated all their wisdom and eloquence, so much so that it is hard to decide whether it has equalled all the Greek discoveries and equipment of learning or surpassed them."[10] The *translatio imperii* from Romans to Germans was accompanied by a similar transfer of *sapientia*. The Germans, symbolized by Albertus Magnus, a thinker

[7] *Conradus Celtis Protucius: Oratio in Gymnasio in Ingelstadio publice recitata, cum carminibus ad Orationem pertinentibus*, Hans Rupprich, ed. (Leipzig, 1932), 12. Cf. *Tusc. Disp.*, V, iii, 8.

[8] Rupprich, *Briefwechsel*, ep. 5, line 43.

[9] *Ottonis Episcopi Frisingensis Chronica sive Historia de duabus civitatibus*, A. Hofmeister, ed. (Hannover and Leipzig, 1912), I, Prolog., p. 8.

[10] *Oratio*, 28. (L. Forster, tr.)

celebrated by German humanism less for his philosophy than for
the happy accident of his nationality, in their turn "amplified and
embellished it."[11]

But, since that happy time when German ambassadors spoke
Greek in preference to Latin, "through the iniquity of the ages and
the change in the times, not only amongst you but even in Italy,
the mother and ancient parent of literature, all the brilliance of
letters has at length faded and all freeborn studies have been put to
flight and overthrown by barbarous upheavals."[12] Italians call all
Germans barbarous drunkards, and this is often sadly true. "It is
our infamy and shame to have received the empire and to neglect the
arts by which it was produced and grew."[13] From the trumpet call
of the Ingolstadt *Oratio* to the foundation of the *Collegium
Poetarum et Mathematicorum* at Vienna, it was Celtis' self-imposed
educational mission to induce the youth of Germany to create an
intellectual brilliance in harmony with their secular pretensions. The
possession of empire, and a possession of wisdom in the past, was
the justification and guarantee of wisdom in the present. As the
Romans had assimilated the *sapientia* of Greece, so now must Germans assimilate the culture of ancient Rome.[14] Let German youth

---

[11] *Conradi Celtis Protvcii Primi Inter Germanos Imperatoriis Manibvs
Poete Lavreati Qvatvor Libri Amorvm* (Nürnberg, H. Höltzel, 1502), fol. A,
12, v is illustrated with Dürer's *Allegory of Philosophy*. See Erwin Panofsky,
Albrecht Dürer, 3rd ed. (Princeton, 1948), Handlist, 350; II, 42. Conveniently
reproduced in F. Winckler, *Dürer, Klassiker der Kunst*, IV, 249. Its general
plan and all details of iconography were supplied by Celtis himself. See
A. Ruland, "Die Entwürfe zu den Holzschnitten der Werke des Conradus
Celtis," *Archiv für die Zeichnenden Künste*, II (1856), 254-260. At the top of
the woodcut are the following lines: "Sophiam me Greci vocant Latini Sapien-
ciam/ Egipcii et Chaldei me invenere Greci scripsere/ Latini transtulere
Germani ampliavere." In Celtis' original draft the last phrase appears as
Germani ampliavere et illustravere. Cf. F. von Bezold, "Konrad Celtis," 108
and Campbell Dodgson, *Catalogue of Early German and Flemish Woodcuts
. . . in the British Museum* (London, 1903), I, 281-282.
[12] *Oratio*, 2.
[13] Rupprich, *Briefwechsel*, ep. 179, lines 137-139.
[14] *Oratio*, 29. "Ita et vos accepto Italorum imperio exuta foeda barbarie
Romanarum artium affectatores esse debebitis."

"lovingly embrace this pristine and lucid consideration of the nature of things; and at last, under the guidance of that antique and true philosophy ... come to their senses and, once the fog has been dispersed and cleared away, turn from old, empty trifles and slippery and foaming verbal controversies to solider, older, and more praiseworthy disciplines."[15] Let them restore the eloquent splendor of the Roman tongue and *prisca illa sapientia et philosophia*: its austere, exemplary virtue and its causal preoccupation with all things divine and human.

God, who constructed the universe with "the highest wisdom and the most admirable and absolute beauty"[16] and who "controls sea, earth, and the vast universe, divided all created things into two parts: the first visible and seizable by the senses, the second invisible to the eye and the unenlightened mind."[17] Human wisdom is the knowledge of all things contained in these two spheres, the sensible human and the intelligible divine, and of their causes.

A constant preoccupation with cause is a fundamental element in Celtis' idea of wisdom. Following the antique precept, Celtis first urges his pupils to investigate the causes of individual things,[18] of things, that is, within the realm of visible sense experience. In an *Ode* appended to the 1492 edition of the *Oratio*, an educational program and a general definition of true philosophy and pristine wisdom in poetic form, he lists some of the causes to be sought: the blowing of the winds, tides, earthquakes, floods, and volcanoes; why the earth produces sulphur and metals and why hot springs restore the sick man's health; the causes of lightning, rain, shooting stars,

---

[15] Rupprich, *Briefwechsel*, ep. 179, lines 65–72.

[16] *Briefwechsel*, ep. 179, lines 33–34.

[17] Karl Hartfelder, *Fünf Bücher Epigramme von Konrad Celtis* (Berlin, 1881), III, 111.

[18] *Epigr.*, II, 54. "Perge, puer, rerum naturae reddere causas."; *Conradus Celtis Protucius: Libri Odarum Quattuor. Libri Epodon. Carmen Saeculare*, Felicitas Pindter, ed. (Leipzig, 1937), *Od.*, I, 11, lines 37–38.

     "Perge consurgens animo volucri
     Singulis rebus reperire causas."

meteors, snow, and hail.[19] He is particularly interested in astronomy and the regularities of celestial motion: "Seek to know the siderial movements and the various orbits of the stars. Begin to recognize the lights of the starry world and why the constellations rise and set. Discuss once more the sun's eclipses and predict the weather to the stolid vulgar—when it will be rainy and windy, when clear, and when snow will be poured out of the North."[20] Finally, he returns in greater length to the medicine of natural magic and secret affinities and asks scholars and poets to be wise in the medicinal virtue of herbs, metals, and gems.[21]

But, beyond the "secret causes of nature," lies the wider area of the purely human, its history and geography. This widens appreciably both the traditional sources of wisdom and its content. Paralleling the extension of the content of wisdom to include the facts of human history is an extension of its sources to include the experience distilled from those facts. Celtis put at the top of the *Allegory of Philosophy* a fragment from Afranius:

> Memorye hyght my mother, my father experience.
> Grekes calle me Sophi, but ye name me Sapience.[22]

He had found the quotation in the *Attic Nights* and, following it, Aulus Gellius' comment that man "must learn wisdom and judgment from the teaching of actual experience, not from what books only, or masters, through vain words and fantasies, have foolishly

---

[19] *Od.*, I, 11. The *Ode* was one of Celtis' most popular works. It was reprinted about 1500 by Winterburg in Vienna as a pamphlet (*Gesamtkatalog der Wiegendrucke*, 6469) and in the postumous 1513 Strasbourg edition of the *Odes*.

[20] *Epigr.*, II, 53.

[21] *Od.*, I, 27, lines 89–96.

[22] See above, note 11. The translation is by Sir Thomas Elyot, *The Boke named the Gouernour*, Henry Herbert Stephen Croft, ed. (London, 1880), II, 367.

represented as though in a farce or a dream."[23] Celtis and his near contemporaries revived this conception. Leonardo da Vinci called wisdom the "daughter of experience";[24] and Sir Thomas Elyot speaks of "Experience whereof commeth wysedome,"[25] and of "practise" which is "of no small moment or efficacie in the acquiringe of sapience, in so moche that it semeth that no operation or affaire may be perfecte, nor no science or arte may be complete, except experience be there unto added, whereby knowlege is ratified, and (as I mought saye) consolidate."[26]

It is characteristic that both Elyot and Celtis identify experience with history and travel. The knowledge of experience, says Elyot, is called example, and is expressed by history.[27] To condemn history is to "frustrate Experience" because "there is no doctrine, be it eyther diuine or humaine, that is nat eyther all expressed in historie or at the leste mixte with historie."[28] Celtis argues that every liberal man should know the histories and deeds of the Greeks and Romans and the antiquities and peoples of Germany. He should fortify this with a firm knowledge of human and physical geography: the topography, climate, rivers, mountains, and peoples of the world, their

---

[23] XIII, viii, 1–3.

[24] *Pensieri*, 40. "La sapienza è la figliola della sperienza." *Tutti Gli Scritti. Scritti Letterari*, Augusto Marinoni, ed. (Milan, 1952), 65.

[25] *Governour*, II, 383.

[26] *Governour*, II, 402–403.

[27] *Governour*, II, 384. Cf. Le Caron, *Dialogves*, 54, r who also finds the source of true wisdom in the lessons of history. "En telz enseignements deuons chercher la vraie forme de sagesse: car l'experience est perpetuée à la posterité pour l'enseigner." For Cardinal Sadoleto, on the other hand, history teaches prudence rather than wisdom. *De liberis recte instituendis liber, Opera omnia* (Verona, 1738), III, 109, col. 2.

[28] *Governour*, II, 385. Cf. *Ibid.*, II, 386–387. "For it [history] nat onely reporteth the gestes or actes of princes or capitaynes, their counsayles and attemptates, entreprises, affaires, maners in lyuinge good and bad, descriptions of regions and cities, with their inhabitauntes, but also it bringeth to our knowlege the fourmes of sondry publike weales with their augmentations and decayes and occasion thereof; more ouer preceptes, exhortations, counsayles, and good persuasions, comprehended in quicke sentences and eloquent orations."

languages, customs, and emotional characteristics.[29] Travel, *priscorum more sophorum*, is the best way to acquire such wisdom.[30] By travel, Aristotle, following Alexander, learned much of historical and natural causation; while Plato got *dogmata sacra* from the Egyptians.[31] "Such was the power of their incredible zeal for the acquisition of wisdom" that to attain it the ancient sages "voluntarily submitted to toils and heat and cold and difficult voyages because they wished to perceive and see with their own eyes what they had discovered with weary effort by close reflection and much reading."[32] By reading, fortified and corrected by the experience of history, observation, and travel, the wise man encompasses a knowledge of all things human and their causes.

Above natural phenomena and the facts of human history and geography, however, above all things visible and perceived by the senses, lies the invisible world of the intelligible. This world of divine things or reasons and immutable forms, which for the Platonists was the only object of wisdom, is for Celtis its second and completing object. It is a knowledge preëminently esoteric and archane; and they are most fittingly called wise who secretly investigate these most hidden things.[33] From sense experience, although it too is in the area of *sapientia*, the wise man bends every effort to rise

[29] *Od.*, I, 11, lines 61–68. Cf. *Oratio*, 31. Celtis himself treated such subjects at length in the geographical sections of the *Quattuor Libri Amorum*, his history of Nürnberg—Albert Werminghoff, *Conrad Celtis und sein Buch über Nürnberg* (Freiburg i. B., 1921)—and in his editions of Hvrotsvitha, Tacitus, and Ligurinus.

[30] *Epigr.*, IV, 43.

[31] *Quattuor Libri Amorum*, IV, 1, lines 35–40. Cf. Elyot, *Of The knowledg which maketh a wise man. A disputacion Platonike*, Kurt Schroeder, *Platonismus in der Englischen Renaissance vor und bei Thomas Eliot*, *Palaestra*, LXXXIII (Berlin, 1920), 14*. "Besides that, I [Plato] am now above the age of fourtie yeres, and have travailed into divers contraies to seke for wisedome."

[32] *Oratio*, 11–12.

[33] Rupprich, *Briefwechsel*, ep. 179, lines 80–83. ". . . verum per abditissimarum explorationem rerum et archano earum scrutinio veteres nominatos fuisse sapientes accepimus."

gradually toward a knowledge of divine things.[34] In his iconography for Dürer's *Allegory of Philosophy*, for example, Celtis returns to the often pictured vision of Boethius, who saw philosophy as a majestic woman richly garbed. "In her right hand she had certain books, and in her left hand she had a scepter," while on the lower part of her dress "was placed the Greek letter π and on the upper θ, and between the two letters, like stairs, there were certain degrees made by which there was a passage from the lower to the higher letter."[35] This is a concrete picture of the ascension, *via* the seven liberal arts, from the practical and prudent active life to a contemplation (θ represents *theoretike* or *speculativa*) of the immutable and divine. Celtis passionately describes the joys of this ascension. "I have always thought that nothing sweeter nor more delightful could happen to human minds in the brief circle of this life than to be free for a contemplation of those things whose knowledge calls souls out of their prisons and speeds them aloft into divine and ethereal movements and loves. Those who have achieved this, their wishes fulfilled and already enjoying their final end, equal to the immortal gods, wander and move about separated and, so to speak, released from the body and see and reflect on that highest felicity and beatitude which the divine oracle promises to all good men and all those zealous for virtue after a life of precise morality. So even while the body lives, by contemplating celestial things and the majesty of the highest creator, they enjoy a certain divine sweetness and security. Oh incredible sweetness, oh blandest and divine

---

[34] Cf. Jakob Locher to Celtis, Rupprich, *Briefwechsel*, ep. 209, lines 16–20. "Haec enim θιλογαδία, qua in sublimes cogitationes rapior, nondum extincta e tuo Delphico atque Palladio sinu primum cepit amplexum et caloris sumpto incremento ad rerum divinarum cognitionem gradatim ascendit." Cf. Ficino, *Opera omnia* (Basel, 1561), I, 761. Plato "veram inquit philosophiam esse ascensum ab his, quae fluunt et oriuntur et occidunt, ad ea, quae vere sunt et semper eadem perseverant. Tot ergo philosophia partes et facultates ministras habet, quot gradibus ab infimis ad superna conscenditur." Quoted by Bezold, "Konrad Celtis," 108, note 226.

[35] *Consolat. Philosoph.*, I, 1 (prose). Cf. Boethius, *In Porph. Dial.*, i. "est enim philosophia genus, species vero eius duae, una quae θεωρητική dicitur, altera quae πρακτική, id est speculativa et activa."

pleasure to banquet with highest Jove on nectar and ambrosia, as the fables of the poets put it, and revel with the gods."[36]

For Celtis, therefore, as for Cicero, wisdom is the knowledge of things divine and human and their causes. Wisdom is a knowledge which begins with a poetic preoccupation with natural causation, the flux of sense experience, and rises to a contemplation of the divine. It is an encyclopedic and arrogant statement: "Whatever is contained in the heavens, in earth or air or sea; whatever may exist in human history and whatever the flaming god causes in the whole world, by philosophy I bear them all in my breast."[37] The content of *sapientia* is a universal knowledge naturally acquired.

Its elements of natural science derive from the rhetoric of the Roman poets. "My fondest prayer," said Virgil, "is that the dear Muses, life's supreme joy, may take me to their choir, their priest, by boundless ecstasy possessed; that they may show heavenly secrets, the stars, eclipses of the sun, ministries of the laborious moon, why the earth quakes, and by what power the fathomless oceans rise, bursting every bound, then sink away to their own bed; why winter suns so swift roll down to ocean's night.... *felix qui potuit rerum cognoscere causas*."[38] Celtis' imitation of this and similar passages in classical poetry indicates no unusual interest in science as such; but it does show a lively interest in and attachment to the facts of sense experience. This is in marked contrast to a common medieval attitude neatly summed up by Augustine in a commentary on these same lines from the *Georgics*. It is not necessary to happiness, he says, to know the causes of things hidden in the most secret recesses of nature's kingdom. What we ought to know are the causes of good and evil.[39] Petrarch, Salutati, and Bruni said the same thing.

---

[36] Rupprich, *Briefwechsel*, ep. 179, lines 37–46.

[37] An epigram by Celtis at the bottom of Dürer's *Allegory of Philosophy*. *Qvatvor Libri Amorvm* (1502), fol. A, 12v.

[38] *Georgics*, II, 477–482, 490. Cf. Ovid, *Metamor.*, XV., 67–72; Horace, *Epistles*, XII, 16–20; and *Sap.* 6:17–21. These references have been assembled by Forster, *Selections*, 84, note 2.

[39] *Enchiridion*, 16.

For Salutati human things had only an ethical significance; for Celtis they also include the individual objects of sense experience.

The metaphysical or "theological" content of wisdom, on the other hand, is a rehandling of certain Neo-Platonic themes. The contemplation of the divine, as well as all divine, and indeed human, causation is reduced to the amorous affinities described by "Hierotheos."[40] Wisdom at this level becomes the contemplation of an immanent God, a "spirit diffused throughout the universe, animating every part" and whom "only pure minds can see and understand."[41] This divine spirit is love, and this "love, which the natural philosophers call fire, water, vapor, or air, I, however, call God Almighty who formed man from the mud and soil of the earth and then implanted in him and in all living creatures, as well as in plants, seeds, and such inanimate things as gems, jewels, and even colors the power and virtue of love, that they might passionately desire and delight in being joined together by a natural kinship and silent amity and attraction."[42]

The universal permeation of nature by this amorous nexus, its identification with God, and the unbroken sapiential ladder from sense experience to the intelligible and divine destroys the traditional distinction between *scientia* and *sapientia*. *Sapientia* is an encyclopedic knowledge of all things: of things human and their individual causes (the old realm of *scientia*); of the intelligible world (the old realm of *sapientia* as metaphysics); and of the creator of both these worlds (the old realm of *sapientia* as natural or revealed theology). It embraces both the divine and human, and culminates in a natural and poetic theology based on Neo-Platonic love theory. There remains, therefore, no opposition between a natural, classical *scientia* and a revealed Christian *sapientia*, nor between a wisdom of this world and a purely Christian wisdom. Here is the essential differ-

[40] Pindter, *Quattuor Libri Amorum*, 116. Cf. F. S. Marsh, *The Book of the Holy Hierotheos* (London, 1927), 238 and Pseudo-Dionysius, *De divinis nominibus*, IV, 15.

[41] *Od.*, I, 5.

[42] Rupprich, *Briefwechsel*, ep. 275, lines 125–132.

ence between Celtis (and with him the humanist movement in general) and the Pauline oppositions of Augustine and his followers. Celtis did retain, of course, a Christian wisdom in the old sense: in the sense, that is, that he was always a pious, active, and indeed credulous Christian.[43] But wisdom is not limited to this area of knowledge and reverence; and it can exist independently of Christian doctrine and grace. Its content is universal, an expansion of Sadoleto's and Sir Thomas Elyot's narrower conception, and its sources are normally human: travel, observation, experience, and reading in the Greek and Roman classics.[44]

In one of her plays the eleventh-century nun Hrotsvitha tells the story of Sapientia and her three daughters, Faith, Hope, and Charity, all lusting for martyrdom at the hands of the Emperor Hadrian, Christian Revelation and the theological virtues baiting the natural virtues of paganism.[45] Celtis was a patriotic editor of Hrotsvitha's works, but his own work was Hadrian's revenge. The greatest antique emperors, he emphasizes, are to be imitated and not despised, "for they were most fervent in the hearing of philosophy and wisdom and always placed a zeal for wisdom before all things."[46] *Sapientia nostra* is superseded here by the Roman clarity of *prisca illa sapientia*.

[43] See his prayers to the Virgin, vigorously defending the Immaculate Conception—*Ars versificandi et carminum* (Leipzig, Martin Landsberg, ca. 1494), fol. C, viii, r; *Od.*, II, 8; and *Epigr.*, I, 19; III, 1—and those asking her to cure him of syphilis (*Epigr.*, IV, 33, 35, 36; V, 1, 4). Cf. his prayers to saints (*Epigr.*, I, 20, 21; III, 24; V, 90 and *Od.*, II, 30), his *Life* of St. Sebaldus (*Od.*, III, 10) and his diatribes against Hus and the heretical sects of Bohemia (*Od.*, I, 27; *Quattuor Libri Amorum*, II, 4; *Epigr.*, I, 64–65, 67–73, 75–76, 78, 81).

[44] One must keep in mind, however, Celtis' ambiguous statement on the illumination of the ancients. *Oratio*, 95. ". . . altum et egregium attingere potentes dum tenuiora tantum sequimur, quasi non apud Platonem et Pythagoram aliosque praecipuos philosophos religionis nostrae quaedam fundamenta inveniantur, quibus pulcherrima luminis naturae et gratiae societas percipiatur."

[45] *Hrotsvithae Opera*, Karl Strecker, ed. (Leipzig, 1930), 207–225.

[46] Rupprich, *Briefwechsel*, ep. 5, lines 23–25.

II

But no sixteenth-century thinker has described the encyclopedic capacities and Promethean nature of the wise man more admirably or in more precise detail than Carolus Bovillus.[47] His *Liber de Sapiente*, written in 1509 and published in February 1511,[48] is the finest Renaissance statement of a wisdom which is the universal knowledge of the perfect man. The wise man, alone among men,

[47] The work done to date on Bovillus is incommensurate with his importance. J. Dippel, *Versuch einer systematischer Darstellung der Philosophie des C. Bovillus* (Würzburg, 1865) remains the only monograph. It is good but dated. A. Renaudet *Préréforme et humanisme à Paris pendant les premières guerres d'Italie (1494–1517)* (Paris, 1916) assembles most of the known biographical facts and has an excellent bibliography of Bovillus' works. But Renaudet's interpretation of his thought, which continues to dominate most reference to him, at least in France, needs revision badly. The following sentence (p. 605) summarizes his conclusions: "Le 1er février 1510/1, Henri Estienne imprime une série d'ouvrages et d'épîtres scientifiques et morales où Bovelles développe une philosophie intellectualiste et illuminée, peu originale d'ailleurs, et qui, dans sa théorie de la connaissance, dans ses méthodes, dans les applications qu'elle tente des mathématiques à l'étude des problèmes fondamentaux, dans sa métaphysique et sa mystique, suit constamment et de très près les doctrines de Nicolas de Cues." The influence of Cusanus has been greatly exaggerated. Their ideas of wisdom are fundamentally dissimilar. J. Uebinger, "Der Begriff docta ignorantia in seiner geschichtlichen Entwicklung," *Archiv für Geschichte der Philosophie*, VIII (1894), 25–32, is a short but important analysis of other basic differences. Ernst Cassirer's *Das Erkenntnisproblem in der Philosophie und Wissenschaft der Neueren Zeit*, 2nd ed. (Berlin, 1911), I, 61–72 and *Individuum und Kosmos*, passim., are the most important pages yet written on Bovillus. The interpretation is very different from Renaudet's. He describes the *De sapiente* (*Individuum und Kosmos*, 93) as "die unmittelbare Weiterbildung und die systematische Durchführung des Grundgedankens von Picos Rede. . . . Dieses Werk . . . ist vielleicht die merkwürdigste und in mancher Hinsicht charakteristischste Schöpfung der Renaissance-Philosophie." See also Bernard Groethuysen, *Anthropologie philosophique* (Paris, 1953; first edition 1931), 190–200.

[48] *Que hoc volumine continentur. Liber de intellectu. Liber de sensu. Liber de nichilo. Ars oppositorum. Liber de generatione. Liber de sapiente. Liber de duodecim numeris. Epistole complures.* (Paris, H. Estienne, 1511). At the end of the *Liber de sapiente* (fol. 148, r.) Bovillus gives details of its composition. "Libri De Sapiente Finis Anno Divine humanationis. 1509 Decimatertia nouembris. Diuine, Increate et intemerate sapientie, Innumere laudes:

is wholly and perfectly a man. He is, says Bovillus, a terrestrial god, and the keys of the universe are in his hands. His wisdom is a knowledge of the whole universe and a natural and humanly created perfection. From darkness he brings light, from potency act, from a beginning the end, from innate capacity the finished work, from a part the whole, and from seeds the fruit. Like Prometheus he seizes the fire of wisdom from the immortal heavens, brings it down to earth, and with its brilliant flame fecundates the natural and universal potentialities within him. He recreates himself. From an ignorant, imperfect, and chaotic being he reforms himself into the wise, perfect, and consummated man.[49]

This conception of wisdom and the wise man ties together important strands of previous Renaissance thinking on wisdom: the exaltation of speculative knowledge so typical of Italian Aristotelians like Bruni and Pomponazzi; the Platonists' idea that wisdom is an esoteric contemplation of divine things; a renewed interest in human things, similar to Salutati's but without his characteristically ethical interpretation of them. Moreover, Bovillus reinforces humanism's insistence that wisdom is naturally acquired, adapting for this purpose Pico della Mirandola's idea of man as a Protean being who has no nature of his own but can freely become all natures and a similar idea—best stated by Pomponazzi and derived, he says, from the third book of the *De anima*—that man can know all things and by knowing them become them.[50] Only one

---

Angelice et humane sapientie, conditrici." The *De sapiente* has been edited by R. Klibansky as an Appendix to Cassirer's *Individuum und Kosmos*. My references are to this edition, noted henceforth as *De sap.*, followed first by the number of the chapter and then by the number of the page in Cassirer. All references to other works, unless otherwise indicated, are to Estienne's edition of 1511.   [49] *De sap.*, viii, 320.

[50] *Petri Pomponatii Mantvani ... de naturalium effectuum causis, siue de Incantationibus* (Basel, 1556), 29–30. "Quinto supponitur ex tertio de anima, quod anima sensitiua cum recipiat species omnium sensibilium, quoquomodo est omnia sensibilia: et intellectiua omnia intelligibilia. Quare cum omne quod est, aut sit sensibile aut intelligibile, humana anima cum utrunque comprehendat, sensum uidelicet et intellectum, ipsa erit omnia: Est enim sensus in actu, sensibile in actu: et intellectus in actu, intelligibile in actu, totum patet ex tertio de anima."

important current of Renaissance speculation on wisdom is missing: the effort of early Italian humanists to transform it into an active moral virtue. Like the Florentine Neo-Platonists Bovillus insists that wisdom is a contemplative virtue opposed to all action or *praxis*.[51] His wise man is uncompromisingly intellectual and solitary. A moralized civic wisdom similar in many points to that of Salutati and Bruni was being developed again in Italy and in northern Europe during Bovillus' lifetime. But this development has a history of its own which left him untouched.

Bovillus defines wisdom as the knowledge one immaterial substance has of another and as the perfect knowledge a single, undivided, and immaterial substance has of itself. All wisdom is immaterial knowledge and all immaterial knowledge is wisdom. Self-knowledge is necessarily immaterial; while the object of wisdom, whether it is defined as self-knowledge or as the knowledge one immaterial substance has of another, is immaterial by definition. Conversely, all self-knowledge and any knowledge one immaterial substance has of another, because it is immaterial, is wisdom.[52]

Immaterial and perfect knowledge is distinguished from material or imperfect knowledge. In all cognition there is a subject or spectator; an object or the thing known; and, finally, the mean between them which is the knowledge the one has of the other. In material cognition the object of knowledge is material, the concrete substances of the visible world, and the knowing subject is the five

---

[51] *Liber propriae rationis*, ix, 4. *In Hoc Opere Caroli Bovilli Samarobrini contenta. Liber Cordis. Liber propriae Rationis. Liber substantialium propositionum. Liber naturalium Sophismatum. Liber cubicarum mensularum.* (Paris, Badius Ascensius, 1523).

[52] *De sap*, xxx, 360. "Omnis enim Sapientia est suiipsius cognitio. . . . Unde fit, ut omnis Sapientia sit immaterialis cognitio et omnis immaterialis cognitio Sapientia." Cf. *De sap.*, xiii, 331. "Omnis itaque immaterialis cognitio cum Contemplatio sit, liquet Contemplationem esse trinam; est enim Contemplatio trium supremorum et precipuorum mundi entium: Dei, Angeli et Anime eviterna et immortalis speculatio."

senses and the *internus Sensus* or imagination.[53] In immaterial cognition, on the other hand, both subject and object are immaterial, both, that is, are immaterial substances. "Wisdom," consequently, "is immaterial both in its subject and object because wisdom originates in immaterial substance and is a knowledge of immaterial substance."[54] As self-knowledge it is the contemplation of an immaterial substance by itself; as the knowledge one thing has of another it must be confined to the contemplation of one immaterial substance by a second or third immaterial substance.

Since wisdom is both immaterial and perfect, it is also triune, for "every consumated and perfect thing is of necessity triune."[55] It is triune, furthermore, in each of its two definitions, as self-knowledge and as the knowledge one immaterial substance has of another. There are three immaterial essences capable of self-knowledge: God, angels, and the rational soul;[56] and the knowledge each has of itself constitutes three corresponding varieties of wisdom: divine, angelic, and human.[57] The human soul, as the first and lowest immaterial essence, is the first to know itself and the first habitat of wisdom. In his prefatory letter to the *De sapiente* Bovillus quotes the definition of wisdom traditionally attributed to Apollo: *O Homo, nosce*

[53] *De sap.*, xi, 327; xiii, 330; 365. Cf. *De sensu*, Praef., fol. 21, r; Exodium, fol. 59, v.

[54] *De sap.*, xxxiv, 374. "Sapientia utrobique, et subiecto et obiecto, est immaterialis. Nam et immateriali substantie Sapientia inest et est immaterialis substantie gnaritudo, scientia, cognitio."

[55] *De sap.*, xxx, 366. "Omne etenim, quod consummatum est et perfectum, est ex necessitate trinum. Sapientia autem perfecta est, trinitas perfecta est, ideoque et Sapientia trina et trinitas trina reperitur."

[56] *De sap.*, xxviii, 357. "Fit iterum, ut trina sit Sapientia, quemadmodum est et trina suiipsius gnaritudo atque scientia. Nam tria sunt immaterialia entia, que in semet flectuntur, in se convertuntur, que suiipsorum capacia et a seipsis agnita sunt: rationalis Anima, Angelus, Deus." Cf. above, note 52.

[57] *De sap.*, xxx, 360. "Sapientia est trina: alia divina, alia angelica, alia humana. . . . Tria autem sunt orbicularia et que se norunt entia: Deus, Angelus, Homo." Cf. *De sap.*, xxxiv, 374.

teipsum.[58] Sir Thomas Elyot found in this maxim a beginning of wisdom; for Bovillus it becomes, momentarily, its single and exclusive definition. "All wisdom is self-knowledge." Foolishness, conversely, is ignorance of oneself.[59] Self-knowledge is the perfect knowledge one part of the same unitary, undivided, and immaterial substance has of its own other part.[60] In man, for example, as Cicero said, self-knowledge is the soul seen by itself; or as Bovillus puts it, *in notione Anime ab Anima.* He compares it to the image which in the *Hieroglyphics of Horapollo* symbolizes eternity: the serpent biting its own tail. As one part of the serpent bites another part of itself, so the human soul, like a circle, turns inward on itself, contemplates itself, and becomes its own perpetual resting place.[61]

Below it, in the sensitive soul of animals, there is no self-knowledge and therefore no wisdom.[62] Animals are capable only of linear and material cognition; but the human *ratio*, the angelic *intellectus* and the divine *mens*, immaterial essences turned inward in self-contemplation, are all capable of orbicular and immaterial cognition. In each of these three "orbes"—the rational, angelic, and divine—one part of the same immaterial substance looks at another part; and the mean between them, or the knowledge each part has of the other, is the act of both, a form of contemplation and its own characteristic and circular wisdom. In the rational soul the intellect, the subject of knowledge, sees the intellectual species of all things in the memory

[58] *De sap.*, Praef., 301. Cf. Cicero, *Tusc. Disp.*, I, xxii, 52. "Est illud quidem vel maximum, animo ipso animum videre: et nimirum hanc habet vim praeceptum Apollinis, quo monet, ut se quisque noscat."

[59] *De sap.*, xxxii, 372. "Si Sapientia, ut diximus, est suiipsius agnitio perfectaque scientia; erit Insipientia sui inscitia et ignoratio." Cf. *De sap.*, Praef., 302.

[60] *De sap.*, xxvii, 355. "Est enim verissima Sapientia suiipsius inspectio atque agnitio, qua in substantia eadem, indivisa, indissecta, una et continua permanente pars partem apprehendit, pars a parte sublabratur, pertrahitur et ad interiora revocatur."

[61] *De sap.*, 356.

[62] *De sap.*, xlvi, 398. "Rursum in Sensu, in muto animali, infra Rationem nulla Sapientia locata est, nullus sui aspectus, nulla sui cognitio. In humana Ratione prima sursum pergentibus occurrit Sapientia, prima sui inspectio, prima eiusdem in seipsum glomeratio." Cf. *De sap.*, xxxv, 375.

which conserves them; while the memory, the object of knowledge, is seen by and presents all things to the intellect. Contemplation is the act of both, the simultaneous inspection and presentation itself, and the knowledge the one has of the other: the intellectual species of all things.[63] God and angels know or contemplate themselves in a similar way. In the divine *mens*, for example, as in the human reason or the angelic *intellectus*, there are two extremes—the subject and object of knowledge, in this case the divine intellect and the divine memory—and the mean term between them, divine contemplation.[64] Human, angelic, and divine wisdom are thus three contemplations: the knowledge which the rational soul, angels, and God have of themselves.

Wisdom describes as well the knowledge these three immaterial essences have of each other: the soul's knowledge of God and angels and the angel's knowledge of God. God knows all things, but He knows all things in himself. Divine wisdom, therefore, remains monistic, indivisible, and exclusively self-contemplative. It is uncreated, infinite, eternal; and in it God has known and magnified Himself since before the beginning of time. In both created wisdoms, on the other hand, are found the beginnings of multiplicity and division. While divine wisdom is monistic, angelic wisdom is dual. The angel knows itself, but it also knows another substance outside itself, God. Human wisdom, lower and more disparate, is triple, formed of the knowledge of all three immaterial essences: the soul itself, angels, and God.[65]

Since six is the first perfect number, it is fitting that there should

---

[63] *De sap.*, xxiii, 349. Cf. *De sap.*, ix, 323. For further details on Bovillus' theory of species see Cassirer, *Erkenntnisproblem*, I, 65.

[64] *De sap.*, xxviii, 357. "...divinus orbis, quo per Deum Deus in Deum fertur, divina Sapientia, Dei a seipso agnitio divinaque Contemplatio nuncupatur; et huius extrema sunt divinus Intellectus, divina Memoria ac divina amborum species."

[65] *De sap.*, xxxiv, 374. "Divina Sapientia omnium est precipua, prima, increata, infinita, eterna, qua Deus ab eterno ante condita secla sibimet arcane innotuit, sibiipsi suffulsit, resplenduit, apparuit. Angelica vero Sapientia est, qua cognitus est ab Angelo Deus et qua Angelus a seipso. Humana porro est, qua ab Anima Deus, Angelus, Anima internoscuntur. Divina Sapientia

thus be six varieties of wisdom, six kinds of immaterial cognition: the knowledge each of the three immaterial essences has of itself and the three possible knowledges they have of each other. The six can be reclassified under three heads, a further perfection: *Mens, Intellectus,* and *Ratio.* "For we define *Mens* as the sight or knowledge of the same thing by itself; *Intellectus* as a thing's knowledge of the things next and closest to it; while *Ratio* we declare to be a meditated knowledge in which the beginning seeks and scrutinizes the end through the middle."[66] There are, therefore, three *Mentes*: the knowledge God has of himself, the knowledge an angel has of itself, and the knowledge the soul has of itself; two *Intellectus*: the angel's knowledge of God and the soul's knowledge of angels; and, finally, one *Ratio*: the soul's meditated knowledge of God.[67] In this classification all possible wisdoms are neatly filed.

The content and nature of human wisdom is now clearer. It is immaterial and a form of contemplation, the soul's sempiternal and immortal contemplation of itself and the two immaterial essences above it: angels and God. In the soul's knowledge of itself man knows all things in the world. By knowing angels and God as well, he perfects and widens this knowledge to a knowledge of the universe. Because, therefore, "the whole universe is the object of the whole man and was created to be known by him"[68] and because the sensible and intellectual worlds link and fuse in him,[69] human

---

monas est et tantum suiipsius noticia, omni alteritate et divisione sublimior. Angelica Sapientia orta et creata a monade dyas est et haud tantum sui, sed alterius, ut Dei, cognitio; et in hac Sapientia prima alteritas primaque divisio contingit. Humana vero Sapientia ultima est Sapientia ac tryas; est enim trium entium cognitio: Anime, Angeli, Dei." Cf. *De sap.*, xiii, 331 and Dippel, *Philosophie des C. Bovillus*, 104–105.

[66] *De sap.*, xxxv, 375. Cf. *De sensu*, vii, 3.

[67] *De sap.*, 376.   [68] *De sap.*, xx, 346.

[69] *De sap.*, xxxiii, 373. "Utramque naturam exprimit, intellectualem atque sensibilem. Collocatus enim, ut diximus, in utriusque mundi speculo: nunc sensuum vehiculo in sensibilem mundum devehitur, nunc vero mente celos exterebrans supercelestia et intellectualia scrutatur, rimatur, perquirit. Sensibilem insuper mundum, ut duximus, in intelligibilem et intelligibilem in sublunarem traducit." Cf. Nicholas of Cusa, *De docta ignorantia*, III, 3: Heidelberg, I, 126–127.

wisdom is an encyclopedic knowledge of all things, created and uncreated, divine and human: the world, the human body and soul, angels, and God, the end of all things.[70] "For the rational soul first collects notions, species, and images of all sensible things in the sublunar world with the help of the body and senses. From these, as the creator of its own species, it constructs, forms, and produces within itself its own proper species, which is the beginning of human wisdom and the soul's knowledge of itself. Then, after attaining self-knowledge, it rises gradually to a simpler and angelic perfection and becomes a participant of angelic knowledge. Finally, ascending still to more sublime things, it finds its consummation in divine cognition and knowledge and participates at last in the truest Wisdom."[71]

Man knows every object of the visible world in his own soul because the soul is a "natural mirror of the universe; and everything in the world exists that he may know it and that it may embellish and illuminate his mind."[72] Man was created outside and facing all things, "separated from the order of all things and placed high above, and apart from, all things, that he might be their center."[73] He is the center of a circle whose circumference is the totality of substantial things. In this favored position the mirror of his soul receives the image of each thing outside him. The world is an object of knowledge; man is the subject of knowledge. In the world are all substantial things. In man is the knowledge of all these things. The world has a maximum of substance, and a minimum of knowledge. Man has the minimum of substance, but a maximum of knowledge.[74]

But although he is the center of the world, surrounded by all objects of knowledge as the firmament surrounds the earth, man is at first and by nature a blank mirror, "rough, unpolished, impure, opaque, empty, reflecting no image."[75] He has nothing; but he is

---

[70] *De sensu*, I, 3–6, fol. 22r–v; VII, 5, fol. 28v.

[71] *De sap.*, xxxiv, 374.   [72] *De sap.*, xix, 342.

[73] *De sap.*, xxvi, 353. Cf. *Physicorum Elementorum Caroli Bouilli Samarobrini veromandui Libri decem* (Paris, Badius Ascensius, 1512), VIII, iii, 7 and *Liber propriae rationis*, i, 12.   [74] *De sap.*, xix, 343.

[75] *De sap.*, xxvi, 354. Cf. *Caroli Bouilli Samarobrini Quaestionum Theologicarum Libri septem* (Paris, Badius Ascensius, 1513), V, 64.

5+

capable of everything. He is ignorant; but, potentially, all knowledge is in him. All things exist in the world outside of him; but all
things may become in him, for he is the world's center. Outside there
is no possibility of becoming: all things already are. Within him
nothing actually exists, but his potency to all things insures their
becoming.[76] "For just as the substances of things subsist in the
world, so their rational brilliance, their sparks, species, or
images live in man. The world may be all things, but it knows
nothing. Man, on the other hand, is slight and almost nothing; but
he knows all things. The world is characterized by substance, man
by knowledge. In the world are all substantial things, in man their
reasons. In the world is truth, in man its similitude."[77]

Man, therefore, passes from ignorance to knowledge, from potency
to act, as the mirror of his soul is polished by and impregnated
with the reasons or species of all things. All things in the substantial
world outside of man are in act. Their acts are their species. Man's
mind, on the other hand, is in potency to these same things. As he
knows them his mind passes from potency to act, and his knowledge of them is the act of both, their species. *Scientia*, which distinguishes man from the *substantia* of the world, is the species, the
act of both the object known and the knowing mind. Imagine, therefore, that all things are outside of man and facing him. These
things are in act, and each is flooding man with the brilliance of
its sensible act or natural species. Imagine next that man is the
focus of each of these innumerable lines of light and can be illuminated by them. Fecundated by *sensibiles actus*, by what Bovillus
calls the *mundana lux*, he reflects the sensible species of all things.[78]
This is the beginning of wisdom;[79] for men "who know the causes
of all things, what and why things are as they are; who know the

---

[76] *De sap.*, 354. Cf. *De intellectu*, I, 1, fol. 3r; II, 3, fol. 4v; II, 17, fol. 5r
and Cusa, *De docta ignorantia*, III, 4: Heidelberg, I, 132.

[77] *De sap.*, xix, 342–343. Cf. *Physicorum Elementorum*, VIII, iv, 5.

[78] *De sensu*, 22r, 3.

[79] *De sap.*, I, 405. "Haud enim mundana lux est Sapientia, sed est Sapientie
initium. Eius vero scientia, quod est precipuum, prestantius et propter se, ut
Hominis, propter quem factus est mundus: hec Sapientia vocitatur."

dimensions, order, number and place of all single things" have the indispensable beginnings of wisdom: a knowledge of individual human things and their causes.[80]

But only the fool looks exclusively at the world. The wise man looks both at the world and inwardly at himself. Like Janus he has two faces: one turned toward the world gathering sensible species; the other turned inward, contemplating intellectual species within himself.[81] These intellectual species, forms which are the end and definition of a plurality of things of the same class, are got by abstraction from sensible species and by what Bovillus, elaborating on the Aristotelian theory of the active intellect, terms a "creation of the mind."[82] For the mind is not merely a passive mirror receiving sensible species, but also a *speculum vivens* which creates its own intellectual species. "Nature is the efficient cause of sensible species. The mind is the efficient cause of intellectual species."[83] Created in this way, intellectual species are stored in the memory where they are contemplated by the intellect. This is self-knowledge: the soul knowing all things immaterially as true intellectual images in itself.[84] This too is wisdom, a *caelum* or firmament of intellectual species, quiddities, or ideas and the intellect's act and consummation.[85]

[80] *De sap.*, xix, 342.

[81] *De sap.*, 1, 405. Cf. Ficino, *Opera*, I, 375 and J. Rohmer, "Sur la doctrine franciscaine des deux faces de l'âme," *Archives d'histoire doctrinale et littéraire du Moyen Age*, II (1927), 73–77.

[82] *Liber propriae rationis*, v, 5; *De intellectu*, V, 7, fol. 9r; *De sap.*, xxii, 348. For discussions of Bovillus' ideas on the transformation of sensible into intellectual species see Dippel, *Philosophie des C. Bovillus*, 79 ff. and Cassirer, *Erkenntnisproblem*, I, 69–70.

[83] *Liber propriae rationis*, ii, 8, 14. "Natura prolatrix est et efficiens causa sensibilium specierum. Mens autem est intellectualium specierum efficiens causa."

[84] *De sap.*, xiii, 330.

[85] *De intellectu*, XII, 8, fol. 16r. "Nam quilibet singularis intellectus, perfici natus est intellectualium specierum multitudine: que illius sapientia litterarius thesaurus nuncupatur."; *Liber propriae rationis*, v, 6. "Vera enim sapientia cum sit maxime inuia et penitus arcana: nimirum sita esse debet in habitu eius speciei, que est omnium praecipua et defaecatissima: et in eius etiam

When the fecund and brightly polished mind is thus fully in act to all things, it is the act itself and species of all things. Man's species is not the species of this or that thing, but the species of all things.[86] He is the "eye of all things," outside them; but seeing, knowing, and judging them all, a natural reflector of the lights and acts of the whole world.[87] By embracing the world and all its acts and species, he becomes the world, a world in miniature, a microcosm of the macrocosm. Only then is man wise, a *Universi speculum*, and the possessor of universal knowledge: the knowledge, that is, of himself and, through this, of all things. For then man "has nothing peculiarly or properly his own, but everything proper to others is common to him. Whatever may be the characteristic property of this or that single object is also a property of man. For he appropriates the nature of all things to himself, sees all things, and resembles the entirety of nature. Swallowing and consuming whatever is in the nature of things, he becomes all those things. For man is not this or that peculiar essence, nor is this or that nature his; but he is all things at once, the meeting place and rational union of all things."[88]

"Man, finally, is the brilliance, light, knowledge, and soul of the

iudicio, cui nullum aliud iudicium dominatur ac praeest. At intellectualis species et mentis iudicium sunt huiusmodi. In his igitur humana sapientia est a nobis vestiganda." Cf. *Physicorum Elementorum*, VIII, vi, 8–9.

[86] *De sap.*, xxvi, 355. "Et si eadem est species, que et omnium dicitur species et naturalis nostri Hominis species: necesse est, ut et nativus noster Homo quoquopacto sit ut omnium potentia; utpote cuius actus est omnium actus, cuius species omnium species, cuius imago omnium imago et cuius denique numerus omnium numerus. Idem est stellarum firmamenti, idem atomorum terre, idem Hominis humaneve speciei et Sapientie numerus: cuius agnitio et deprehensio est et sui et universorum gnaritudo atque scientia. Sicut enim est eadem Hominis et universorum species—nam que Hominis est, omnium est, et que est omnium, est Hominis—: ita et eadem utrorumque scientia, unica, par gnaritudo."

[87] *De sap.*, 355. "Est igitur Homo ultima, suprema et precipua sensibilis mundi creatura, sita et collocata extra omnia tanquam omnium potentia et concurrentia; luminum insuper et actuum mundi naturalis umbra et ut quiddam mundi medium."

[88] *De sap.*, xxiv, 350–351. Cf. *De intellectu*, V, 3, fol. 11, v.

world; while the whole world is as the body of man."[89] As *Anima mundi* man's relation to the world parallels the relation of his soul to his body. As his soul knows the body, so does man know and judge the world. Together man and the world form the *universum*, and the soul of this universe is the whole man and its body is the world.[90] Man is linked to the world as form to matter in a single substance, the *universum*. Man is the form of the world, the act and species of the world, the knowledge of the universe. As a soul is necessary for the continued subsistence of man, so is man, and especially the wise man, who is the truest soul of the world, all the more necessary for the subsistence and completion of the universe. Since man is the form of the world, he is in the fullest and most literal sense the species of all things in the universe. And this species, which is also the *numerus* and act of man, is *sapientia*.[91]

III

Bovillus' wise man belongs to an élite. "The wise man, who knows the secrets of nature, is himself secret and spiritual. He lives alone, far from the common herd. Placed high above other men, he is unique, free, absolute, tranquil, pacific, immobile, simple, collected, one. He keeps to himself, needs no one, abounds in every good. He is perfect, consummated, and happy.... He alone has the capacity to govern kingdoms because, knowing all things, he respects the natural order and the rank of every man, rendering to each his own and thus maintaining equality and justice.... The

[89] *De sap.*, xix, 343. Cf. *De sap.*, xxi, 347. "Est enim Homo mundi Anima; mundus vero et quicquid sub celo visitur, Hominis est ut corpus." Cf. *De sensu*, I, 8, fol. 22, v.

[90] *De sap.*, xxi, 347. "Et huius Universi Anima est totus Homo, corpus vero mundus."

[91] *De sap.*, xxvi, 354. "Quicquid firmamento inest, fieri in terra potest: sicut et quicquid est in mundo, fieri potest in Homine. Etenim precipua Hominis species, cuius habitum Sapientiam esse docuimus: haud huius vel huius est species, sed aliquo pacto species omium." Cf. *De sap.*, xxii, 347 and Cassirer, *Individuum und Kosmos*, 95.

keys of the universe are in the hands of the wise man."[92] He has, indeed, the characteristic inaccessibility and remote unconcern of Aristotle's God. Proudly isolated, secret, and dealing in secrets, he is a member of an avant-garde coterie, specializing in a wisdom alien to the vulgar and carefully kept from it. Like Pico della Mirandola, Conrad Celtis, or Mutianus Rufus, the Erfurt humanist who was so self-consciously esoteric that he wrote nothing but letters, he throws no holy things to dogs nor pearls to swine, but reserves wisdom for an initiated few.[93] Magnificently elevated, self-sufficient, free, happy, attuned to the natural order, he is the just and fit ruler of the world.

So great, indeed, is the dignity of the wise man that he escapes any fixed position in the chain of being. Bovillus, like Pico, imagines him, not as a stationary and passive link in a static hierarchy, but as a free agent dominating a wide area of possibility. Man has immense innate potentialities. To the extent that these are activated he can ascend or descend the chain of being at will. He was created outside of nature, apart from all things, higher than all things and in their center. He may become all things, and so pass from potency to act; or he may remain nothing, his potentialities atrophied.[94]

[92] *Metaphisicum introductorium cum alio quodam opusculo distinctionis nonnullorum omnium communium quae ad metaphisicam spectant.* (Paris, J. Petit, 1503/04) e, i, r–v. Quoted by Renaudet, *Préréforme et humanisme à Paris*, 420, note 2.

[93] Pico della Mirandola, *Oratio de hominis dignitate*, Edizione Nazionale, E. Garin, ed. (Florence, 1942), I, 154–156. Carl Krause, *Der Briefwechsel des Mutianus Rufus* (Kassel, 1885), ep. 11, p. 13. "Scimus enim mysteria non esse vulganda, sed esse vel supprimenda silentio vel per quaedam fabularum atque aenigmatum involucra tradenda, ne suibus demus margaritas." For Conrad Celtis see above, note 33 and *Oratio*, 79–80. ". . . poetae, qui suis figuris et idoneis fabulis ita naturas rerum transtulerunt, ut sacrarum rerum notio vulgo occulta esset, scientes inimicam esse naturae apertam et nudam expositionem sui, ideo eam sub honestis operimentis et sacramentali quodam velamine enuntiari debere. Quod si vulgus quaedam arcana, ut philosophi, intelligeret, difficile eorum impetus coerceri posset." See George Boas's Introduction to *The Hieroglyphics of Horapollo*, Bollingen Series, XXIII (New York, 1950) for a discussion of Renaissance esotericism.

[94] *De sap.*, xxvi, 353.

There are men, for example, who merely exist, like rocks. There are others, "vital" or "vegetable" men, who add life to mere being and, like trees, living but insensate, suck a greedy but unconscious nourishment from the earth. A third human type is the sensual man. He wallows in the luxuries of sense experience like the horse. Above all these, finally, is the learned, virtuous, and rational man. Only he, by adding intelligence to being, life, and sensation, is really and fully a man; and he alone can be considered upright, wise, happy, and blessed.[95] Man can descend to the sensual prison of animals and, further, to an unconscious vegetation or the mere objective existence of a stone; or he can ascend to a full human perfection, or, further, to the rarified intelligence of angels. Man is defined, not by a specific nature, but by a freedom to become any or all natures. Man can be less than a man without destruction—he is then merely a fool; and more than a man without blasphemy.

Outside of the "order of all things," free to become all things, possessing, therefore, the "keys of the universe," the wise man is a second and secular god. Imitating Prometheus, he scales the heights of angelic intellection and rules the earth like another god. "A wise man is the true and consummated end of all material things enclosed by the firmament and (as many think) a kind of terrestrial and mortal god."[96] He resembles the divine Prometheus also in his creative power; for the wise man is his own artificer.[97] He recreates himself in the divine image, he deifies himself. The English theologian and educator John Colet, like many medieval mystics, had also described man's "deification"; but he made it clear that only Christ can purify, enlighten, and justify men that they "may be holy, wise, and good, and, being made like God, may become gods."[98] Nicholas of Cusa noted that Hermes Trismegistus had called man a second

---

[95] *De sap.*, ii, 307–308; vi, 316–317.

[96] *De sap.*, xix, 341. Cf. *De sap.*, vii, 318. "Vivit denique in terris ut Deus alter: eterni, primi naturalisque Dei—a quo et Substantiam et Virtutem mutuavit—vera, precipua et substantialis imago."

[97] *De sap.*, xxxi, 369.

[98] *Enarratio in Primam Epistolam S. Pauli ad Corinthios*, J. H. Lupton, ed. and tr. (London, 1874), 171.

god, but he interprets this in terms of his own mystical epistemology. Man creates "images of the images of the divine understanding" and is consequently deified by his intellectual capacity, once illuminated and reformed by the Word, to reflect relative images of the divine.[99] Bovillus secularizes these essentially mystical conceptions. Deification in Colet and Cusa comes from without and above man. For Bovillus deification is the result of a naturally achieved perfection, a passage from potency to act, a willed development of all human potentialities. The wise, divine, and Promethean man is the natural end and consummation of the natural man and his own creation.

The wise man, finally, is a *res perfecta*, "the undiminished, whole and perfect man."[100] Like every perfect thing he is composed of form and matter. His matter is the natural man, his form the virtuous and rational man, the man by art. To have a human body and a rational soul is to be a man by nature. The baby, the fool, and the wise man are all men in this sense. But to be fully and perfectly a man is to consummate by personal effort the natural man in the man of virtue and reason, to be at once a man by nature and a man by art. Nature gives man his matter and the potentialities inherent in that matter. Man himself must create his form and activate his potentialities. By nature man is simple; he makes himself, by a conscious exercise of will, a composite being, a being that is blessed and good, virtuous and rational. From nature come seeds of perfection, innate capacities. By art, by hard work, self-cultivation, and self-formation, these seeds are brought to fruition. "Nature," for example, "has endowed man with a special strength of reason. But he himself, obeying the rule of reason in all things, seeks to be rational in the living of his life. He makes reason his guide, and does nothing except by it. He is glorified by its radiance and adjusts his own mind, acts, and every movement to its measure."[101] Similarly, nature has endowed man with the capacity for intellectual virtue. But man himself must activate this capacity, transform an

---

[99] *De Beryllo*, vi: *D. Nicolai de Cvsa Cardinalis . . . Opera* (Basel, 1565), 268.

[100] *De sap.*, vi, 317.

[101] *De sap.*, 317.

intellectual potentiality into the active knowledge of all things in the universe. By nature, in short, man is imperfect, unconsummated, and a fool; by art only does he become wise: "The angel is perfect by nature; man is perfected by art."[102]

The wise man, because he is the end and perfection of the natural man, is in fact twice a man, "a man by nature and a man by intellect; a man in matter, a man in form; a man in potency, a man in act; a man in his beginning, a man in his end; a man in being and a man in form; a man finally both inchoate and perfect."[103] He is a man by nature, because of his rational soul, and a man by virtue, because he is wise: a *Homo-Homo*.[104] Within him is every human potentiality and every human perfection. Wisdom, as the form and species of man, the intellectual virtue which activates the natural man as he rises gradually from ignorance to universal knowledge, defines that perfection. The wise man is the natural man reduplicated by art, the fruit, end, and wisdom of the natural man. As a living being he embraces within himself all possibilities of being, from rocks to angels and can become them all. As a knowing intellect his object is the totality of things divine and human, from the disparate particulars of the sublunar world and their causes to the Form of forms which is God, and he can and does know them all. The wise man is perfect, and wisdom is the universal knowledge

---

[102] *De intellectu*, I, 5, fol. 3 v.

[103] *De sap.*. vi, 317. "Accipe igitur Sapientis consummatique viri vestigia ex re huiusmodi tota, integra atque perfecta sive ex perfecto, toto et hoc aliquid ente, quod utrinque quidem ens est: ens inquam in potentia et ens in actu; ens in principio, ens et in fine; ens in materia, ens et in forma; ens in occulto, ens in aperto; ens inchoatum, ens perfectum. Est enim Sapiens integer, totus ac perfectus Homo. Homo inquam a natura et Homo ab intellectu; Homo in materia, Homo in forma; Homo in potentia, Homo in actu; Homo ex principio, Homo quoque ex fine; Homo existens, Homo et apparens; Homo denique inchoatus, Homo et perfectus."

[104] *De sap.*, xxxi, 369. Cf. *De sap.*, xxii, 348. "Artis vero Homo humanave species Arte progenita dyas est et primi quedam Hominis emanatio, Sapientia, fructus et finis. Cuius habitu, qui a natura Homo tantum erat, Artis fenore et uberrimo proventu reduplicatus Homo vocatur et Homo-Homo."

5*

which perfects him, a second *humanitas* and the true species and image of the man by art.[105]

As a self-achieved "humanity" this new wisdom is independent of any peculiarly Christian presuppositions. Because it is a naturally acquired virtue, it implies no opposition of grace and nature or of reason and an illuminated intellect—in clear contrast here to the various wisdoms of the Middle Ages, Nicholas of Cusa, the Florentine Neo-Platonists, and the Reformers. Wisdom is innate in the natural man and brought to mature perfection by him. No human incapacity and no compensatory grace intervene between the natural man, ignorant but potentially wise, and the man consummated and perfected by a wisdom which is at once his own species and the species of all things in the universe. Wisdom is a universal knowledge of the divine and human, and man's reason is potent and adequate to know it. Wisdom is man's end and perfection, and the perfect man embraces the Promethean encyclopedia as his natural and defining prerogative.

In the *De sapiente* Bovillus has created a Renaissance culture hero, heroic in his self-achieved perfection, his universality of knowledge, his esoteric isolation and self-sufficiency, and his capacity for ruling men. The medieval notion of the wise man was a static conception. He was a man whose perfection came to him as a gift of grace and whose properly sapiential knowledge was confined to divine things. He was rarely a self-consciously isolated thinker, but pursued knowledge as a member of the corporate body of the learned engaged in mastering received texts in the interest of a common and received end. He frequently described wisdom as self-knowledge, but the end of self-knowledge was to determine with precision his own place in a fixed and static hierarchy. Bovillus' wise man, on the other hand, is fundamentally dynamic. For him self-knowledge is a process of absorption by which he becomes all things by knowing them in himself. His wisdom is a perpetual becoming, a lifelong

[105] *De sap.*, xxii, 348. "Unde manifestum est Sapientiam esse quandam humanitatem et primi nostri, indefecati naturalisve Hominis imaginem veramque speciem seu artis Hominem ex primo, naturali Homine et ipso mundo felici congressu progenitum."

passage from potency to act. His perfection is actively self-achieved, for the wise man re-forms himself, and from the given matter of the natural man creates himself in wisdom. Even his esotericism is dynamic, as a revelation of his consciousness of change, his sense of novelty and innovation, and of his isolated progress toward an end fixed by and for himself: the universal knowledge of the perfect man.

Chapter 5

Sapientia Nostra

The late fifteenth century and the first half of the sixteenth century was a period of religious enthusiasm and reforming zeal. Paralleling the tentative secularisms of humanism ran a current of profound spirituality and mystical renunciation, a European movement without national or sectarian bias. Wessel Gansfort and the young Luther in Germany, John Colet in England, Savonarola in Florence, John Mombaer of Brussels, a late flower of the mystical piety of the Brothers of the Common Life, Marguerite of Navarre, and the circle around Jacques Lefèvre d'Etaples at Meaux: all these sought a more vibrant and personal religious life, a purity and simplicity to be found only by a return to the texts of Revelation, a total evacuation of self, a passive, almost feminine receptivity to the divine. They found their inspiration in the Pseudo-Dionysius, Augustine, the medieval mystics, and above all in the passionate and annihilating spirituality of Paul whom, as Lucien Febvre has finely said, "each true and passionate Christian of that age thought he himself had discovered and carried firmly closed in his heart like a private treasure and his source of ardour and a generous life."[1]

One problem—which they knew to include all others—dominated them: man's relation to God. They solved it by attributing as much as possible to God and as little as possible to man. Their judgment of the natural man is superb in the Pauline simplicity of its renunciations. All, says Colet, that "belongs absolutely and essentially to man (who is nothing if not weak, foolish, evil, vain, lost and nought; whose power is weakness, his wisdom folly, his will malicious, his acting an undoing, his accomplishment destruction) all, I say, that

---

[1] *Autour de l'Heptaméron. Amour sacré, amour profane*, 2nd ed. (Paris, 1944), 53.

goes to make up man is condemned with one voice and one judgment of the Spirit throughout the entire Holy Scriptures of God."[2]
"It is not only the privation of a property of the will," emphasizes
Luther, "nor only the privation of light in the intellect, of virtue in
the memory; but the absolute privation of all righteousness and of
the power of all strengths, of body and soul, of the whole man
interior and exterior. Further there is a positive inclination to evil,
a disgust for the good, a hatred of light and wisdom, a delight in
error and darkness, a flight from and abomination of good works,
a race toward evil."[3] And Calvin concludes: "The mind of man is
so entirely alienated from the righteousness of God that he cannot
conceive, desire, or design anything but what is wicked, distorted,
impure, and iniquitous; that his heart is so thoroughly envenomed
by sin, that it can breathe out nothing but corruption and rotten-
ness; that if some men occasionally make a show of goodness, their
mind is ever interwoven with hypocrisy and deceit, their soul inwardly bound with the fetters of wickedness."[4]

This is a view of man systematically hostile to the dignities with
which some Renaissance humanists were endowing him. It is an
ascetic rejection of *humanitas* and the world. The result is a depreciation of the powers of natural reason, a denial of the freedom of the
will, and a forcible insistence on man's inability to cooperate in his
own salvation.

Colet frequently emphasizes the weakness and insufficiency of
natural reason. Reason is the light of the soul, a participation in the
divine light and reason of which it is the lowest emanation. The
fall, however, brought a radical deterioration, leaving the light of
man's intellect "obscured and almost extinguished." Reason became

[2] *Enarratio in Primam Epistolam S. Pauli ad Corinthios*, J. H. Lupton,
ed. and tr. (London, 1874), 247. Noted henceforth as *Cor.* My translations of
Colet are based on those of Lupton. Page references are to the Latin text.

[3] *D. Martin Luthers Werke. Kritische Gesamtausgabe* (Weimar, 1883——),
LVI, 312. All references to Luther are to this edition, noted henceforth as
Weimar.

[4] Quoted by E. M. W. Tillyard, *The English Renaissance: Fact or Fiction?*
(London, 1952), 23; H. E. Fosdick, *Great Voices of the Reformation* (New
York, 1954), 218.

a "dense gloom," a "blindness," full of "fickleness and incapacity," weak and feeble, "purblind and sightless before the light of God and divine things," plunged in the waves of this world.[5] As a result men of themselves can have neither true knowledge nor true wisdom, for they are foolish, ignorant, and bad.[6] For Luther, too, human reason is wholly deformed and incapable of knowing hidden and invisible things. Although "synteresis" insures a potential aptitude for the wisdom of God, the unaided intellect is chained in darkness; and man inevitably sins when he tries to achieve any true knowledge without the aid of grace.[7]

It was precisely in order to furnish this grace, a spiritual illumination of the mind of man, that the Word was made incarnate. Every true notion must consequently be ascribed to Christ, for all truth is a necessary function of divine illumination. "The ground which is uncultivated and receives no rain from heaven," says Lefèvre d'Etaples in the Preface to his *Commentary on the Epistles of Paul*, "produces nothing fit for human consumption, only thorns, prickles, thistles, and useless herbs. In almost the same way, human minds which have not received the divine ray can produce nothing which is not more harmful than profitable and are incapable of giving souls a vivifying nourishment. Indeed, works of an intelligence deprived of grace from above are worth scarcely more than thorns and thistles."[8] When, therefore, Lefèvre's disciple, Marguerite of Navarre, speaks of the infidelity of reason and its ceaseless war against the Faith,[9] she is only taking the next simple and inevitable

---

[5] *Enarratio in Epistolam S. Pauli ad Romanos*, J. H. Lupton, ed. and tr. (London, 1873), 163. Noted henceforth as *Rom*. Cf. *Cor*., 168, 180 and Eugene F. Rice, Jr., "John Colet and the Annihilation of the Natural," *Harvard Theological Review*, XLV (1952), 141–163.   [6] *Cor.*, 246.

[7] Weimar, I, 148. Cf. Weimar, I, 36 and LVI, 355.

[8] Prefatory epistle to Guillaume Briçonnet, *Epistolae Divi Pauli Apostoli* (Paris, Henricus Stephanus, 1512), a, i, v. Cf. *Ibid*. "Mentes autem humanae de se steriles sunt, quae si se posse credunt, praesumunt: et si quicquam pariunt, infructuosum est, graue, opacum et potius contrarium menti quam vitale pabulum animae vitaeque consentaneum."

[9] Marguerite de Navarre, *Dialogue en forme de vision nocturne*, Pierre Jourda, ed., *Revue du Seizième Siècle*, XIII (1926), 29.

step: an assertion of the necessary and permanent hostility of grace and human reason. Explicitly Colet takes the same step. "Human reason," he says in an extreme statement, "is the enemy and opponent of grace."[10]

Parallel to this depreciation of natural reason is a tendency to deny the freedom of the will. Despite hesitations and embarrassment, Augustine's solution of the problem remained archetypal: Adam was able not to sin, man possessed by grace is not able to sin, and man unaided by grace can merely choose between different degrees of sin. In limping *terza rima* but with a mystic's passion, Marguerite of Navarre describes the incarceration of man's pristine freedom in the prison of sin. In the disordered state of nature after the fall man is a slave. The condition of liberty is grace:

> Franc Arbitre luy est lhors redonné,
> En luy treuve sa liberté perdue,
> Par trop avoir en péché sesiourné.[11]

Luther says the same thing. Alone the human will is in total bondage, and it cannot love the good nor will a righteous act. Only grace, purely gratuitous and just, can open the will to a freedom in which it is unable to sin.[12] Colet, despite certain inconsistencies,

---

"Mais aussy vient de Raison, qui entretient
Entendement en infidelité,
Qui contre Foy sans cesser contrevient.
Sans quelle Foy, pour dire verité,
Prudence, sens, humaine sapience,
C'est follie et tout vanité."

The poem probably dates from November, 1524: Pierre Jourda, "Sur la date du Dialogue en forme de vision nocturne," *Revue du Seizième Siècle*, XIV (1927), 150–161.

[10] *Epistolae B. Pauli ad Romanos Expositio Literalis, Opuscula quaedam theologica*, J. H. Lupton, ed. and tr. (London, 1876), 263. "Humana ratio inimica et adversaria est graciae: legem suam constituentes legi Dei non sunt subjecti."

[11] *Dialogue en forme de vision nocturne*, 24.

[12] Weimar, LVI, 235, 237.

is equally explicit. He repeats Augustine's antimonies: "Without grace, indeed, there is no liberty; and yet in grace there is nothing but liberty"; or, "unless a man will, he does not receive the light; and unless he is enlightened, he does not will to receive it."[13] Freedom is God's gift to a will created to receive it. Gratuitously, by an "arbitrary election," God's grace mysteriously selects certain souls for salvation. They themselves contribute nothing toward their election "lest the plan and purpose of God seem to depend on the will and deeds of men."[14] On the contrary, those who love God love Him because he has first loved them. Inscrutably, for, as John says, "the Spirit bloweth where it listeth," the gaps left by the fallen angels are filled by the elect whom a sweet and irresistible grace has drawn out of the formless iniquity of the natural state.[15]

Such emphasis on the weakness of the chief faculties of the human soul, reason and will, is only a special instance of a larger assertion: the radical inability of man to cooperate in his own salvation. Sixteenth-century theologism generally felt and discussed this problem in terms of a dichotomy of faith and works, of human merit and grace. Against a background of Pauline Christianity—the dramatic opposition of flesh and spirit and the emphasis on a total, generous, and gratuitous redemption through Christ—it erected a profoundly dualistic vision of the world and of man's relation to God which satisfied a basic emotional and pietistic need: the secret, sweet passivity of a total dependence on God. Doctrinally this old, almost mythical vision, which opposes man, powerless to contribute to his own salvation, and the arbitrary plenitude of grace, was formulated as the justification by faith alone. Its chief scriptural sources are two

[13] *Ioannes Coletus Super Opera Dionysii. Two Treatises on the Hierarchies of Dionysius*, J. H. Lupton, ed. and tr. (London, 1869), 183. The quotations are part of an excursus on free will independent of the Pseudo-Dionysius.

[14] *Rom.*, 163.

[15] *Rom.*, 142. Frederic Seebohm, *The Oxford Reformers*, 3rd ed. (London, 1887), 36 ff. compares Colet's views on free will to those of Savonarola. He denies that Colet's position can be described as Augustinian. A. Hyma, "Erasmus and the Oxford Reformers (1493–1503)," *Nederlandsch Archief voor Kerkgeschiedenis*, N.S. XXV (1932), 102 correctly emphasizes their similarity to Luther's lectures on Romans.

Die ewig Weyszhait

Wisdom and Fortune

Die Ler der Wisheit

IE NE SCAY.

PAIX ET PEV

DE LA
SAGESSE
TROIS LIVRES.
PAR
PIERRE CHARRON
Parisien Docteur
es Droicts.
Troisiesme edition reueüe
et augmentée
M.DC.XIIII.

A PARIS.
Chez David Douceur Libraire Iuré ruë Sainct
Iacques a l'enseigne du Mercure arresté.

Auec Priuilege
du Roy.

L. Gaultier
fecit

Allegory of Wisdom

celebrated texts of Paul: "For by grace are ye saved through faith; and that not of yourselves: it is the gift of God: Not of works, lest any man should boast." And again: "Therefore we conclude that a man is justified by faith without the deeds of the law."[16]

Much that is profound and beautiful in sixteenth-century religious writing is a rich embroidery on these texts. Already in a prayer to Jesus by the young Erasmus, the sinner implores a gratuitous and unmerited salvation: "It is a great thing, I know, that a wretched worm asks of Thee, not only beyond his merits but beyond prayers and understanding. . . . Therefore, not for my merits, which are none or evil, but of Thyself I beseech Thee."[17] For Marguerite of Navarre the only valid human merit finds its origin in the passion of Christ, whose grace sustains and unites man to Himself. Alone man is totally unprepared and can no more rise than stone or wood. He has no natural merit, his works are valueless and generally incited by sin; and justification and salvation, gratuitous gifts, never rewards, flow from divine grace through faith in Christ. Works are nothing, faith is all. The only good work is a good and simple heart, full of a faith tried and revealed by the love of one's neighbor.[18]

The assertion of the justification by faith alone is a conscious avoidance of the scandal which the confrontation of man's contingent being with God's omnipotence must inevitably raise. In abandoning man, created by God but wrecked by his own withdrawal of love, to the uninhibited exercise of the divine mercy, it is at once wholly logical and emotionally sound. Luther, and after him the

---

[16] Eph. 2:8-9; Rom. 3:28. Cf. Rom. 1:16-17.

[17] *Precatio Erasmi Roterodami ad Virginis Filium Jesum. Opera Omnia*, Joannes Clericus, ed. (Leyden, 1703-1706), V, 1213 D.

[18] *Dialogue en forme de vision nocturne*, 9, lines 97-99; 23, lines 502-504; 25, lines 544-546; 27, lines 604-606. Cf. Lefèvre d'Etaples' commentary on Eph. 2:8-9, *Epistolae Divi Pauli Apostoli* (Paris, 1512), 165 r. "Simus igitur erga deum animo semper gratiarum actione pleno, simus fideles. Nam gratia eius per fidem saluati simus: non saluati ex nobis neque ex operibus nostris, sed dei gratia. Gratia autem, donum est, non opus. Et ne etiam fidem qua mediante justificamur nostram esse credamus: etiam et ipsa est dei donum. Nichil igitur nobis: sed omnia deo tribuere debemus, vt non in nobis, non in operibus gloriemur: sed in sola dei gratia et misericordia."

vast majority of sixteenth-century Protestant reformers found a durable peace in this abandonment. They sought salvation not in any personal merit, good deeds, or any conscious exercise of will, but in the inflexible predestination of God. Before the immutability and omnipotence of God's will every act of contingent being is irrelevant. The elect do not merit salvation. They are saved only and necessarily by the inscrutable mercy of God. "This doctrine," cried Luther, "may seem hard and cruel, but it is full of sweetness..."; for it teaches us to seek humbly all assistance and all salvation from without, through faith in Christ the Redeemer.[19]

II

A religious sensibility which spontaneously minimizes nature in order to exalt grace will tend to deny all validity to human wisdom and resolve the traditional antagonism of "our Christian wisdom" and that of the philosophers by eliminating natural wisdom altogether. A woodcut in Sebastian Brant's *Narrenschiff* (1494) pictures this purely Revelational wisdom as a crowned, winged woman preaching in a church (*Sapientia clamitat.* Prov. 8:1). The arm of God in a cloud points at her head, divine illumination *desursum descendens*; while in her hand she holds a staff on the top of which is perched a haloed dove, *Spiritus domini spiritus sapientiae*, transmitting its inspiration to the audience at her feet. Wisdom, this emblem suggests, is a gift of God and the result of no human effort or learning. It is a revealed knowledge of divine things understood in an explicitly Christian sense.[20]

John Colet has outlined such a Christian wisdom. Christ is the wisdom of God, *sapientia tandem, quasi humanata in persona humana.*[21] Man's wisdom is knowledge of Him. The wise man knows "God and divine things," the "heavenly verities," and "things invisible." He is a *divinarum rerum contemplator.*[22] Scrip-

---

[19] Weimar, LVI, 91, 89, 382.

[20] Sebastian Brant, *Das Narrenschiff. Faksimile der Erstausgabe von 1494* (Strassburg, 1913), 58, 309.

[21] *Cor.*, 171, Cf. *Rom.*, 216.

[22] *Hierarchies*, 242; *Cor.*, 202; *Rom.*, 165.

ture is the source of wisdom, and its content is the short, simple, and perfect doctrine of Christ, a doctrine of faith, that all men should believe and trust in God and in His messenger Jesus Christ and confess their faith in Words.[23] Wisdom, therefore, comes only from God; it can be known only by faith, not by reason; and it is a product of divine illumination. "Illumination consists in faith in what is revealed, which is our wisdom."[24] All other wisdom is really foolishness, for "wisdom without faith is in truth a lack of wisdom and a degeneration from true wisdom to what is lower and worse." Colet calls it *tenebricosa* and *demonica*, and says that it is opposed to divine wisdom and despised and rejected by Christ.[25]

The Reformation idea of wisdom is very close to Colet's. Properly speaking, Luther says, only God is wise; and in its strictest sense *sapientia* is the Word of God or Christ.[26] He uses traditional Scotist distinctions to make this identification more precise. The names we attribute to God are either personal and relative or essential and absolute, the latter applicable to all three Persons of the Trinity, the former to one of the three without reference to the others. *Sapientia* is a *nomen personale* or *relativum* applied to Christ.[27]

The name denotes a form of contemplation. Wisdom is God contemplating in His Word all things before their becoming (the Ideas in His mind considered as exemplary causes), above their becoming (the universals of medieval realism existing above and apart from the objects in which they are individuated), and in their becoming (the Aristotelian forms of individual objects).[28] Uncreated wisdom is the serene contemplation of the world of form.

From another point of view, it is the active manifestation of God's formal principle to men and angels. In his *Commentary on Proverbs*

---

[23] *Rom.*, 169.

[24] *Hierarchies*, 240.

[25] *Rom.*, 192; *Cor.*, 171, 203, 238.

[26] Weimar, I, 36. "... incarnatum est verbum, sapientia Patris...."; Weimar, XXXIX (2), 25. "Filius Dei dicitur sapientia et virtus Dei."

[27] Weimar, IX, 20–21. Cf. *Ibid.*, 38 and Paul Vignaux, *Luther Commentateur des Sentences (Livre I, Distinction XVII)* (Paris, 1935), 33.

[28] Weimar, LVI, 440. "Ideo Sapientia Dei est, qua in se ipso contemplatur omnia, antequam fiant et supra quam fiant et intra quam fiant."

Melanchthon describes a Wisdom which reveals and glorifies the
Father in the marvelous order of the created world; in the promulga-
tion of the Word, its assumption of human nature and its resurrec-
tion; in the reparation of men and the conservation of the Church;
and in miracles like the flood or the crossing of the Red Sea. The
most important objectification of Wisdom in this sense (after the
Incarnation itself, of course) is the Word of God in Scripture. For
wisdom, Melanchthon continues, is not only the Word of God
revealed in the creation, in the salvation of man and in the Church,
but also in the Law and the Gospel.[29] Luther describes the Gospel
in the same words Paul used to describe Christ, *sapientia et virtus
Dei*;[30] and Melanchthon, commenting on the use of the word
wisdom in the book of *Proverbs*, makes it clear that the Old Testament too is a concrete manifestation of God's Word. *Lex Dei est
sapientia aeterna et immutabilis in Deo, revelata in doctrina Legis.*
It is a wisdom which teaches us what kind of men we should be and
what things we ought and ought not to do. It demands our conformity to the Wisdom and will of God which is manifest in the
Word, promising rewards to the obedient and damning those who
fail in that conformity which is perfect obedience.[31]

Human wisdom, on the other hand, that part of it at least which
is true wisdom, is knowledge of God—*Vera sapientia est cognitio
dei*[32]—or knowledge of Christ, the Word of God.[33] It must be distinguished from *scientia*, which is the knowledge of temporal things
(this is Augustin's distinction), and from *prudentia*, which judges
earthly things, deciding whether they are just or unjust, good or

[29] *Opervm Omnivm ... Philippi Melanthonis* (Wittenberg, 1562), II, 886–
887.

[30] Weimar, LVI, 165.

[31] Melanchthon, *Opera*, IV, 437. Cf. *Ibid.*, IV, 439. "Vna est Lex moralis
aeterna, quae est aeterna sapientia et voluntas in Deo, cuius suae sapientiae
radios Deus in creaturas rationales transfudit, et quam sapientiam Deus
expressit in Decalogo, et eius declarationibus saepe repetitis in scriptis
Propheticis et Apostolicis."

[32] Weimar, XVII (1), 39.

[33] Weimar, XXII, 325.

bad.[34] Luther calls it the contemplation of eternal things and the "notion [*notitia*] of things unknown to reason and world, that is, of things heavenly and spiritual."[35] What he means by heavenly things is clarified by Melanchthon's remarks on the word *notitia* in his *Definitiones multarum appellationum* where he defines wisdom as a *notitia vera*, "which knows the things that God wants us to look at and think about, as it is said in Deuteronomy 4: This is your wisdom, to hear the precepts of God."[36] Luther himself goes on to make explicit this identification of wisdom and revealed theology. "When you talk of wisdom," he says, "what you mean is the doctrine which teaches how to know God, which shows what his will, counsel, and intention are, and which includes all the articles of faith and how to become just in God's eyes, etc."[37]

Clearly, the wise man is the Christian; and the content of wisdom is Christian doctrine, the articles of faith or the *Credo*. Its primary source—by the doctrine of *sola scriptura*, indeed, its only source—is Scripture. "Wisdom is . . . the high, heavenly, hidden teaching of the Gospel of Christ." From it man learns to know the will of God, and this knowledge makes him wise.[38] The first problem, therefore, that a man faces in his effort to become wise is the nature of his assent to Revelation.

Luther's attitude is authoritarian. He demands an assent to Revelation without the aid of reason, condemning the search for motives of credibility and the effort to clarify and understand articles of faith like the Trinity. Scripture cannot be understood rationally, and he attacks Thomists and Scotists for their arrogant attempt to do so. "For the Spirit alone understands Scripture rightly and according to God's intention."[39] Scripture can be understood only through

[34] Weimar, LVI, 440. "Quod ad sapientiam pertinet eternorum contemplatio, Sed ad scientiam temporalium rerum cognitio." Cf. Weimar, XVII (2), 389.

[35] Weimar, XXXIX (2), 262.

[36] *Opera*, I, 353. Cf. Deut. 4:6.

[37] Weimar, XXII, 182. Cf. Weimar, XVII (2), 389.

[38] Weimar, XXII, 381. "Weisheit aber ist . . . eben die hohe heimliche verborgene Lere der Euangelij von Christo."

[39] Weimar, LVI, 336.

grace, prayer, and faith; and true faith is an assent to its mysteries unaided and unclarified by reason. Luther considered it an unworthy thing for human reason to be mixed up with divine Revelation; and, like John Colet, he was most unwilling "to have it thought that the truth was believed through the persuasion of men rather than through the power of God."[40]

He worked passionately, therefore, for a return to a purity of sapiential faith uncontaminated by philosophy. His writing is filled with attacks on the "subtleties" of the scholastic theologians and their profanation of mystery. Erasmus has reported Colet's similar hostility to Aquinas: "Why do you extol that writer to me? If he had not been full of arrogance, he would never have defined everything so rashly and so overbearingly; and without something of a worldly spirit he would not have contaminated the whole doctrine of Christ with his own profane philosophy."[41] Luther probes to the source and condemns the use of Aristotle's fallacious metaphysics and philosophy in theology.[42] This improperly mixes the human with the divine, diminishing the divine to human size and capacities. It claims to explain theology and to fortify the faithful by furnishing motives of credibility. In fact, it perverts it by falsely stripping Revelation of its mystery. Man must assent to the articles of theology as he assents to Scripture, by faith alone.[43] Before such mysteries the understanding fails.

As in Nicholas of Cusa, incomprehensibility is a cachet of distinction. The impenetrability of the Trinity becomes almost a guarantee of its virtue. Unlike Aquinas or Scotus who, while never trying to demonstrate the Trinity, once believing try to understand it—*fides quarens intellectum*—Luther insists that it be believed in the purity

[40] Colet, *Cor.*, 171.

[41] P. S. Allen, *Opus Epistolarum Des. Erasmi Roterodami* (Oxford, 1922), IV, ep. 1211, lines 438–441.

[42] Weimar, LVI, 349. Cf. H. Denifle, *Luther und Lutherthum* (Mainz, 1904), I, 587.

[43] Weimar, LVI, 6. " 'Fidei' dicit [Paulus], non Sapientie per rationes et experientias probande. Non enim intendit probare, que dicturus, Sed simpliciter sibi vult credi vt habenti auctoritatem diuinam neque ad disputandum de fide et iis, que credenda sunt."

of its Augustinian statement. It is ineffable and incomprehensible, and no effort should be made to show that it is compatible with reason or to taint its incomprehensibility by analysing it in terms of Aristotelian metaphysics. Philosophical concepts are a product of carnal wisdom, frivolous and useless, while any addition to faith in its simplicity is most certainly a figment of the human imagination.[44] Christ is the Wisdom of God; the doctrine of Christ is the wisdom of man. To the Scriptural and theological sources of this wisdom the human mind must bend passively. The wisdom of the Trinity, the *principium* of life and thought, is a gift of grace, to be believed quite simply. Before this sapiential treasury man becomes aware of the scandal of his reason and accepts humbly the gratuities of the divine.

The only viable way to become wise is therefore a spelling out of I Corinthians 3:18-19. "Let no man deceive himself. If any man among you seemeth to be wise in this world, let him become a fool, that he may be wise. For the wisdom of this world is foolishness with God." God, says Luther, "saves no one but sinners, makes learned no one but the simple and foolish, gives birth only to the dead—not those indeed who merely imagine or claim to be these things, but only those who really are and know it."[45] He who sincerely knows himself a fool is in fact a wise man. Similarly, those who boast of their strength, beauty, and nobility are in fact and in the sight of God, weak, deformed, and ignoble.[46] The condition of wisdom is ignorance, full consciousness of being a fool, the absence of all intellectual pride, and the knowledge that man, of himself, can never be wise. Stripped of all conceit and self-confidence, man must subject himself truthfully to God and look to Him for reformation and the power of discerning and judging all things rightly.

If the first stage in the acquisition of wisdom is the acute realization that, of himself, man is nothing, the second is the search outside

---

[44] Weimar, IX, 62. "Cum enim ista nemo viderit, quicquid supra fidem additur certissimum est figmentum esse humanum." Cf. *Ibid.*, 31 and Vignaux, *Luther Commentateur des Sentences*, 9ff.

[45] Weimar, LVI, 427.

[46] Weimar, LVI, 12.

himself for divine illumination. This illumination can come to him only from God, as an intellectual grace and a total re-formation by the Spirit and the Word, the wisdom of God. For wisdom comes only from God and is God's free gift. It is a virtue infused from above, *desursum descendens*; the noblest gift of the Holy Spirit, renewing and transforming all things. *Ego dabo vobis os et sapientiam.* Luther interprets Christ's promise by identifying *sapientia* and sacred theology and emphasizing that it is a divine gift from heaven poured into us through the Holy Spirit and not a philosophic invention of human reason.[47] "For God wants to save us by a justice and wisdom which is not inherent, but external to us, which originates and comes not from us but from without, and which does not spring from the earth, but comes from heaven."[48] To become wise the very Word of Justice and Wisdom is necessary, and this is the Word of Faith.[49] From it alone comes the total re-formation in the Spirit which makes the acquisition of wisdom possible. Natural man has the form of carnal wisdom, a wisdom hostile to God. He must abandon this form and take on a new and spiritual form by destroying all carnal attachments and conforming himself, through faith, to the Word.[50] For only the Word will make him wise.[51] Conformed to the Word and Wisdom of God through faith, he is, like it, just, true, wise, good, gentle, and chaste.[52]

Luther demands that religion encompass every good, that every virtue be included in it and subordinated to it. He recognizes no virtue, no probity, no wisdom which does not have its source and definition in Revelation. True wisdom, therefore, must be defined

[47] Weimar, XXXIX (1), 260, 262; XXII, 182, 381.

[48] Weimar, LVI, 158.

[49] *Ibid.*, 406. "Quia Caro et sapientia carnis nullo modo est capax Iustitie et sapientie Dei, Idcirco necesse est ipsum verbum Iustitie et sapientie, quod est verbum fidei."

[50] *Ibid.*, 329–330.

[51] *Ibid.*, 409. Cf. *Ibid.*, 68–69. "Igitur sola fide dicitur: 'Quoniam iniquitatem meam ego cognosco,' quia sequitur: 'Incerta et occulta sapientie tue manifestasti mihi.' Hec sunt absconditissima legis: cognitio, que nunquam perfecte cognoscitur, Sed manifestatur, Vt credatur."

[52] *Ibid.*, 330.

as a revealed knowledge of Christian doctrine in the purity of its Scriptural and credal statement. It is a theological virtue in the realm of faith. Its content is the *Credo*, and it is received passively as a gift of grace, beyond all rational exercise.

Luther reinforces these assertions by two important statements of what wisdom is not. He denies, first, that the naturally accessible truths of natural theology can be accepted as wisdom. In the second place, he denies the sapiential character of metaphysical knowledge. By thus rejecting areas of knowledge which many of his predecessors, contemporaries, and successors considered true wisdom, he emphasizes the radically Christian content of *sapientia*, its Revelational character and its inaccessibility to the unilluminated reason.

Aquinas had considered the naturally accessible truths of natural theology an important part of true wisdom; and the possibility of their acquisition had been frequently justified by a classic text from Paul's *Epistle to the Romans*: "For the invisible things of him from the creation of the world are clearly seen, being understood by the things that are made, even his eternal power and Godhead."[53] Commenting this text, Luther does not explicitly deny the possibility of such knowledge; he does deny its usefulness and, except in a limited and pejorative human sense, its truth. The human mind can know the disparate particulars of sense experience with reasonable certainty and proceed unaided from them to some knowledge of the divine. Reasoning from created things, *naturaliter ex effectibus*, the ancient philosophers, although they were ignorant of the creation, could ascend to the knowledge of God's existence and know certain of his attributes: that He is one, unchanging, and eternal; good, beautiful, just, and mighty. Thus, man "in this world can to a certain degree understand the things of God, which are beyond sight and sense."[54]

This knowledge is natural, autonomous, and certain; but it is also insufficient, profitless, dangerous, true only in a limited human sense, and therefore unusable as a basis for a natural theology or the natural acquisition of wisdom. For Luther, always sensitive to the wickedness of man and the frailty of his reason, it is a knowledge

[53] Romans 1:20.
[54] Weimar, LVI, 174. Cf. *Ibid.*, 176–177.

which, although true in itself, only leads downward through four stages of perdition when received by men who do not possess and are not guided by faith. The first of these stages is ingratitude. Received by the *vetus homo*, knowledge of God only increases his pride. He refuses to worship God in his pure and nude reality, but reconstructs Him according to his own human image and his own carnal wishes and desires. He worships no God but a figment of his own imagination, and transforms the truth of God into a lie. Sunk thus in his own thoughts and imaginings, careful only of his own intentions and efforts, he feeds on himself alone and on creatural goods, seeking nothing higher than his own glory, pleasure, and utility. This is vanity, the second stage of his fall; and it plunges him at once into spiritual blindness, the third stage. Here empty of all truth, he wanders foolishly in darkness. The result is error toward God and his final perdition. Deep in sin and idolatry he worships no real God, but a foul creation of his own—Jupiter or some other. He has relinquished God and is now drawn into every devilish wickedness.[55]

Luther denies that metaphysics—and philosophy in general—is wisdom for much the same reasons that he condemns natural theology. All philosophical knowledge acquired solely by natural reason is useless and a *sapientia carnis* opposed to true wisdom and to God. It is useless because the only important task of man on earth is to open himself humbly to regeneration and salvation. It is dangerous because it is an infraction of the Augustinian rule of *uti non frui* and because it draws man from the contemplation of God to an exclusive interest in the temporal and creatural. The study of creatures is justified only if they are considered from the point of view of God and a future life, *secundum quod future sunt*. Any consideration of the natural world per se is wasted effort. Luther condemns physics, the study of motion, and metaphysics, the study of *essentia* or *quidditates et qualitates*, as a loss of precious time better devoted to more transcendent objects. "We conclude, therefore, that the man who studies the essences and operations of creatures

[55] *Ibid.*, 178–179.

rather than their longings and expectations of a future life is without doubt a blind fool who does not even know that creatures are only created beings."[56] The creature can be fruitfully studied only from the point of view of his relation to God, not the causal relation which can unite him to God in the natural realm, but the supra-rational relation of redemption in the area of grace. One must see him only in his groans, expectations, and anxieties, "that is, full of hatred for what is and longing for that which is not yet."[57]

Philosophy is the knowledge of what is. In contrast to true wisdom it is at once, following the Augustinian distinction, *scientia* and a corrupt form of wisdom. If true wisdom is "the contemplation of eternal things," *scientia* is the knowledge of created things outside of God.[58] Its point of departure is a sensible experience of the visible, and it proceeds by rational and experimental demonstration. Luther identifies it with *sapientia humana*, *sapientia carnis*, and a *sapientia corporalis*, under which he classifies philosophy and the liberal arts.[59] Such knowledge is the province of those outside the faith who are ignorant of God and a future life, of men wise in visible things. It is a wisdom of this world whose contaminated source is natural reason. It is no true wisdom. "Those therefore who are wise in and concerning visible things (as are all those outside the Faith and those who are ignorant of God and a future life) understand nothing and are wise in nothing, that is, they are neither intelligent [*intelligentes*] nor wise [*sapientes*], but foolish and blind. And though they may think themselves wise men, yet they have become fools. For they are wise, not in the wisdom of secret, hidden things, but of that which can be found in a human way."[60]

Melanchthon, in spite of his humanistic leanings, also says that any knowledge found in a human way is folly. For him too *sapientia carnalis* and *sapientia rationis* are the same.[61] The whole of

---

[56] *Ibid.*, 371–372.   [57] *Ibid.*, 371.
[58] *Ibid.*, 440. "Scientia autem est eorum, que sunt extra Deum et creata."
[59] *Ibid.*, 362.
[60] *Ibid.*, 237. Cf. Henri Strohl, *L'Evolution religieuse de Luther jusqu'en 1515* (Strasbourg and Paris, 1922), 162.
[61] *Opera*, III, 716.

philosophy and human wisdom deals with terrestrial, fleeting things: civic virtue, good health or bodily strength, power, wealth, and pleasure. It never talks about the will of God or eternal light, wisdom and justice. Instead it teaches a low shrewdness in increasing one's own power and wealth without regard to the means.[62] Athens under Solon and Pericles, the Rome of Fabius, Scipio, and Laelius were rich in human wisdom. But what use was their universal wisdom without true knowledge of God? Ignorant of their eternal end, they never asked God for aid and counsel nor did they know that justice which gives eternal life. In the end their wisdom was destructive of their country and of themselves. Their reliance on human wisdom brought down dreadful calamities on Themistocles, Theramenes, Pericles, Cicero, and many others; while a similar confidence has spawned innumerable heresies since the time of the Apostles—clear evidence that God hates our trust in human wisdom and wants to rule us by His Word alone.[63]

Just as natural theology, then, inevitably sinks into idolatry, so does an autonomous philosophy produce a wisdom whose chief characteristics are pride, vanity, and error. It is sunk concupiscently in the visible, its end in man and not in God. It places the *summum bonum* in creatures rather than in God,[64] thus enjoying the created more than the Creator and determining what is good and bad according to the vanities of human judgment. All rebellion against God originates in this carnal wisdom. It is the greatest barrier between man and God. Proudly unsubjected to God, human wisdom flows from the unbridled reason and a dangerous self-confidence in which men seek salvation in their own wisdom and justice and reject the word of God. "For carnal wisdom, which the vulgar call *Sinnligkeit*, is a form of sensuality, a servitude to one's own judgment, that is, the reason is wise and dictates what seems right and good to it. But it is unable to do this; and should seek from God, that it may be taught by His Spirit, not what seems right and good, but what

---

[62] *Opera*, II, 886; III, 650.   [63] *Opera*, II, 887; III, 661–662, 736.

[64] Weimar, LVI, 76. "Denique Iob. 3. Maledixit hunc diem sapientie, Quia Deo contraria est et facit bonum apparere aliud quam summum illud, quod Deus est, et frui eo, quod est creatura."

in fact is right and good." For the Word, the Wisdom of God, was made man precisely "in order to remove and annihilate this most evil wisdom of ours which is full of vanity, error, and sin."[65] All autonomous philosophical knowledge is thus by its very nature opposed to God. It is sterile as a source of wisdom.

Metaphysical wisdom—a natural knowledge of eternal things and the second important area of natural wisdom set up by Aquinas— is impossible for other reasons. Without grace it is impossible to pass from particular to universal in any field. Aristotle had noted that "all men suppose what is called Wisdom to deal with the first causes and the principles of things."[66] But Luther, because there exist for him no autonomous secondary causes in a world penetrated by the divine, denies that one can proceed from the sensible object to its invisible cause. Thus, "all those are fools who, like Aristotle, seek the knowledge of things through their causes, for they are incomprehensible."[67] Reason is equally powerless to perform similar operations in the realm of ethics. It is capable of knowing particular goods, but cannot know any good *in genere et universali*. It can know only what it has judged good and useful from its restricted, human point of view. Grace alone can lift it to the *summum bonum* and enable it to judge all lesser goods by its standard.[68] In the same way it is impossible for the unaided reason to pass from visible to invisible things, from the particulars of sense experience to universals or the ideas in the mind of God. Luther has a mystical epistomology, a fundamental skepticism immediately rescued by grace. The natural man is a nominalist. Grace enables him to become a realist. By reason alone man can know only particular things without significant interrelations and apart from their intimate connections with the divine.[69]

---

[65] Weimar, I, 34. Cf. Weimar, LVI, 212–213. "Sapientia enim nostra non solum verbis Dei non credit neque subiicitur, Sed etiam Verba Dei non esse putat, sed sese verba Dei habere credit et veracem esse presumit. Sicut Iudeorum et hereticorum et omnium ceruicosorum hominum est insipientia."

[66] *Metaph.*, I, 1, 981b, 28–29.   [67] Weimar, LVI, 116.

[68] Weimar, LVI, 355–356. Cf. Weimar, I, 36.

[69] Weimar, I, 35. See also Weimar, LVI, 407; IX, 83, line 9 where he speaks of the *error realistarum*; and Strohl, *L'Evolution religieuse de Luther*, 167, 170–171.

He needs divine help to know invisible things. This is the more necessary because Luther equates invisibles with the truths of Christian doctrine, which at once transforms them from objects of metaphysics into objects of theology.[70] And naturally acquired knowledge of objects of theology is both useless and ultimately false.

Luther concludes that wisdom is exclusively Christian. He opposes true wisdom, attainable only by faith or the mystic's seizure, spiritual and a gift of grace, to human or earthly wisdom, to all wisdom carnally acquired by natural means. The one is in the province of the *vetus homo*; the other in that of the *novus homo*. One is wisdom in the sight of man; the other is wisdom in the sight of God. One is *sapientia spiritus*, the other *sapientia carnis*; and *sapientia carnis* is "hostile to God because it is not from God but from the devil." Consciousness of possessing such wisdom is pride; its content an arrogant inanity. The human intellect is blind to the things of God, and in His sight the wisdom of the world is foolishness. *Sapientia vera*, *sapientia nostra*, on the other hand, is a wisdom of the spirit; and since the fall of man the presence of the spirit is determined solely by a gratuitous gift of divine grace.[71] The truly wise man thus finds his only adequate foundation in Christ. His roots are in God, and he derives the nourishment of wisdom and goodness through them alone. He seeks the wisdom-giving knowledge of secret, hidden, and invisible things in Revelation and is conscious that only the man reformed by faith and divine illumination can attain and contemplate them.

The search for wisdom is thus indistinguishable from the search for salvation. Just as man is incompetent to cooperate in his own salvation, so too is he powerless to attain true wisdom without the help of God. Before God, man is an untilled field full of weeds and thistles, a virgin bride before the bridegroom, a lump of soft wax in the hands of a modeler. He has no free will, no effective, autonomous intellectual power, no true wisdom. He is without form —contingent, mutable, and powerless. But to his formlessness is opposed the formal fecundity of Gods grace, which repairs his

---

[70] Weimar, III, 176.   [71] Weimar, LVI, 76.

reason, frees his will, makes him wise, and gratuitously saves him. Opened finally to this destructive but redemptive penetration of the divine, the carnal formlessness of human wisdom is replaced by a new and spiritual form which is a gift of grace.

III

Calvin's idea of wisdom is a modified restatement of Luther's. It sums up with elegance and simplicity the sixteenth-century revelational conception of wisdom and the wise man.

All true and solid wisdom is twofold: knowledge of God and knowledge of oneself. The former teaches not only that God is one and to be worshiped and adored by every man; but also that in Him is the fountain of all truth, wisdom, power, and holiness. All participation in these essentially divine attributes and virtues must be humbly sought by man from God, with praises of the divine mercy and its gifts. Knowledge of oneself, on the other hand, is the fully conscious realization of one's own weakness, misery, vanity, and hideousness. It leads one, first, to an earnest humility, self-abasement, and a distrust and hatred of oneself; and second, it illuminates a desire, based on the consciousness that man is empty and devoid of goodness, to seek God, the treasure house of all good. Hence, and this knowledge is the core of wisdom, "from the consciousness of our own misery, blindness, vanity, wickedness, and corruption we recognize that true greatness, wisdom, truth, justice, and purity is located nowhere but in God. Thus our own evils urge us to contemplate the goodness of God; and we cannot seriously aspire to Him before we have begun to be absolutely disgusted by ourselves."[72] Wisdom is thus primarily a knowledge of God and divine things whose necessary preliminary basis is a knowledge of the human condition: the absence of all human good and man's deplorable depravity since his fall.

[72] *Christianae Religionis Institutio,* I, 1: *Ioannis Calvini Opera quae supersunt Omnia,* Guilielmus Baum, Eduardus Cuntiz, Eduardus Reuss, eds. (Braunschweig, 1863–1900), I, 279. "Tota fere sapientiae nostrae summa, quae vera demum ac solida sapientia censeri debeat, duabus partibus constat:

The insight that wisdom is first and essentially an attribute of God and that human wisdom is an unmerited gift of grace is the foundation of the Calvinist conception. For Calvin, as for Luther, Colet, or Lefèvre d'Etaples, wisdom is the Word of God, supervising the creation and all God's works, but itself generated outside of time and before the creation of the world.[73] Preëxistent and buried thus in the opacity of the Trinity, it is, as Paul rightly says, mysterious and hidden. Remembering their own weakness, therefore, human beings must acknowledge that the light of wisdom, covered as it is by a deep mist, is properly and literally called inaccessible.[74] Only the grace of God, by divine illumination or an infusion from above, *desursum descendens*, can redeem a human folly irremediable by man's unaided efforts and make him wise. Such wisdom, and this illustrates a triumph of the virtue of God over the flesh, comes *per Dei gratiam* and solely as a gift of the Holy Spirit. Like salvation it is totally unmerited and its sole source is the divine mercy.[75]

---

cognitione Dei, et nostri. Illa scilicet, quae non modo unum esse Deum ostendat, quem ab omnibus oporteat coli et adorari, sed simul etiam doceat, illum unum omnis veritatis, sapientiae, bonitatis, iustitiae, iudicii, misericordiae, potentiae, sanctitatis fontem esse, ut ab ipso et expectare et petere universa ista discamus, praeterea cum laude et gratiarum actione accepta illi referre. Altera autem, quae, nostram nobis imbecillitatem, miseriam, vanitatem, foeditatem ostendendo, primum nos in seriam humilitatem, deiectionem, diffidentiam, odiumque nostri adducat, deinde quaerendi Dei in nobis desiderium accendat, nempe in quo repositum sit omne bonum, cuius ita inanes et vacui deprehendimur."

[73] *Rel. Christ. Institutio*, 481.

[74] *Institutio Rel. Christ.* (*1559*), I, xviii, 3: *Opera*, II, 171. "An quia propter hebetudinem sensus nostri multiplex apparet Dei sapientia (vel multiformis, ut reddidit vetus interpres) ideo somnianda nobis est in ipso Deo aliqua varietas, quasi vel consilium mutet, vel a se ipso dissideat? Imo, ubi non capimus quomodo fieri velit Deus quod facere vetat, veniat nobis in memoriam nostra imbecillitas, et simul reputemus, lucem quam inhabitat, non frustra vocari inaccessam, quia caligine obducta est."

[75] *Commentarius in Epistolam Posteriorem ad Corinthios*, I, 12: *Opera*, L, 17–18.

Hence the notion, verbally classical and charged with antique overtones, but now clear in its real meaning, that the origin and half the content of wisdom is self-knowledge. For Calvin self-knowledge is the knowledge of human depravity and weakness and the consequences of this for man's relation to God. Wisdom in this sense is simply the knowledge that of himself man is a fool and must therefore attribute no good to himself but seek every moral and intellectual virtue from God. The wisdom of self-knowledge, since it reveals no more than a negative abyss, is only a proper state of mind, an as yet unfulfilled capacity to be wise. It has no relation whatever to the dignity of the antique conception. It is rather the confession of ignorance, folly, and impotence; a form of ascesis which becomes the condition on which, if God is merciful, man may receive wisdom: a reinforcement and explanation of the assertion that all true wisdom comes to man gratuitously as a gift of the Holy Spirit.

Positive wisdom, true wisdom, therefore, is a divine gift and must be defined as a knowledge of divine things inaccessible to natural reason. Calvin echoes the traditional Augustinian distinction between *sapientia* and *scientia*, but with modifications. He defines *scientia* as a knowledge of holy things and *sapientia* as the perfection of this knowledge. *Sapientia* is, of course, knowledge of a much higher order, and its content is the most secret and sublime revelations.[76] It is a *Christi scientia*, a knowledge of Jesus Christ, the whole doctrine of salvation, and of the "secret mysteries of the Kingdom of God" derived from a humble and illuminated perusal of the

---

[76] *Commentarius in Epistolam Pauli ad Corinthios I*, XII, 8: *Opera*, XLIX, 499. "Quod ad differentiam istorum donorum (pertinet): scientia vel cognitio et sapientia varie in scripturis sumuntur: sed hic accipio tanquam minus et maius, sicut ad Colossenses, capite 2, 3, ubi etiam iunguntur, quum tradit Paulus reconditos esse omnes thesauros in Christo sapientiae et scientiae. Scientia ergo rerum sacrarum intelligentiam mihi significat: sapientia vero eius consummationem. Aliquando prudentia quasi media inter ipsas ponitur: et tunc peritiam applicandae ad usum aliquem intelligentiae significat. Sunt quidem valde affines, sed tamen vides in coniunctione discrimen. Sit ergo scientia mediocris cognitio: sapientia vero revelationes magis arcanas et sublimes contineat."

6+

Gospels.[77] In the moral realm the wise man is he who, having laid aside all pride and confidence in himself, has been borne upward by the authority of God, whose mind is filled only with God, and who considers nothing righteous but what He has prescribed.[78] The result is a Christian philosophy wedded to the Gospels as its chief source, a Christian wisdom whose content is a knowledge of the Trinity and Christian doctrine, whose preoccupations are faith, love, God, the remission of sins, grace, the nature of justification, and true works.

Such wisdom is a *sapientia* of the spirit. But Calvin speaks also of a wisdom of the world, a human or carnal wisdom, and it is his relative moderation here which distinguishes his views from the hermit-like denunciations of Luther and Colet. Spiritual wisdom is absolutely hidden to the natural man. Human wisdom, on the other hand, and here it is indistinguishable from the normal definition of *scientia*, is all knowledge acquired by the unaided reason, all knowledge which can be in man without the illumination of the Holy Spirit, whether by the power of his natural intelligence, from the teachings of experience, or from a cultivation of the liberal arts.[79] Such wisdom is neither false nor necessarily opposed to spiritual wisdom. It is, however, subservient, and, as philosophy is the handmaiden of theology, so also is human wisdom the handmaiden of spiritual wisdom. As in Aquinas, the higher perfects and consummates the lower; or, more precisely, in the terminology of Augustine, the knowledge which comprises human wisdom is to be used and not enjoyed. It is a means, not an end; and in itself is of negligible importance. Philosophy and the liberal arts have an authentic place.

[77] *Commentarius in I Cor.*, 325.

[78] *Commentarius in Acta Apostolorum*, X, 21: *Opera*, XLVIII, 234. "Hoc est vere sapere, dum exinanita omni confidentia et correcta pertinacia nos Dei autoritas ad se rapit, mentesque nostras sic occupat, ut nobis nihil rectum sit, nisi quod illa praescribit."

[79] *Commentarius in I Cor.*, 234. "Hic per sapientiam intelligit quidquid comprehendere potest homo, tam naturali ingenii facultate, quam usu et literis atque artium scientia adiutus.... Proinde quidquid intelligentiae in hominem cadit absque spiritus sancti illustratione, id sub mundi sapientia continetur."

They form the privileged area of natural reason; they are gifts of God and good of their kind. Still, they must be used only, that is, they must be subject always to the Word and Spirit of God.[80] Separated from God, made the occasion for self-confidence and pride, they are pernicious and become a wisdom carnal in the Pauline sense: a radical folly, pure vanity, damnable, and opposed to God. For human wisdom is totally incapable of penetrating the divine. Its sole value is supplementary and utilitarian, and if it is perverted into an end, the blindness and disorder of loves which results is the beginning of spiritual death.

IV

The Reformation idea of wisdom has three fundamental characteristics. First, wisdom is an intellectual virtue, a form of knowledge, an attribute of the intellect rather than of the will. Second, because its content is Christian by definition, it is inseparable from Revelation. It is a knowledge of divine things, understood as the Trinity and the *Credo*. Its source, finally, is wholly external to man: God as He reveals himself in Scripture or by the direct action of grace.

This wisdom is unashamedly revelational. No trace of metaphysics disfigures it, no philosophy profanes it. As a knowledge of the essential points of Christian doctrine it is revealed and, with the aid of grace, firmly believed. If one could overthrow the poverty of words, one would see that it is not even a form of knowledge. It is certain, but cannot be demonstrated; it is true, but cannot be known. It must be believed and then perfected by love. *Illuminatio in fide est revelatio, quae est sapientia nostra*, said Colet; and Luther drives the point home in a perfect definition: wisdom is the knowledge that Christ became incarnate, was crucified, died, and was resurrected from the dead for our salvation.[81]

---

[80] *Commentarius in I Cor.*, 360.

[81] Weimar, III, 176. "Est enim intellectus cognitio vel notitia sensus Christi, de quo Apostolus 1. Corinth. 1. et 2. excellenter docet, quoniam 'Sapientiam loquimur inquit absconditam in mysterio, quam nemo principum huius seculi cognovit.' Et est breviter nihil aliud nisi sapientia crucis Christi, que gentibus stultitia et Iudeis scandalum est, scilicet intelligere, quod filius dei est incarnatus et crucifixus et mortuus et sucitatus propter nostram salutem."

This conception of wisdom is a commonplace of post-Augustinian Christianity. Given a new vigor by the Reformation, it dominates important areas of sixteenth-century speculation. Not only Protestants urge it. It can be found in the Spanish mystics and in the Hymns of Ronsard. It was widely held in French Catholic circles at the end of the Renaissance.[82] It returns with renewed emphasis in Pascal and the Jansenists of Port Royal. A striking page of Guillaume Budé's *De asse* reveals its most intimate message. Antiquity, he remarks, was convinced that the wise man formed himself, that *sapientia* was a naturally acquired virtue, that it depended on man alone to be what he was or wished to become. But we Christians, taught by Scripture, know better: that man cannot reform himself to wisdom without the intervention of God, that God, who inclines our wills to good and evil, is the sole source of real wisdom.[83] This is a perceptive contrast of Christian and antique ideas of wisdom. It makes equally clear the essential difference between the Medieval-Reformation idea of wisdom and the various definitions of Renaissance humanism.

[82] Pierre Charron, *De la Sagesse*, Amaury Duval, ed. (Paris, 1820–24), II, 148–151.

[83] *De Asse, et partibus eivs, libri V* (Lyons, 1550), 737–738. "Haec est in uita humana summi boni medulla, quam ueluti thesaurum in sacrario sapientiae conditum, tot philosophorum classes omnem lapidem molientes (ut est in prouerbio) inuenire nequiuerunt. Existimabant enim non ex deo sed ex sese ita aptum sapientem esse, ut in eo plane situm esset an ipse talis esset. Nos autem ex sacris monumentis accepimus arbitrium tantum nostri iuris esse, rectam autem firmamque animi constitutionem muneris esse diuini, sed ita promiscui, ut nulli recte atque ordine id petenti negetur.... Atenim haec de sapientia in confesso sunt apud omnes qui se probatae et uerae persuasionis tenaces uideri uolunt. Quis enim negare audeat quae oraculorum instar habent? Sed quae nos hodie studia literarum uocamus, nihil eo pertinent. Quid enim literis priscis cum studio sapientiae, quae a Christo genus ducit?"

Chapter 6

The Transformation of Wisdom from Knowledge to Virtue

The Reformation idea of wisdom was the last major reassertion of the medieval Christian conception. It was a living ideal in the sixteenth century; but it faced powerful and ultimately destructive competition from the more secular enthusiasms of humanism, from ideas best represented by Bovillus and Pierre Charron.

Bovillus represents strikingly that group of Renaissance thinkers who found wisdom in knowledge. His wisdom is a universal *scientia*, an intellectual virtue, and a form of contemplation. Charron's *De la Sagesse* is a corresponding and ideal summary of the arguments of those who found wisdom in virtue. His wisdom is a precise and particular prudence, a moral virtue, and a code of action. Bovillus identified *sapientia* and *scientia*; Charron identifies *sapientia* and *prudentia: Ainsi nous disons que sagesse est preude prudence, c'est-à-dire preud'hommie avec habilité, probité bien advisé.*[1]

This transformation of wisdom from contemplation to action, from a body of knowledge to a collection of ethical precepts, from a virtue of the intellect to a perfection of the will is humanism's chief contribution to the development of the idea of wisdom in the century between Bovillus' *De sapiente* and Charron's *De la Sagesse.* The result was a moral wisdom appropriately symbolized by the Minerva of Mantegna in the Louvre, that severe and armored virgin in aggressive pursuit of the passions and vices of the soul.

The transformation of wisdom from knowledge to virtue is, of course, a moralizing process evident in humanism from the beginning. Petrarch had said that wisdom was inseparable from virtue;

[1] *De la Sagesse* (Paris, 1836), 702.

and Salutati had gone further in the direction of identifying wisdom and prudence than anyone was to go before the middle of the sixteenth century. But this development was not continuous or linear. The early efforts of Italian humanism to associate wisdom with moral virtue and civic action relaxed in the second half of the fifteenth century; and even in the next century humanists in Italy and the North continued the earlier effort only in part. They paid scant attention, for example, to any kind of wisdom tied specifically to civic action. On the other hand, they did increasingly concern themselves with the relations of wisdom and virtue and wisdom and worldly success. *Sapientia* remained for them the quality men most prize; but they asked again not what they must *know* to *become* wise, but what they must *do* to *be* wise. Like Socrates they wanted to "call philosophy down from the heavens and set her in the cities of men and bring her also into their homes and compel her to ask questions about life and morality and things good and evil."[2] They transferred wisdom from heaven to earth.

Their motives for doing this, the terms of the problem they were trying to solve, the assumptions on which their new solution rested are all suggested by three texts originating in France between 1530 and 1580. The first is Guillaume Budé's *De Philologia*. It is a dialogue between Budé and Francis I, and it opens with a comparison of *sapientia* and *prudentia*. Budé is disturbed by the fear that he has given too much time to the pursuit of wisdom and not enough to acquiring prudence. The king is astonished. Isn't wisdom, he asks, the knowledge of true, honorable, and useful things and their causes: to call a man wise, isn't that to call him prudent too?[3] Not necessarily, Budé replies. Properly speaking, wisdom is an intellectual virtue, *mentis et intellectus exacta quaedam constitutio et absoluta*; and Budé defines it, in the traditional way, as a contemplation of sempiternal things, of things which remain ever the same and cannot change. Prudence, on the other hand, he compares to the *ius gentium*. It is a knowledge of mutable things and of things which virtuously regulate human life. Because of the majesty of its name

[2] Cicero, *Tusc. Disp.*, V, iv, 10–11.
[3] *De philologia libri II* (Paris, Badius Ascensius, 1532), V, r.

—and in itself—wisdom is nobler than prudence, for it contemplates nobler and more elevated things. But prudence is more useful and appropriate to men; while wisdom without prudence is useless and ridiculous.[4]

Because they knew high, admirable, and divine things Aristotle rightly called Anaxagoras and Thales wise men; but, again rightly, he denied that they were prudent. For, since they were ignorant of the order of human goods and of things conducive to a good life, this knowledge was of no use to them. Prudence, as Cicero said, is a certain art of living; and no ignorance is more damnable than that of how to lead a righteous, useful, and orderly life. We have given philosophy a serious and splendid name and call it the pursuit of wisdom because it seeks a knowledge of all things divine and human. We call it prudence, however, only when it benefits men and helps them achieve a richer, ampler, and more fruitful existence, which is, after all, the customarily desired end of all living men.[5]

It is a deplorable commonplace to observe men who are deeply learned and technically "wise" with barely a trace of philosophy in this more richly ethical sense. Who has not experienced, exclaims Budé, the rude lack of humanity, the meanness and parsimony of such men. They are said to be learned, and no doubt they are; but

---

[4] *De philologia*, V, r. "Verum sapientia proprie virtus est, contemplatrix rerum sempiternarum, atque earum quae semper eodem modo se habentes, non admittunt mutationem. Cum interim prudentia in iis percipiendis occupata sit, quae mutabilia quidem ipsa, sed tamen ad humanam vitam agendam conducibilia esse manifestum est, duntaxat vt est comparata iure gentium vita. Ac tametsi sapientia cum nominis maiestate, tum re etiam ipsa dignior sit prudentia, nam digniora excelsioraque contemplatur, hominibus tamen vtilior est commodiorque prudentia."

[5] *De philologia*, V, v. "Certe quidem nulla maior esse potest aut damnosior inscientia, quam vitae, recte, commode, atque ordine constituendae. Ita haec quam graui nomine ac specioso vocamus philosophiam quasi studium sapientiae, quod rerum vtique humanarum intelligentiam diuinarumque con-sectatur, et praefert, sapientiae quidem titulum sibi tueri potest, non item prudentiae: nisi hominibus vna quoque id praestet, vnde conditionem quisque suam vberiorem facere amplioremve possit: quem fere finem esse videmus omnium more hominium viuentium."

the generality of men do not consider them honest or provident. Really prudent men, indeed, have almost come to the conclusion that wisdom and prudence are mutually exclusive, that men seduced by the promises of wisdom and the magnificence of its name become utterly useless to society and to themselves. Their lives are disordered and often immoral, their private affairs languish, and their improvidence strips them of any protection against poverty, disgrace, or an unexpected change of fortune. Wisdom, disassociated so ostentatiously from prudence, becomes empty and jejune, almost a vice; and frugal, careful parents, bent on an orderly, prosperous life, have begun to forbid their sons all commerce with the Muses and philosophy.[6]

Budé has posed the problem: the contemporary gap between prudence and wisdom, knowledge and morals, contemplation and action. Louis Le Caron, a poet and lawyer of the next generation,[7] begins with the same problem. But his more radical criticisms of a purely intellectual and contemplative wisdom not only define the problem more clearly; they also make explicit those more dynamic assumptions of what the ideal life and ideal man should be on which its solution was to rest.

In 1556 Le Caron published a vulgarization of Sadoleto's *Phaedrus* —but one stripped of Inghirami's Machiavellian definition of virtue, his extremism, his egoistic and preremptory formulas. "Who," he asks in this dialogue, "could imagine a man monstrous enough to be able to know and judge things truly without a committed experience of human life. The world is the true theater in which the man who wishes to be called noble and virtuous should exercise himself. Wisdom must be sought in the world, and man must bend his every effort to the world's utility."[8] Solitude breeds brutishness, but wisdom distills itself in the company and assembly of men. Its defining ideals must therefore identify themselves harmoniously with those of a living society. The common life of men should be

[6] *De philologia*, V, v–VI, r.

[7] See the *Dictionnaire des lettres françaises. Le seizième siècle* (Paris, 1951) for a short biography and the relevant literature.

[8] Louis Le Caron, *Les Dialogves* (Paris, 1556), 52r.

the wise man's mirror. From it he should decide what to imitate and what to avoid, constructing thus an empirical wisdom, practical rules of conduct based on the mores of his age, a kind of prudence stripped of any element of the esoteric.[9] Molière is still advocating it vigorously a century later;

> Mais je tiens qu'il est mal, sur quoi que l'on se fonde,
> De fuir obstinément ce que suit tout le monde,
> Et qu'il vaut mieux souffrir d'être au nombre des fous
> Que du sage parti se voir seul contre tous.[10]

Thus the wise man, precisely because he is no longer isolated from the community, should be active in public affairs and successful in his own calling. He should be provident, respect the security of his family, live fully and handsomely. Like his predecessors, Le Caron symbolizes the insufficiency of a nonprudential wisdom by Anaxagoras, who left his fields deserted and untilled to contemplate the stars. He should have stayed, and in the framework of his individual agricultural success, furthered the public good.[11]

The older wisdom, Budé had said, was no help and frequently a hindrance to an ample, satisfying, and honorable material existence. By denying legitimate self-interest and ambition, frugality, foresight, political activity, and the moderate acquisition of fame and wealth, it forcibly contradicted new assumptions of what the ideal man should be. Le Caron makes these assumptions explicit in specific value judgments: that the active life is more suitable for man than isolated contemplation; that man's end is virtue, not knowledge; that an active and successful burgher is worthier of praise than an improvident and frivolous philosopher. The ideal man, that is, unlike either the medieval monastic or Bovillus' Promethean hero, should no longer be isolated in knowledge, but an active, useful

---

[9] *Dialogves*, 51r–v. Cf. *Ibid.*, 52v. "[La sagesse] n'est autre (a mon auis) que la science, discretion, prudence, ou industrie (si mieux-aimez) d'avoir le contentment des choses plus estimées et desirées de la multitude des hommes, avec lesquelz on frequente."

[10] *L'Ecole des Maris*, Act I, Scene 1.

[11] *Dialogves*, 55v.

6*

member of society; no longer a specialist in the esoteric, but a man in open harmony with the ideals of his time; no longer an idle dreamer, but a success in his career and calling.

The traditional intellectual conceptions of wisdom, as Budé and Le Caron were uncomfortably aware, were no longer in harmony with this active, bourgeois ideal. How out of harmony they were and how necessary, therefore, the increasingly active and utilitarian meanings given wisdom in the sixteenth century is underlined by Ronsard's *Des vertus intellectuelles et moralles.* This is an oration on a question set by Henri III: are the moral virtues more worthy of praise, more necessary and more excellent than the intellectual virtues? Ronsard in his turn praises Socrates for bringing philosophy out of the clouds, setting her into the cities of men, and thus "transforming contemplation into action." He goes on then to assert the superiority of the moral virtues. He admits that if any man could possibly combine in himself both moral and intellectual virtues, he would be another god and possess the highest good. But this is unthinkable because action prevents contemplation and contemplation prevents action. It is better, therefore, to choose the nobler, more useful, more necessary activity, and the one more proper to the successful conduct of politics and business. Since it is the active life and the moral virtues which instill moderation and self-control, which make us virtuous, solid citizens, we should choose them rather than amuse ourselves with vain trifles.[12]

For many of the intellectual virtues, and *sapientia* among them, are vain and useless. Conrad Celtis had exhausted his eloquence urging German youth to investigate the causes of human and divine things: the motion of the stars, meteors, comets, snow, rain, and hail. Ronsard mocks this as useless effort, remarking that "God has

---

[12] *Des vertus intellectuelles et moralles. Discours prononcé à l'Académie du Palais par Ronsard en presence de Henri III. Œuvres complètes,* Gustave Cohen, ed. (Paris, Bibliothèque de la Pléiade, 1950), II, 1037–1038. The Oration was given in the late 1570's For further details see Frances A. Yates, *The French Academies of the Sixteenth Century* (London, 1947), 31–32, 108–109 and Ed. Fremy, *L'Académie des derniers Valois, 1570–1585* (Paris, 1887), 225–230.

put such curiosities in man's mind only to torment him." Bovillus defined wisdom as the universal knowledge of a new Prometheus; but Ronsard quotes Cato the Censor who had stigmatized the introduction of so many sciences and so much knowledge as the central cause of Roman decline. Sadoleto prized wisdom because it contemplated only divine and immutable things; Ronsard maintains that it is no great virtue "to amuse oneself by contemplating an object which cannot deceive or change." Much nobler, on the contrary, is to manage, govern, and moderate the mutable and passionate. The intellectual virtues, after all, undermine the active life; they are for the lazy, for "hermits and other such fantastical and contemplative people." But what use is contemplation without action? None, no more than a sword in its sheath or a knife which cannot cut. "I conclude, therefore, that since the moral virtues make us more charitable, humane, just, moderate, firmer in the face of danger, more sociable and obedient to our superiors, they are to be preferred to the intellectual."[13]

When Budé regrets having pursued wisdom at the expense of prudence, when Le Caron praises as wise men free of the esotericism and vanity of the philosophers, men who are good citizens and prudent fathers, when Ronsard prefers the moral to the intellectual virtues, they are renewing Salutati's criticism of intellectual, contemplative conceptions of wisdom, and they are doing this from assumptions of what the ideal life and the ideal man should be very close to his. They make two major points: first, that wisdom as an intellectual virtue has no necessary relation with moral virtue and therefore does not guarantee the probity of the wise man; and, second, that a purely contemplative wisdom isolates man, denies the active life, legitimate self-interest, frugality, foresight, political and business activity, that it is no help to an ample material existence. Sixteenth-century humanists in Italy and the North met these criticisms, not by rejecting wisdom, but by redefining it, by transforming it from a knowledge of divine things or of divine and human things and their causes to a code of ethical precepts, indistinguishable from

[13] *Des vertus intellectuelles et moralles*, 1038–1039.

prudence, on how to live well and blessedly. The result was an active, moralized wisdom more obviously in harmony with many contemporary needs and an ideal man who, as Le Caron put it, "should excell all men in courage, intellectual subtlety, and by a careful and skillful application to his calling; who should accommodate himself to all men, do nothing the result of which will cause him to repent, owe his prudence to no one, never neglect affairs of state and consider no life higher than one devoted to great and public things."[14]

I

When Budé answered his own most important criticism of wisdom as an intellectual virtue by saying that the pursuit of wisdom must be inseparable from virtue, he was quoting Petrarch; and from Petrarch's *De sapientia* to Charron's *De la Sargesse* this insistence on the desirable coexistence of wisdom and virtue is an important constant of humanist thought. But by the early sixteenth century it had become rather more than a pious wish. In the works of Erasmus and in those of his contemporary, the Spanish humanist Juan Luis Vives, it is the first step in an identification of wisdom and prudence. Erasmus and Vives define what they mean by wisdom both negatively and positively. Positively, they revive the traditional idea of *sapientia est pietas*, and then go on, more fundamentally than Petrarch, to transform this idea into an ethical category. Negatively, they analyze, on the basis of humanistic criteria, what wisdom is not. Both agree that it is not scholastic theology, metaphysics, or physics. Their final position tends to be an implicit identification of wisdom and prudence.

Negative criticism of disciplines which have nothing to do with moral judgments clears the ground for this conclusion. Erasmus shares with Petrarch, Salutati, and Bruni the common humanist prejudice against science. In the golden age men "had too much piety to search out, with a profane curiosity, the secrets of nature; to investigate the dimensions, motions, and influences of the stars,

---

[14] *Dialogves*, 53r.

or the hidden causes of things; deeming it a sacrilege for mortal man to try to know more than is proper to his station."[15] Even more presumptuous and less wise are metaphysicians, who, "though they are ignorant even of themselves, and on occasion do not see the ditch or the stone lying across their path, because many of them are blear-eyed or absent-minded; yet they proclaim that they perceive ideas, universals, forms without matter, primary substances, quiddities, and ecceities-things so tenuous, I fear, that Lynceus himself could not see them."[16] A worse labyrinth still is the wisdom of scholastic theology, that inextricable tangle of realists and Nominalists, Thomists, "brawling" Scotists, "stubborn Occamists," and "invincible" Albertists. They speak with unclean lips about holy things, "which are rather to be worshiped than expounded," dispute about frivolous subtleties by the profane methods of the heathen, define things arrogantly and defile the majesty of sacred theology by "silly, sordid terms and sentiments."[17] This kind of speculation, far from yielding wisdom, is an obscurantist cult which hides true philosophy and religion from the people. Like metaphysics, it tends to become an empty playing with words, a matter of "quiddities," "instances," and "formalities" with little or no relation to a human reality. Its symbol is Epimenides, who, the story goes, slept in a cave for forty-seven years. When he came out, he thought the world was a dream. Metaphysics, scholastic theology, and physics are unreal in the same way.[18] They are not sapiential sciences.

Vives agrees. In his *Praelectio in sapientiam* (1522) he looks for a wise man among the masters of the University of Paris. The first one he meets is a grammarian interested only in the exact date of Virgil's death or in whether Sallust wrote *omnes homines* or *omneis homines* at the beginning of his *Cataline*. He talks to a poet next because Horace and Strabo said that poetry was the earliest wisdom; but the poet's mind is full of nothing but foolish and confused

[15] *The Praise of Folly*, Hoyt Hopewell Hudson, tr. (Princeton University Press, 1941), 44.

[16] *Praise of Folly*, 77. [17] *Praise of Folly*, 82–83.

[18] P. S. Allen, *Opvs Epistolarvm Des. Erasmi Roterodami* (Oxford, 1906), I, ep. 64, lines 21ff.

mythology, which he calls *sacra theologia* because Ennius called poets saints. Then he turns to a logician and a physicist. One is a windbag, the other a fool. The philosopher he interviews is such a simpleton that Vives breaks out furiously: "These men are monstrosities and neither learned nor wise."[19] A rhetorician, an astrologer, a physician, and a lawyer follow in turn, none of whom is any wiser than his predecessor. At last, when Vives has almost been forced to admit that wisdom cannot be found among men, he meets a sober theologian. He does tell him what wisdom is.

It is fitting that a "sober" theologian be the mouthpiece for Vives' and Erasmus' idea of wisdom; for if the subtleties of scholastic theology yield little wisdom, the same cannot be said for a simple, positive theology based on Scripture. Such piety is wisdom. Vives, for example, says that absolute wisdom is the Son of God and human wisdom is knowledge of Him. It begins in a fear of God and develops through self-knowledge to the contemplation of Christ. God increases and perfects it by the gift of Charity. Compared to it, *sapientia mundana* is corrupt, damned, a pure folly in the eyes of God.[20] In the *Enchiridion Militis Christiani* Erasmus defines a comparable wisdom as *precatio et scientia*, knowledge of the law of God activated by prayer, the Erasmian equivalent of *sapientia est pietas*.[21] It is a kind of manna raining from heaven and is got by an "ardent study of Holy Scripture." Its content is *Christi doctrina*, a set of *salutares opiniones* corresponding to Petrarch's "true opinions" about God.[22] At the end of the *Praise of Folly* Erasmus calls this Christian wisdom a kind of madness, a divine folly which leads the soul away from visible, corporeal things to the invisible and divine, until it is "wholly rapt away in the contemplation of things unseen" and seeks and loves only the supreme good which is God.[23] Such knowledge alone is white as snow, pure and free of any blemish.

[19] *Opera; quibus omnes ipsius lucubrationes, quotquot unquam in lucem editas voluit, complectuntur* (Basel, 1555), I, 298–299.

[20] Vives, *Opera*, I, 300. Cf. *Ibid.*, II, 94.

[21] Annemarie and Hajo Holborn, *Desiderius Erasmus Roterodamus Ausgewählte Werke* (Munich, 1933), 29.

[22] Holborn, 30–31.   [23] *Praise of Folly*, 120 ff.

This wisdom is no rustic piety. It is a *sancta eruditio* rather than a *sancta rusticitas*, a *scientia* whose source is not only Scripture but the classics also. Erasmus warns his readers against those who oppose learning on the authority of Paul's *scientia inflat*, or say that immortality was promised to the innocent not to the learned, and that if you know Christ well you need know nothing else. It is ignorance, not learning which causes pride; for, like Socrates, the more a man knows the more he knows that he does not know.[24] Therefore, men should not spurn what is gentile merely because it is gentile. The classics have important uses. They form an elegant style, useful for an eloquent propagation of religious truth.[25] They are filled with moral precepts and examples whose Christian meaning can always be disclosed by a sufficiently allegorical ingenuity; and since the full weight of their salubrious meanings can be brought to bear only by allegory, they teach men to prefer the spirit to the letter, and thus make an ideal introduction to the study of Scripture.[26] More than this they are a positive help in understanding Scripture because a competent knowledge of physics, mathematics, and history, for example, is indispensable for a proper interpretation of Holy Writ. The classics, in short, contain many truths (all of which are necessarily compatible with Christianity[27]); and it is therefore "useful to taste the whole of gentile literature if it is done moderately . . . during a suitable period of one's life (in one's youth), with caution and selectivity, merely pausing with them on one's forward progress, not remaining there, and finally, above all, if all are ultimately referred to Christ."[28]

Like Petrarch's *docta pietas*, Erasmus' and Vives' idea of wisdom is a profoundly Christian conception. Wisdom is a bundle of truths about a Christian God derived from Scripture and the classics. It

---

[24] *Liber apologeticus Desiderii Herasmi Roterodami in quo refelluntur rationes inepte barbarorum contra poesim et literaturam secularem pugnantium*, Albert Hyma, *The Youth of Erasmus* (University of Michigan Press, 1930), Appendix B, 288.

[25] Allen, I, ep. 49, lines 91–94.   [26] Holborn, 32.

[27] Holborn, 35, line 33. "Christi autem esse puta, quicquid usquam veri offenderis."   [28] Holborn, 32.

comes from God, directly in the case of Scripture; indirectly, via an illumination predating the birth of Christ, in the case of antique literature. But Erasmus and Vives, too, and more powerfully and radically than Petrarch, transform this revealed, intellectual virtue into a naturally acquired moral virtue. The transformation is effected by draining the terms of their initial theological definition of wisdom of almost all Revelational meaning. In the end only ethical meanings are left.

Wisdom, Erasmus had said, is a knowledge of *salutares opiniones*, of things which will assure man of salvation. But these things, as the preface to the 1518 edition of the *Enchiridion* makes clear, are nothing but a good, pure, simple life.[29] Erasmus goes further. *Sapientia* is a knowledge of God; but it is the knowledge of a God whose "very nature is Virtue" and who is the "parent and author of all virtues." Christ is *sapientiae auctor* or, better still, Wisdom itself; but what one must know of Him is His law, which supplements the Mosaic law.[30] And this law is crystallized in the actions of a human Christ. From a knowledge of Christ, wisdom becomes an active imitation of Christ, whose life on earth was a consciously exemplary moral pattern. Wisdom thus flows from a God whose central attribute is virtue, from a Scriptural Revelation described as a code of conduct, and from a Christ whose function was livingly to illustrate that code. From a knowledge of *salutares opiniones* he transforms it into the active practice of those virtues opposed to *stultitia* and *malitia*, the generic names for vice of the Stoics and Christians respectively, and calls it, in phrases which remind one of Salutati, *absoluta probitas* and *virtus cum eruditione liberali coniuncta*.[31]

Vives' *Introductio ad sapientiam* (1524) gives an excellent and fuller picture of wisdom as moral virtue. "True wisdom," he says, "consists in judging things correctly, so that we may estimate a thing at its true worth, and not esteem something vile as though it were

---

[29] Allen, III, ep. 858, line 97. "... qui [Christus] a nobis praeter puram simplicemque vitam nihil exigit."

[30] Holborn, 29, 38.

[31] Holborn, 38; *Liber apologeticus*, 315.

precious or reject something precious as though it were vile, nor condemn what should be praised or praise what should be condemned."[32] To be wise is, first, to have true opinions about things and, second, to translate this knowledge into action by desiring only honorable things and avoiding the base, choosing good and rejecting evil, by making the appropriate choice so customary a part of our nature that we cannot be tempted to do evil. Vives epitomizes the double character of this wisdom in two phrases: *veras habere opiniones* and *bene agere.*[33]

This is another way of saying, with Erasmus, that wisdom is a combination of virtue and learning. The function of *eruditio* is to have "true opinions" about things. The most important of these is that virtue is the noblest of all things; and it defines virtue as "respect for God and man, worship of God, love of man and the desire to do good."[34] Its further function is to know what is good and what is bad in order that we may virtuously follow the good and flee the bad. *Eruditio*, in short, instructs the will. Virtue, on the other hand, is a habit of the will which causes it to act on this instruction. Wisdom unites the ethical insights of learning with the practice of virtue. It consists of moral precepts and the actions which obey them.

The *Introductio ad sapientiam* is an elementary collection of the most important of these. One precept, for example, commands us to treat the body as a servant rather than a master. This is a rule of action based on a correct appraisal of the relative value of body and soul. Another tells us to master the affections and passions and defines the wise man as a person who has been able to do this. Others are rules for controlling the tongue; do not boast, do not flatter, do not lie, gossip, or slander. There is a section on man's behavior to himself; on how he ought to treat other men ("You must love all men and so behave even to unknown men that they will feel you are the friend of all mankind"); on charity ("The wisest master and author of our life has given us one rule of life: to love

---

[32] *Opera*, II, 70. [33] *Opera*, II, 70–71.
[34] *Opera*, II, 71.

one another, knowing that if we love, our life will be most happy and need no other laws"); and, finally, on man's duties to God. Knowledge of God and the action such knowledge instructs and guides is the height of wisdom. "To know [the Christian religion] is perfect wisdom; to live according to it is perfect virtue; but no man truly knows it who does not live it."[35]

Salutati, too, defined wisdom as virtue based on ethical knowledge; but he went on to insist that this virtue is a gift of God exclusively. Erasmus and Vives tend to see virtue as a natural human acquisition. This does not mean that they were not also perfectly aware that wisdom comes from God. Wisdom, virtue, and knowledge, says Vives, all come from above. Even Plato and Socrates, because they were illumined by "that small ray of light which the divine goodness has denied to no one," told their pupils that they must hope to receive wisdom from God and not from men. But God does not reward the lazy, and so we must exert every effort of our own to excel in the study of literature and virtue.[36] Erasmus agrees that we must ask God for wisdom—just as we ask Him for our daily bread, our clothing, shelter, and everything else we need to survive in the world. This does not mean that we do not have to work for it. God, he suggests, helps those who help themselves.[37]

Erasmus goes further. The ancients knew nothing about the Christian God, but they did know much about the rules of ethics and the good life. In terms of moral wisdom they were wise, and this wisdom was self-achieved. John Colet always insisted that man could never reform himself and that his wisdom came to him directly from Revelation. For Erasmus the insights of wisdom are natural products of human reason. That Cicero, for example, was wise and that this was true wisdom is plain from the panegyrical preface to the *De officiis*. It too is an enchiridion, and its teachings are sufficient to combat every vice. Conrad Celtis promised a blessed life to the follower of Ciceronian ethics; Erasmus promises immor-

---

[35] *Opera*, II, 78–79. Cf. *Ibid.*, I, 258.

[36] *Opera*, I, 7–8; II, 78, 850.

[37] *Liber apologeticus*, 326. "Hac ratione quoque sapientiam postulamus, at ita ut de humana industria nihil diminuamus."

tality, almost making antique virtue a sufficient condition of salvation and denying the name of Christian to those who lead evil
lives.[38] This emphasis on the sufficiency of ethics for salvation, and
the opening of the whole field of necessary ethical knowledge to
the natural reason, is the source of Erasmus' tendency to define
Christianity as an ethically blameless life,[39] of his semi-Pelagianism
and his invocation of St. Socrates. Like Celtis, but from a renewed
ethical point of view, an initial identification of *sapientia* with
Revelation gradually gives way to a *prisca sapientia* whose primary
source is the natural reason of the classical moralists.

II

Vives and Erasmus went about as far in the direction of moralizing wisdom as it was possible to go without actually identifying
wisdom and prudence. Logically, this was the next step in transforming wisdom from knowledge to virtue and the neatest possible
answer to criticisms like Budé's of purely intellectual conceptions
of wisdom. A few humanists were already taking this position as
early as the end of the fifteenth century. Geiler von Keisersberg, for
example, explicitly identified wisdom and virtue in one of the
sermons on Sebastian Brant's *Narrenschiff* he gave in Strassburg
Cathedral in 1498–99. "To learn wisdom," he said, "is to learn the
virtues; to learn the virtues is to perform virtuous acts; and to perform virtuous acts is to perform acts which are according to right
reason." He defined wisdom, therefore, as a *collectio omnium
virtutum*.[40]

But a fusion of wisdom and prudence only became common as the
sixteenth century went on. A curious illustration of the tendency in

[38] Allen, I, ep. 152, lines 46–48. "Hic fons ille diuinus honestatis in quatuor
riuulos se diuidit, qui potus non solum vocalem, vt Aonius ille, verum etiam
immortalem faciat."

[39] Compare Colet's definition: "Christiani sunt homines, qui gracia Dei
vocantur mirifice, ut sanctificentur, sanctique delectabiles sint filii Dei pulchri
in Christo Jesu pulchrificante." *Epistolae B. Pauli ad Romanos Expositio
Literalis, Opuscula quaedam theologica*, J. H. Lupton, ed. and tr. (London,
1876), 203.

[40] *Nauicula siue speculum fatuorum* (Strassburg, 1511), IX, F.

this direction is the popularity of the Pseudo-Virgil's *Vir bonus*.[41] It was printed in most collected editions of Virgil, Sebastian Brant adapted it for the last chapter of the *Narrenschiff*, the indefatigable Geiler von Keisersberg wrote a sermon on it, Bonaventure Des Periers translated it. It is a dull poem, but its moralism and its identification of the wise man and the good man appealed to humanists and helped to justify their efforts to push on beyond Erasmus and Vives to a purely ethical conception of wisdom. In Bonaventure Des Periers' translation, for example, the wise man is called an *homme de bien*.

> Il est semblable à la sphère arrondie
> De l'univers, tout en soy recueilly
> Et par dehors tant rondement poly,
> Qu'un brin d'ordure il ne peult amasser.
> Son passe temps est de soy compasser
> Les longues nuitz de l'hyver chassieux,
> Et, aux grandz jours de l'esté gracieux,
> A donner ordre au bastiment de soy,
> Que tout à poinct et à la bonne foy
> De jour en jour il estoffe et cimente,
> Qu'il n'a pas peur qu'il se jette ou desmente,
> Ou qu'au droict coing ayt une gauche pierre,
> Tant bien l'assiet au plamb et à l'esquierre.[42]

His wisdom is a code of conduct whose chief rules are moderation and self-control. It is a bastion of virtue built by himself, ordered and controlled by continuous self-examination. Every evening before he goes to bed the wise man reviews his day. He examines each word, each act, condemning the vicious and congratulating himself on the virtuous. "I have done that," he will say to himself, "but this remains to do. I have lost so much, but I have gained this or that." He is a moral accountant, prolonging the double-entry book-

[41] For the Latin text see *Appendix Vergiliana sive Carmina Minora Vergilio Adtributa*, R. Ellis, ed. (Oxford, 1907).

[42] *Œuvres françoises de Bonaventure Des Periers*, Louis Lacour, ed. (Paris, 1856), I, 82.

keeping of his business day in an accurate calculation of his ethical solvency. "Haven't I tried to acquire something it would have been better not to want? Oh malicious fool, to have more greatly loved by far a bit of profit than an honorable man should!" Thus he notes his departure from the moderate norm and censures his loss of self-control, his passions, the "appetite of my foolish nature." He recalls wounding words or offences given, repents, and vows correction—corrections determined by *l'avis de prudence et droicture*.[43]

This is the standard of a wisdom indistinguishable from prudence. It retains those activist preoccupations insisted on by Le Caron: that it usefully contribute to action in the world, to success in public and private life, and to the dignity of a comfortable material existence. But it insists now that the active life be also a good life and that success be pursued virtuously. It becomes, in short, a code of personal ethics, a moral guide to an active life of successful virtue.

In his *De sapientia* the Italian mathematician and philosopher Cardanus (1501–1576)[44] has discussed wisdom as an active moral virtue at greater length, and much more picturesquely than any thinker before Charron. Had he lived in 1663 when the collected edition of his works was published, he would have been considered an *extravagant*: extravagant in his superstitions—his divinations and auguries, miraculous cures, occult experiments, and the proclaimed presence of a familiar guardian demon; extravagant in his ambiguous and tormented sexual life, his passionate gambling, his touchy vanity; extravagant finally, in his unmeasured ambition and sense of persecution. In his youth he composed a special prayer: "Lord,

---

[43] *Œuvres*, 82–83.

[44] All important biographical facts can be found in Cardanus' own fascinating autobiography, *De propria vita*, Jean Dayré, ed. and tr., *Bibliothèque de l'Institut français de Florence*, 1er série, XI (Paris, 1936) and in Oystein Ore, *Cardano. The Gambling Scholar* (Princeton University Press, 1953). Two important analyses of his thought are J.-Roger Charbonnel, *La Pensée italienne au XVIe siècle et le courant libertin* (Paris, 1919), 274–299 and Henri Busson, *Les Sources et le développement du rationalisme dans la littérature française de la Renaissance (1533–1601)* (Paris, 1922), 231–241. Charbonnel gives a detailed bibliography. The most recent book on Cardanus is Angelo Bellini, *Gerolamo Cardano e il suo tempo* (Milan, 1947).

in Thy infinite goodness grant me a long life, wisdom, and health of mind and body." When, in a dream, the Virgin and St. Martin of Tours promised him tranquillity and eternal life, he was sure that his request had been granted. He saw himself henceforth as a new Prometheus, persecuted and dishonored for teaching wisdom to mortals.[45]

Cardan mirrors every variety of Renaissance wisdom. In the confused mass of the ten folio volumes of his works he defines it variously, calling it piety and theology, metaphysics or a knowledge of pure forms, a universal human knowledge which includes every liberal and mechanical art.[46] He defines it finally, as the art of living long and virtuously. It is this definition which he ultimately accepts.

Wisdom as piety or theology he calls, like his predecessors, divine wisdom. With the exception of certain pagan religious virtuosi—the Sybils, for example—it is scarcely found in the wicked—*Quoniam in malevolam animam non introibit sapientia, nec habitabit in corpore subdito peccatis*—or in men who do not worship the true God. It is inseparable from true faith, and its human representatives should be sought among the prophets and Apostles, the doctors, preachers, and martyrs of the church. Its source is divine illumination. Seek it, therefore, not in any exercise of the human will but in a gratuitous, spontaneous gift of God.[47] Its content, and its cause, is a knowledge and contemplation of God and a love of Him. The infallible sign of its possession is to keep the divine law—Love God

---

[45] *De propria vita*, xxii: Dayré, 51–52.

[46] Cf. "De sapientia multiplici et speciebus eius," *Paralipomenon*, XVIII, vii: *Hieronymi Cardani Mediolanensis Philosophi ac Medici Celeberrimi Opera Omnia*, Carolus Sponsius, ed. (Lyons, 1663), X, 584, col. 1–2. "Est [sapientia] quidem a lumine intellectus: alia a disciplina per demonstrationem, alia per notitiam multarum rerum, alia quasi diuinitus inducta, alia quasi composita ex arte atque iudicio, alia per solertiam, per quam coniectamur, et non est perfecta, nisi postquam facta fuerit necessaria."

[47] *De sapientia: Opera*, I, 499, col. 1–2; 501, col. 1–2; 501, col. 1–2; 500, col. 1. "Namque quid clarius est, quam quod dona gratuita sint? diuina autem sapientia donum dei est: si igitur cum omnia fecerimus, merito dicere possumus, serui sumus inutiles, sapientia Dei spontaneum donum Dei erit, nulla arte, vel inuentione paratum."

with all thy mind and thy neighbor as thyself—and to spurn all human things—wealth, friends, sons and relatives, power and glory —for these are sordid in comparison with divine things. Its fruit is the greatest security and happiness man can find in this life.[48] Divine wisdom begins in a fear of God. It is consummated in the happiness of contemplating Him and in the security of a revealed knowledge of personal immortality.[49]

Cardanus' divine wisdom recapitulates the fundamental characteristics of any wisdom defined as piety or the knowledge and love of God. Others of his definitions reflect the vigorous survival of wisdom as a revealed knowledge of divine essences, as a natural knowledge of the "divine things" of metaphysics, and as the encyclopedic knowledge of all things divine and human. Thus he calls wisdom the contemplation of God as supreme essence or infinite form and of those essences which flow from Him, a contemplation achieved with His help.[50] Cardanus sounds here like a conventional theologian. Elsewhere he restates views closer to Plato's and Aristotle's. Wisdom is then a naturally acquired intellectual knowledge of metaphysics and the noblest of the intellectual virtues. In contrast to *scientia*, which, as Aristotle says, is a knowledge of sensible things,

---

[48] *De sap.*, 501, col. 2. "Dei dilectionem sequitur legis etiam diuinae custodia: quamobrem sapientiae diuinae fructus, causa, et signum, ex his manifesta sunt. Siquidem causa est Dei cognitio, dilectioque, ac cum illo vt ita dicamus collocutio. Signum autem vt legis diuinae mandata seruet, humanaque omnia spernat, quae ad diuina cum comparantur, sordida sint: opes, amici, filij, parentes, affines, potentia, gloria, caeteraque huiusmodi. Fructus est diuturna, secura, ac summa foelicitas, quae homini in hac vita possit contingere." Cf. *Ibid.*, 499, col. 2.

[49] "De humana perfectione," *Paralipomenon*, II, vii: *Opera*, X, 448, col. 2. "Ergo cognoscere Deum et contemplari, vtraeque sunt partes ipsius felicitatis: nam si haec Deorum est felicitas summa, et ipsi soli beati sunt; felicitas summa etiam hominis in hac vita, quae est summa perfectio et sine errore, est ipsum contemplari et cognoscere. At in securitate est cognitio immortalis animi: ergo sapiens felicissimus est vtrisque his iunctis." Cf. *De sap.*, 499, col. 2. "Est igitur vera sapientiae divinae diffinitio, legis custodia, timorque excelsi."

[50] *Paralipomenon*, II, vii: *Opera*, X, 448, col. 2. "In sapiente ergo tria sunt quae complent felicitatem: contemplatio optimi entis cum his quae ab eo pendent: cognitio perpetuitatis propriae naturae, et auxilium Diuinum."

sapientia is a knowledge of intelligible forms, of things without any sensible accident.[51] It is a certain, natural knowledge of the highest and most secret things: Ideas, axioms, first principles, and the reasons of things.[52] But, and here Cardan joins and goes beyond Bovillus and Conrad Celtis, wisdom is also a *universa cognitio humana*, a knowledge of things both human and divine, good or bad, intellectual, rational, and sensible.[53] It includes the seven liberal arts and the three traditional parts of philosophy: physics, metaphysics, and ethics. It can be extended to include the mechanical arts. *Sapientia* is then the extraordinary mastery of any such art. Phidias and Apelles were wise in this sense.[54]

---

[51] *De rerum varietate*, VIII, xlii: *Opera*, III, 159, col. 1. "Aristoteles autem diuidit notitiam simplicem in duo genera: aut enim est eorum, quae sensibus quoquomodo subiacent, vocaturque scientia; aut quae non subiacent, diciturque sapientia." Cf. Aristotle, *Metaph.* I, 2, 983a, 6–7; *Eth. Nic.*, VI, 5, 1140a, 24–1140b, 30.

[52] *De rerum varietate*, VIII, xlvi: *Opera*, III, 177, col. 1. "Eorum [sapientes] autem delectatio est, vel in cognitione altissimarum rerum, vel secretarum, aut in opere secundum virtutem: vnde probus homo, idem qui et sapiens." Cf. "De sapiente," *Paralipomenon*, XVIII, i: *Opera*, X, 577, col. 1. "Sapientiae verbo intelligimus quamcunque notitiam certam, velut intellectum, qui est ingenita facultas, principia solo nomine cognoscendi proprio lumine." See also *De subtilitate*, xiv: *Opera*, III, 584, col. 1. "Est autem sapientis officium pulchras primo dubitationes proponere: ac etiamsi fieri potest vtiles inde solutiones, causamque afferre, et nihil circa causae redditionem absurdum dicere.... Quoniam ex se, aut sensibus habet, quae primo nouit, aut ex his cognoscit: palam igitur quod non possint esse plura: alia autem aliis principia sunt sensu cognita, aut consequentia. Mens autem in his non laborauit: aeterna enim est, velut et species. Aeternorum autem quaedam non mutantur vt Deus; quaedam successione, vt coelum, alia circuitu. Species igitur immotae sunt, sed non vt supremi intellectus, verum vt mens: non laborat igitur mens, quia in tempore non est, imo contemplatio ipsa animum exhilarat, et iuuentutem producit. Viuimus enim tantummodo dum contemplamur, quoniam vita ea vera sola est, quae diuis conuenit sempiterno aeuo, talis autem haec sola in nobis."

[53] *De sap.*, 503, col. 2. "... nam omnis praeclara cognitio seu boni seu mali, seu vt diximus in mente seu oratione seu in operatione sit, sapientiae apud nos vt etiam antiquo tempore nomen habet."

[54] *De sap.*, 503, col. 1–2. "... sapientiam in artibus esse quandam excellentem rationem illarum, vt si Phidiam statuarium, Apellem pictorem sapientem

Each of these definitions asserts that wisdom is a form of knowledge and an intellectual virtue. There is, however, a second definition which asserts that wisdom is a mode of action and a moral virtue; and this is the definition, Cardan says, men prefer.[55] Without explicitly rejecting his other definitions, he therefore devotes his chief attention to this. He calls it *sapientia naturalis*. Like many of his other discoveries, natural wisdom was first revealed to him in a dream. "It seemed to me," he recalls in his *Autobiography*, "that my soul was in the heaven of the moon, separated from the body, alone and mournful. I heard my father's voice saying: 'God has made me your guardian spirit. The air here is full of souls which you do not see, just as you do not see me; and to them you can not speak. You will stay in this heaven seven thousand years, and the same number in each sphere until the eighth, when you will enter the Kingdom of God.' I interpreted this dream as follows: my father's soul is my guardian spirit...; the moon represents grammar; Mercury geometry and arithmetic; Venus music, divination, and poetry; the Sun moral philosophy; Jupiter natural science; Mars medicine; Saturn agriculture, botany, and other lesser arts; the eighth orbe an epitome of all the arts and sciences, various studies, and natural wisdom. After that I will rest with God."[56]

Natural wisdom, in this celestial ladder of values, is above the knowledge of all particular sciences and on the threshold of the Kingdom of God. Nothing in life is more useful or necessary. It is the mother of every good, and we should pursue it with all our strength. It is synonymous with human happiness and with every good which brings such happiness.[57] "It is, for example, repose, tranquillity, modesty, temperance, order, change, joy, theatrical

---

appellemus: vtrique enim eorum in sua arte nihil defuit quo ab omnibus earum artium studiosis non probarentur."

[55] *De sap.*, 495, col. 1. "Verum et sapientiae plures aliae sunt diuisiones, alia enim tantum scire docet, alia etiam agere: et haec apud homines in maiore precio habetur."

[56] *De propria vita*, xxxvii: Dayré, 102–103.

[57] *De sap.*, 492, col. 1–493, col. 1.

performances, social intercourse, sleep, eating and drinking, riding and sailing, contemplation, education, piety, marriage, banquets, an orderly memory of past events, elegance, water and fire, hearing music, the pleasures of sight, conversation, stories and histories, liberty, self-control, little birds, puppies and cats, the consolation of death and the thought that time passes equally for both the happy and the miserable, the succession of good and bad fortune, the expectation of unforeseen events, the exercise of a profession one has mastered, the multiplicity of change and the whole of this vast universe. Where is there any evil in this abundance of wise and beneficent things, for all are full of hope?"[58] A single formula sums of this happy wisdom: *bene ac diu vivere*; and a single and identical sapiental rule: *ut diu ac bene vivas*.[59]

III

A man is wise, and because he is wise he is also happy, if he lives virtuously and for a long time. Wisdom is a collection of precepts designed to make man virtuous and prolong his life. Half moral, half medical, its uses are to embellish the mind, preserve the body, and dominate fortune. It is a method of action, of fighting "against those evils which can be uprooted by art and effort," and of "creating or retaining good things." Wisdom teaches us to avoid the evils of body and soul and to cultivate their goods. And in the face of evils no man can control, against a capricious fortune unmanageable by virtue or any medicine, wisdom is a form of consolation.[60] It is thus the method, or *ars*, of a happy life, a rule of physical and moral conduct which dominates the ravages of time, life, and fortune. It fights evil, creates good, and consoles man for any necessary torments of the human condition.

A long life is necessary for happiness. As the art of living for a long time, wisdom is a group of precepts which involves both the

---

[58] *De propria vita*, xxxi: Dayré, 80.

[59] *De sap.*, 479, col. 1. Cf. *Ibid.*, 503, col. 2. "Erit autem vt diximus vna sapientiae ratio, vt diu ac bene viuas."

[60] *De sap.*, 503, col. 1.

body and soul. It encourages good health and, looking beyond mere physical existence, the prolongation of one's personal life in children, fame, and the hope of immortality.[61] A certitude of personal immortality would surely be the best possible guarantee of living long as well as virtuously. Such certitude, unfortunately, is impossible. In his treatise on the immortality of the soul Cardan has listed fifty-four objections to the soul's immortality and forty-nine arguments favoring it.[62] His own conclusion, not unlike Cicero's in the *De Senectute*, seems to have been that the human soul, in so far as it is individuated in matter and inseparable from it, is mortal. The *mens* or *anima intellectiva*, on the other hand, that suprapersonal part of the soul which participates directly in the world soul and is extrinsic to man and his body, survives his death. This is no personal immortality or the survival of the moral personality, but an anonymous immortality, a continuity *in globo* of intellectual activity in which individual sparks of the world soul rejoin it after a temporary sojourn in the individual souls of men.[63]

But even if personal immortality is uncertain and from some points of view, indeed, unlikely, a significant precept of natural wisdom still urges man to hope at least that he will live again after death. This hope is not irrational. No one can prove that immortality is possible, but then no one can prove that it is not. Cicero rightly said that those who teach the immortality of the soul cannot be proved wrong. Prudently refusing to commit himself entirely on this

---

[61] *De sap.*, 497, col. 1.

[62] Busson, *Sources et développement du rationalisme*, 234.

[63] *De rerum varietate*, VIII, xlii: *Opera*, III, 156, col. 1. "Mens est sempiterna substantia, imago verarum rerum a materia secretarum, extrinsecus homini adveniens." Cf. *Ibid.*, 159, col. 1. "Hoc autem est cognituram seipsam mentem quid sit, et vnde profecta: immortalis enim natura, est mens atque anima intellectiua. In his vero quorum pars a toto distinguitur, totum immortale esse potest, partes autem corrumpi, vt in elementis, et singularibus specierum animalium aut stirpium. Quamobrem omnes, qui naturaliter locuti sunt, animam statuentes immortalem, vnam esse dixerunt, vt Theophrastus, Themistius, et Auerroës. Vt igitur vna et in toto, perpetua est, conjunctaque superiori mente: et ita extrinsecus aduenit: vt cujusque anima, et cuique propria, et in corpore, mortalis." Cf. Cicero, *De Senectute*, xxi, 77–78.

question, the wise man will keep a strong hope in immortality. "To affirm the soul immortal is not only pious and prudent, but blameless as well and the cause of a multitude of goods."[64] Such hope will fortify man's security and peace of mind, lay firm foundations for his happiness, teach him patience and humility, and sharpen his zeal for virtue. To retain a sure hope of immortality is the first precept of wisdom.

A surer form of longevity is nevertheless the prolongation of one's personal life in children and fame. We have been given, Averroës once said, a frail and miserable nature which cannot guarantee the perpetuity of the individual man; but we have been given as well, and in potent abundance, the virtue of generation. "A great care, therefore, is incumbent on the wise man: to prolong his own life by the propagation of offspring and to see also that they live gloriously and happily."[65] In the lives of his children and his children's children the wise man will assure his own continuation.

Wise men, however, are not great lovers; and their children rarely resemble them.[66] At best a son propagates only the image of his father's body. Fame, on the other hand, is a spiritual longevity and propagates the image of his mind. Fame is the surest immortality, and to live long is to survive in the memory of men. Measured in years, the longest life is short if it has been spent in unproductive leisure; while the shortest physical life is long to eternity if it has produced things of beauty and merit. "The longest life is one which has left great, glorious, splendid deeds chronicled in the eternal monuments of history."[67] The central precept of wisdom, insofar as it concerns longevity, is therefore less concerned with physical existence than with liberty—a freedom from foolishness, envy, fear, importunate desires, and the domination of fortune—and with works, *inclytis factis et virtutibus*, the creation of beautiful statues

---

[64] *De sap.*, 520, col. 2.   [65] *De sap.*, 509, col. 1.

[66] *De subtilitate*, XII: *Opera*, III, 558, col. 2. "Sapientes autem ob contemplationem ad Venerem minus sunt prompti, quoniam spiritus ob studium resoluuntur, ferunturque a corde in contrariam partem genitalium, scilicet versus cerebrum, et ob id, et debiles, ac maxime sibi dissimiles generant filos.

[67] *De sap.*, 506, col. 1.

and pictures, the authorship of great books.[68] Absolutely, our time is short. We live wisely and for a long time if we use every moment of our lives in doing and creating famous things which will propagate our memory to the end of time.[69]

The wisdom of longevity, finally, includes those lesser precepts, moral and medical, which prolong human life in the literal sense. Its first rule is to avoid disease and care for it well. Its second is moderation in all things. Do not eat too much, do not drink too much. The simpler foods and drinks are best for preserving bodily health and mental keenness: milk, honey, and olives. Be moderate also in the passions, avoid violent emotion, fear, and unseemly enthusiasms. The third rule of wisdom in this matter is to retain as much bodily humidity as possible. Since humidity is necessary for a long life, the wise man expends it parsimoniously. He refrains from overexercise, excitement, immoderate love making; and, an absurd culmination, recalling that ants live preternaturally long because they defecate so rarely, he goes to the toilet as seldom as possible.[70]

By guarding his health, by having children, by creating future fame in a life of brilliant accomplishment, by a prudent and pious hope of immortality man correctly and sagely follows the first injunction of Cardan's recipe for wisdom: *ut diu ac bene vivas*. It is not the more important injunction, however; and like the ancients we should prize living well above living long. Better still, leave the length of life, like immortality itself, to hope; but bend every conscious and active effort to living well and embellishing the soul with prudence and every virtue. For longevity, compared with virtue, is a small part of wisdom; while virtue, which indeed includes good health, is the core of wisdom and its very meaning.[71]

[68] *De sap.*, 507, col. 1. Cf. *Ibid.*, 506, col. 2.

[69] *De sap.*, 511, col. 2.   [70] *De sap.*, 504, col. 1.

[71] *De sap.*, 519, col. 2. "Neque vero haec tantum placebunt, quae ad diuturnitatem spectant, quam ad bene viuere, atque ideo etiam longiora quam par sit existimabuntur. Quoniam bonum et malum sentimus, diu esse non sentimus, sed in ampla spe collocamus: ob hoc, cum non minus diu quam bene esse optent homines, bene tamen viuere omni industria quaerunt, diu viuere negligunt."

Virtus est vitium fugere, Horace said. The man is virtuous who flees vice. There are three vices which particularly block the path to wisdom and a blessed life; fear, envy, and avarice. Fear, for example, is utterly useless; no vice is more harmful to man. It convulses the body, confuses the mind, and robs man of all happiness and security. The wise man avoids fear by confidently foreseeing and then parrying danger. Envy, which also destroys the possibility of security and happiness, must be similarly avoided. Any man who envies the goods of another loses forever his own peace and repose. For envy has no end or limit. It can never be satisfied, just as gluttony is never satiated nor lust appeased. "The greatest benefit of wisdom and its highest praise, therefore, is that it flees this monster." Avarice, wisdom's third major enemy, is the mother of a multitude of crimes —of tyranny, cruelty, injustice, pillage, and war. "It incites men to scorn the gods, break their plighted word, forsake glory, violate modesty, corrupt the law, betray their friends, hate and abandon their relatives and family; it weakens their health and shortens their lives."[72] Avarice is at once an unmeasured desire for wealth and the refusal of liberality. But it is money's only viable function to be liberally used to embellish virtue. The wise man, therefore, flees avarice as he flees envy and fear, assuring himself happiness and security by keeping open the path to virtue.

Although fear, envy, and avarice are the principal obstacles to wisdom, there are other lesser vices to be overcome. Anger, for example, is a vice which the wise man combats by the virtue of tranquillity. Tranquillity is "both the token and cause of wisdom. For if someone is dominated by anger or any other passion of the soul, however prudent he may be by nature, he can never be wise." Foolishness is another. The fool is a hypocrite. He talks of things he knows nothing about as if he did, he is virtuous in words but not in deeds. As a magistrate, he punishes cruelly, thinking that men will call him just; as a man of business he is avaricious, thinking that men will call him prudent. The wise man, on the other hand, weighs his words, discusses only what he knows, and makes a

---

[72] *De sap.,* 520, col. 1–522, col. 1.

virtue of silence. In his dress and style of life he reflects precisely what he is, no more and no less. His virtues are unostentatiously active, and every aspect of his life radiates the essence of wisdom, a prudent and balanced judgment.[73]

Sexual love, finally, is a disturbing passion. Is it, like anger or folly, a vice incompatible with wisdom? Its physical effects, as Cardan has already noted, can be bad. Its moral effects, however, are often admirable. It can tame the violent, make stingy men generous, the timid bold, the cruel merciful, solitary hermits civil gentleman, the irreligious pious, and teach the mute to spout with eloquence. Anticipating Marivaux's *Arlequin poli par l'amour*, Cardan tells the story of Cimon, a Greek shepherd, stupid, fierce, unbroken to society, whom love for Iphigenia made elegant, well-mannered, sociable, bold, eloquent, and gallant. He concludes that a moderate love is suitable for the wise man. It will prolong his youth, sweeten his heart with joy, and make him apter for every accomplishment.[74]

To moderate the passions and flee vice—avarice, envy, fear, anger, and foolishness—is thus the central principle of wisdom. Its positive obverse is to pursue virtue and insure an honest probity in every act: *morum sanctitas et animi virtus*.[75] Such wisdom must be learned actively. It is a form of ethical erudition. Like Ronsard, Cardan derives the moral virtues from experience and practice: and makes a correct education responsible for their effective inculcation. Children are not naturally bad. Injustice, perfidy, mendacity, cruelty are not innate in them. They are, on the other hand, naturally intemperate and violent: and this lack of measure, once allied to a bad education, leads directly to vice. Man's nature, in short, is

[73] *De sap.*, 523, col. 2. "Quamobrem nihil tam sapiens vitabit, quam vel vt de re incerta vel ancipiti vel ignota loquatur. Studebit taciturnitati, laudabitque illud Xenocratis: loquutum fuisse poenituit saepius, tacuisse nunquam. In vestitu, risu, et ambulatione decorem seruabit: Nam his praecipue tamquam indiciis sapiens a stulto dignoscitur, vt Salomon inquit: non quod haec ad rem ipsam plurimum conducant, quae extranea sunt: sed quod sine iudicio et animi trutina recta, quibus maxime sapientia ipsa constat, haec non possint reprehensione carere."

[74] *De sap.*, 524, col. 1.   [75] *De sap.*, 525, col. 1.

naturally prone to virtue rather than vice; but unless education, habit, and the example of good things reinforce this natural inclination, he will inevitably drift into a vicious life. Natural wisdom, therefore, is first the absence of vice; but it is second the presence of virtue, acquired by example, reason, and meditation and reinforced by habitual exercise.[76]

The nature and sources of Cardan's wisdom are now clear. Its fundamental preoccupation is the assurance of a long, good, and blessed life: the virtue of the soul, good health, accurate sensory perception, the consciousness of a life of probity, honesty, love, and friendship.[77] It can be defined as the conservation of body and soul. Its content, and its source, is then a naturally acquired mixture of two traditional disciplines: medicine and ethics. Medicine conserves the body, while ethics conserves the soul. So conserved the wise man has achieved five specific goals: his mind is learned and virtuous, his bodily strength is intact and his person beautiful, he enjoys the good and pleasant things of life and exhibits an honest probity in all his acts.[78] Wisdom, in short, is a rule of happiness and security, a set of precepts insuring health, virtue, and an honorable success in life.

IV

Colet, Luther, Sir Thomas Elyot, Jacques Lefèvre d'Etaples and his pupils Josse Clitchove and Bovillus, all assumed that wisdom was a form of knowledge. They asked the question: what must man know in order to be wise? Their answers inevitably describe a wisdom defined by its intellectual content, whether this is the Second Person of the Trinity, disembodied Platonic Ideas, angels, universal

[76] *De sap.*, 525, col. 1. Cf. Ronsard, *Vertus intellectuelles et moralles*, 1035.

[77] *De sap.*, 519, col. 2– 520, col. 1. "Ergo naturalis sapientiae institutum, quod ad beatam pertinet vitam, animi virtutes, bonam valetudinem, integritatem sensuum, conscientiam rectae vitae, honestatem et amorem, quem amicitiam nuncupamus amplectitur."

[78] *De sap.*, 520, col. 1. "Quinque enim scopi esse videntur illius qui naturali sapientia praeditus est, animum eruditione et virtute excolere, corporis vires seruare, vitae commoda praestare, personae decorem tueri, honestatem sic in cunctis operationibus praeferre, vt nihil iure reprehendi queat."

forms or species, or the mutable particulars of sense experience. Their wisdom is a theoretical science and an intellectual virtue. Petrarch, Salutati, Vives, and Erasmus, Inghirami, Le Caron, and Cardan asked a different question: what must man do in order to be wise? From their answers gradually emerges a more active, "useful" wisdom, a naturally acquired moral virtue designed to guide man's life in the world. Their wisdom is a practical science and a collection of ethical, medical, and worldly precepts.

This progressive transformation of the idea of wisdom from contemplation to action and from knowledge to virtue defines its final secularization. It is secularized in its source, in its object, and in its end. Its source is no longer God but man or Nature. Wisdom is no longer necessarily Christian and a gift of grace; it is purely human and a perfection of the natural man, naturally derived from the dictates of the autonomous human reason, experience, contemporary ideals and practice, and the Greek and Roman moralists. It is acquired by active practice and consolidated by habit. The object of wisdom, in the second place, is no longer God or "divine" things; nor is its content any speculative science. On the contrary, it focuses exclusively on living men in their concrete relations with each other; and its content is the practical rules which govern those relations. As such, it is the same as prudence and the chief of the naturally acquired cardinal virtues. Its end, finally, is no longer a solitary, contemplative blessedness but mundane happiness and a good and successful life: to live, in Cardan's phrase, long and well; to enjoy good health, longevity, and the affectionate remembrance of posterity; to be a success in political life and in one's own calling; to be, finally, moderate and self-controlled, know oneself, and inform each act with probity and virtue.

Chapter 7

Pierre Charron and the Triumph of Wisdom as a Moral Virtue

Pierre Charron's *De la Sagesse* is the most important Renaissance treatise on wisdom.[1] It is an extraordinarily representative work. Montaigne is the chief source, but Charron also draws on the most interesting ideas of other contemporaries: Bodin, Justus Lipsius, and du Vair. J. B. Sabrié, Charron's biographer, rightly calls it "the philosophical *Summa* of humanism at the end of the sixteenth century."[2] First published in 1601,[3] amply and stimulatingly argued, the *De la Sagesse* successfully concludes the transformation of *sapientia* from contemplation to action and from knowledge to virtue. In it Charron systematizes humanist speculation on wisdom

[1] Charron was born in 1541 and died in 1603. On his life and work see Gabriel Michel de la Rochemaillet, *Eloge véritable ou Sommaire Discours de la vie de Pierre Charron, Parisien, vivant docteur ès droicts* which prefaces the *Traicté de Sagesse* (Paris, David Le Clerc, 1606) and J. B. Sabrié, *De l'humanisme au rationalisme. Pierre Charron (1541–1603). L'Homme, l'œuvre, l'influence* (Paris, 1913). Full bibliographies in Sabrié, in Henri Busson, *La Pensée religieuse française de Charron a Pascal* (Paris, 1933) and in the *Dictionnaire des lettres françaises. Le seizième siècle* (Paris, 1951).

[2] Sabrié, *Charron*, 281.

[3] *De la Sagesse livres trois* (Bordeaux, S. Millanges, 1601). Charron prepared a substantially revised second edition before his death. "Je sçay que ce livre est diversement pris. Il y a des choses un peu hardiment dites; c'est pourquoy je l'ay reveu et corrigé, et en plusieurs lieux je l'ay adouci." (L. Auvray, "Lettres de Pierre Charron à Gabriel Michel de la Rochemaillet," *Revue d'histoire littéraire de la France*, I (1894), 322–323). This is the *De La Sagesse trois livres. Seconde edition reueuë et augmentée* (Paris, David Douceur, 1604). I have used the edition of Amaury Duval (3 vols., Paris, 1820–24) which includes the *Petit Traicté de Sagesse* as well. Unless otherwise indicated references are to this edition, noted as *Sag.*, followed first by the numbers of the book and chapter, then by the volume and page.

from Petrarch to Cardanus and makes sharply explicit its secular assumptions. This book is the triumph of wisdom as a naturally acquired moral virtue.

The result is a purely human wisdom. As though to emphasize this, Charron explicitly refuses to consider more transcendent and contemplative varieties of *sapientia*. He alerts his readers on the first page of the Preface to what were even then unusual limitations on his subject. I will not, he says, understand wisdom "subtly, in the arrogant and pompous sense of theologians and philosophers, who love to describe things which have never yet been seen and lift them to such a degree of perfection that human nature is incapable of them except in imagination."[4] He will not, that is, describe wisdom as the perfect knowledge of divine and human things; nor as metaphysics, the principles, first causes, and reasons of things; nor, following the theologians, as an infused knowledge of religious truth. Such wisdoms are purely speculative. They can, and do, exist without probity, utility, action, and use. They flee the world and the company of men.[5]

But Charron aims at men committed to the world. He wants to instruct them in the active virtues of public, private, and business life, not turn them into monks, theologians, or professional philosophers. He confines himself, therefore, to "human wisdom," which is

[4] *Sag.*, Preface (1601): I, xxxi.

[5] *Petit Traicté de Sagesse*, I, 4: *Sag.*, III, 263–264. "... les Philosophes la font [la sagesse] toute speculatiue, disent que c'est la cognoissance des principes, des premieres causes et plus hauts ressorts de toutes choses, et enfin de la souueraine, qui est Dieu, c'est la Metaphysique; cette cy reside toute en l'entendement, c'est son souuerain bien et sa perfection, c'est la premiere et plus haute des cinq vertus intellectuelles, qui peut estre sans probité, action, et sans aucune vertu morale. Les Theologiens ne la font pas du tout tant speculatiue qu'elle ne soit aussi aucunement pratique, car ils disent que c'est la cognoissance des choses diuines, par lesquelles se tire vn iugement re reglement des actions humaines, et la font double: l'vne acquise par estude, et est à peu prez celle des Philosophes que ie viens de dire: l'autre infuse et donnée de Dieu. *Desursum descendens*. C'est le premier des sept dons du Sainct Esprit. *Spiritus Domini spiritus sapientiae*, qui ne se trouue qu'aux iustes et nets de peché. *In maleuolam animam non introibit sapientia*." Cf. *Sag.*, Preface (1601): I, xxxi.

active not contemplative, moral not intellectual, a humanly achieved perfection, "a rectitude, a beautiful and noble formation of the whole man within and without, in his thoughts, words, actions, and every movement." Charron calls this wisdom *preude prudence*, an *habile et forte preud'hommie*, a *probité bien advisée*, the "excellence and perfection of man as man."[6] In it three fundamental tendencies of Renaissance wisdom become explicit; humanism, secularism, and moralism. By its concern for the dignity of man and its vital re-appropriation of an important variety of ancient wisdom, Seneca's *est enim sapientia in naturam converti*, Charron's idea of wisdom is humanistic. It is secular because it clearly and consciously dis-associates wisdom and Revelation. It is moralized when Charron identifies wisdom with an autonomous ethic, the naturally acquired cardinal virtues; prudence, justice, fortitude, and temperance.

I

The particular character of Charron's idea of wisdom is evident at once in the invidious distinction he draws between *science* and *sagesse*, *scientia* and *sapientia*. There is no novelty, of course, in a distinction of wisdom and knowledge. It had been made by everyone who had discussed either wisdom or knowledge. But Charron not only distinguishes them; like Montaigne, but more consistently, he makes them mutually exclusive. He advances two propositions: "first, that knowledge and wisdom are very different things and that wisdom is better than all the knowledge in the world, as the sky is better than the whole earth, or gold than iron; second, that, not only are they different, they are almost never found together. Usually they are mutually exclusive—the learned man is rarely wise, the wise man is generally unlearned. There are, of course, exceptions, but these are rare and great souls, rich and happy. There were such men in antiquity, but practically none can be found any more."[7]

---

[6] *Sag.*, Preface (1604): I, xlii; *Sag.*, Preface (1601): I, xxxii.

[7] *Sag.*, III, xiv: III, 87. Cf. Etienne Gilson, *René Descartes. Discours de la Methode. Texte et commentaire*, 2nd ed. (Paris, 1947), 94.

Compared to wisdom, knowledge is a "small and sterile good." It does not help to make our lives happier or more contented. Think of the men and women who live pleasantly and happily without ever having heard of *science*. And, if our lives are troubled and unhappy, it brings no consolation. It merely sharpens the consciousness of misfortune; and to such an extent that "the evil is lodged in the soul more by knowledge than by nature." It is no help, furthermore, in making us virtuous. On the contrary, it makes *preud'hommie* more difficult. Knowledge spawns enemies of innocence, and a desire for it was the devil's first temptation, the beginning of all evil. There are more *gens de bien*, more men who excel in every sort of virtue, among the simple and ignorant than among the learned. Knowledge, in fact, is not only vain, but positively harmful. It can make us more polished and eloquent, but it often robs us of virtue.[8]

Knowledge, therefore, is quite different from wisdom. *Science* is servile, base, and mechanical, a heterogeneous erudition got from books. Its content, stored in the memory, is scraps of information on all possible subjects, all of it borrowed from some external authority. Wisdom, on the other hand, is essentially one's own, a natural gift formed and cultivated by man himself. *Science*, again, is proud, presumptuous, arrogant, opinionated, and quarrelsome. *Scientia inflat.* But wisdom is modest, restrained, and peaceful. Knowledge, finally, is either a feat of pure memory or an empty speculation. It can do nothing but talk vainly and play with words. Wisdom, however, just as Salutati and Bruni, Le Caron, and Ronsard had insisted, is active. It controls, manipulates, and governs all things. "Knowledge and wisdom, therefore, are two very different things; and wisdom is much more excellent, more to be prized and esteemed than knowledge. For it is necessary, useful in every enterprise, universal, active, noble, honorable, gracious, and happy; while knowledge is particular, unnecessary, scarcely useful,

---

[8] *Sag.*, III, xiv: III, 88–91. Cf. Montaigne, "Apologie de Raimond Sebond," *Essais*, Albert Thibaudet, ed. (Paris, Bibliothèque de la Pléiade, 1940), II, xii, pp. 467–469.

inactive, servile, mechanical, melancholy, opinionated, and presumptuous."[9]

But not only are they different, they are almost never found together. History gives spectacular examples of this. The greatest states have flourished without learning. For the first five hundred years of her history Rome was valiant, virtuous, and ignorant. No sooner had she begun to embellish herself with learning than corruption, civil war, and ruin set in. Sparta had no "professors of literature"; and this school of virtue and wisdom easily defeated Athens, the most learned city in the world, the school of every science, the home of the Muses, that *magazin des philosophes*. But if ancient history is clear proof that wisdom flourishes concomitantly with ignorance, the contrary is equally true. Continuing Budé's criticisms of the isolated, foolish, and unvirtuous learned, Charron finds his examples of knowledge without wisdom closer to home in the contemporary products of the school and universities. No one is more inept, foolish, more impotent before the simplest practical situation than these men. Their absurdity has become proverbial. Hence the expression for a thing badly done is *faicte en clerc*. Knowledge addles them, hits them on the head like a hammer, and leaves them fools and imbeciles. "There are many people who would be wiser if they had never been to school. Their brothers, who stayed at home and did not study, are much wiser."[10]

[9] *Sag.*, III, xiv: III, 93. Cf. *Sag.*, I, lxiv: I, 433–434. "Les uns l'estiment tant [la science], qu'ils la preferent à toute autre chose, et pensent que c'est un souverain bien, quelque espece et rayon de divinité; la cherchent avec faim, despence, et peine grande.... Je la mets beaucoup au dessoubs de la preud'hommie, santé, sagesse, vertu, et encores au dessoubs de l'habileté aux affaires: mais après cela je la mettrois aux mains et en concurrence avec la dignité, noblesse naturelle, vaillance militaire; et les laisserois volontiers disputer ensemble de la presseance." Cf. Montaigne, "Du pedantisme," *Essais*, I, xxv, p. 148.

[10] *Sag.*, III, xiv: III, 95–97. Cf. Ronsard, *Des vertus intellectuelles et moralles, Œuvres complètes*, Gustave Cohen, ed. (Paris, Bibliothèque de la Pléiade, 1950), 1037–1039; Montaigne, "Apologie de Raimond Sebond," *Essais*, II, xii, p. 479; and "Du pedantisme," *Essais*, I, xxv, p. 145.

Properly understood, therefore, wisdom is not knowledge at all. Charron's is the culminating attack on all intellectual speculative varieties of wisdom in favor of an active, virtuous prudence. To those who had defined wisdom as the knowledge of the principles and first causes of things Charron replies that "the causes and prime mover of things are unknown, their seeds and roots are hidden. Human nature can not, and should not, try to find them."[11] Sir Thomas Elyot located wisdom in a knowledge of ideas, "forms," "species," numbers, and figures. "But who," asks Charron, "will believe that Plato put forward his Republic and his Ideas, Pythagoras his numbers, Epicurus his atoms as gospel truth? They merely enjoyed exercising their minds with amusing and subtle inventions."[12] Such things have never yet been seen, they are unknowable, human beings can grasp them only in imagination. Humanist *eruditio*, finally, the universal knowledge of all things divine and human is *pedantisme* and the very opposite of wisdom. All purely intellectual and speculative wisdom, in short, whatever its definition, is, first, impossible to attain and, second, useless, vain, culpably inactive, and destructive of virtue.

II

Charron's distinction between wisdom and knowledge is a function of his contrasting estimate of the powers of the two chief faculties of the soul, will and intellect. Sharpening a common humanist tendency to skepticism in knowledge and Pelagianism in the moral life, he says that the intellect is weak and fickle, incapable of knowing any ultimate truth, while the will is potent, efficacious,

---

[11] *Sag.*, II, 1: II, 284.

[12] *Sag.*, II, ii: II, 47. Cf. *Ibid.*, 50–51. "Si l'on veust que je m'assujettisse aux principes, je diray comme le curé à ses paroissiens en matiere du temps, et comme un prince des nostres aux secretaires de ce siecle en faict de religion, accordez-vous premierement de ces principes, et puis je m'y sousmettray. Or y a-t-il autant de doute et de dispute aux principes, qu'aux conclusions, en la these qu'en l'hypothese, dont y a tant de sectes entre eux, si je me rends a l'une, j'offense toutes les autres."

and entirely in man's own control. Charron is a skeptic.[13] "It is a curious fact," he remarks, "that although man naturally wants to know the truth and tries every possible means to attain it, he cannot attain it. This is not his fault—for truth is beautiful, lovable, and knowable—but the fault of human weakness, which is incapable of accommodating such a splendor. Man is potent in desire, but weak to seize and keep."[14] He is born to search for truth, but only God, in whose breast it dwells, can possess it. Man never understands anything completely and in its true purity. He turns here and there, circles aimlessly about the appearances of things, chooses now the true now the false. He lacks all real power of discrimination. He can have approximations, even probabilities, but no certainty.[15] His devise, like the one Charron had carved over the door of his own house at Condom, must be *Je ne sçay*.

The reason for man's inability to have certain knowledge of the truth is the weakness of his rational faculties. In the first place, his

---

[13] Not a Pyrrhonist. "Ie responds [to critics who accuse him of Pyrrhonism] premierement, q'il y a difference entre mon dire et l'aduis des Pyrrhoniens, bien qu'il en ait l'air et l'odeur, puisque ie permets de consentir et adherer à ce qui semble meilleur et plus vraysemblable, tousiours prest et attendant à receuoir mieux s'il se presente." (*Petit Traicté de Sagesse*, IV, 4: *Sag.*, III, 308.) Yet one should not take Charron's disclaimer too seriously. His major sources, to be sure, are the skepticism of Montaigne's *Apologie de Raimond Sebond* and the defense of Academic skepticism in Cicero's *De Academica*. However, there are important affinities with Sextus as well. But cf. Sabrié, *Charron*, 291 and Heinrich Teipel, *Zur Frage des Skeptizismus bei Pierre Charron* (Elberfeld, 1912), 42 ff.

[14] *Sag.*, I, xxxix: I, 257.

[15] *Sag.*, I, xv: I, 126. Charron, however, does not always speak so lightly of man's intellectual power. While not necessarily contradictory (capacity for knowledge is not knowledge), the different tone of the following passages should be noted: "Cet entendement (ainsi l'appellerons-nous d'un nom general) *intellectus, mens, nous*, est un subject general, ouvert et disposé à recevoir et embrasser toutes choses, comme la matiere premiere, et le miroir de toutes formes, *intellectus est omnia*. Il est capable d'entendre toutes choses." (*Sag.*, I, xv: I, 116.) And again: "Son action est la cognoissance et l'intelligence de toutes choses: l'esprit humain est capable d'entendre toutes choses visibles, invisibles, universelles, particulieres, sensibles, insensibiles. *Intellectus est omnia*." (*Sag.*, I, xiv: I, 110.)

senses are deceptive and untrustworthy. Weak and unreliable in themselves, when stirred by the passions of anger, love, or hate, they see and hear things with no relation whatever to objective reality.[16] His understanding, in the second place, is as fickle and uncertain as his senses. It is without order or measure, always in motion, completely undisciplined. It produces dreams, bizarre imaginings, visions, arbitrary constructions of every sort; and these it calls reality. The mind, in short, forms its own truth by frequently missing and distorting the simple truths of the objective world.[17] Experience, finally, the third possible avenue to truth, is useless because there are no constants in human experience. Events are always different. "There is nothing so universal in nature as diversity; nothing so rare, difficult, and almost impossible as similarity."[18] No wonder then that there is no agreement whatever on the most crucial matters; on the immortality of the soul, for example, or the truth of the Christian religion. The vast diversity, indeed contradiction, of opinion among even the wisest and most learned men is the sure and final proof of the relativity of human truth and the weakness of man's intellect.[19]

The will, on the other hand, is free and powerful. For this man should be grateful because on it depends almost his entire dignity and well-being. "The will alone is really ours and in our power. The rest, understanding, memory, imagination, all this can be taken from us, altered, troubled by a thousand accidents; but not the will."[20] For the will is free and autonomous. It has the power of choice. By motions of the will the soul projects itself outward, fastens onto and lives in the things chosen and beloved. It bears its name and is called virtuous or vicious, spiritual or carnal, according to the nature of the chosen object. It follows that the will ennobles itself by loving worthy and elevated things; degrades itself by loving lesser, worthless things. As a wife is known by the quality of her

---

[16] *Sag.*, I, xi: I, 91.

[17] *Sag.*, I, xv: I, 115–116, 118–119, 120–121.

[18] *Sag.*, I, xxxix: I, 258. Cf. Montaigne, "De l'experience," *Essais*, III, xiii, p. 1034.

[19] *Sag.*, I, xvii: I, 141.   [20] *Sag.*, I, xviii: I, 142.

husband, the will is known by the splendor or baseness of its loves.[21] The power to know the truth with certainty and precision is not in man's control; but the ability to distinguish good from evil, the freedom to choose the good and reject the evil, the power, finally, to be virtuous or bad—these are innate capacities of the will. For Luther and Calvin both will and intellect were feeble and iniquitous. For Charron neither is iniquitous, the intellect is weak, and the will defines the dignity of man. Man is ignorant, but he can be virtuous.

Since Petrarch's essay *On His Own Ignorance* and Nicholas of Cusa's *De docta ignorantia*, the notion of ignorance had played an important part in the development of the idea of wisdom. Used in the framework of a religious philosophy emphasizing illumination and grace, it enforced, as in Cusa, a reassertion of the transcendence of wisdom and its inaccessibility to the unaided reason. But it could serve a very different purpose. When the idea of ignorance, understood now as a general intellectual skepticism, was combined with an assertion of the autonomous power of the will, it became a lever by which wisdom was transferred from the weaker to the stronger faculty, from intellect to will. For the intellect is not only weak, but *science*, the result of intellectual activity is useless and bad. The will, on the other hand is strong, and *sagesse* is good and useful. In order to tie wisdom firmly to the will, Charron has only to define *sagesse* as a moral virtue. He does this by calling wisdom *preud prudence* and *preud'hommie*, by identifying, as Bonaventure des Periers had done before him, the wise man and the *homme de bien*. Charron's wisdom will be an explicit ethic.

III

The beginning of wisdom is self-knowledge, *Nosce teipsum*. The antique injunction, originated by the gods, carved in golden letters over the entrance to Apollo's temple at Delhi, repeated by the seven wise men and by Socrates, receives a final interpretation from Charron. To know oneself is to know one's strength and weakness,

---

[21] *Sag.*, I, xvii: I, 144. Cf. *Ibid.*, 143.

to recognize one's faults and remedy them, to know one's necessities and provide for them, to realize, finally, the misery of the human condition and try to repair it. By knowing himself man will learn his central place in the hierarchy of being, that, "like a fabled animal, he is made up of hostile contradictions. For the soul is like a little god, the body like a beast, a dung heap."[22] He will learn, and much better than from any book, the nature and strength of the body's passions. He will understand the composition of his soul; the splendor, and weakness, of the intellect; the dignity and power of the will. He will conclude that the nature of wisdom is based on these characteristics of the soul; that the weakness of the intellect determines the first component of wisdom, complete intellectual liberty, a liberty defined as a tolerant and universal skepticism; and that the second component of wisdom, which flows from the dignity and potency of the will, its ability to choose the good and its power to rule the passions, is a universal *preud'hommie*, an active prudence, a harmony and self-control reducible to a constant, serene practice of the naturally acquired cardinal virtues. Charron's conclusion is in unexpected agreement with Pascal: *Il faut se connaître soi-même: quand cela ne servirait pas à trouver le vrai, cela au moins sert à regler sa vie, et il n'y a rien de plus juste.*[23]

The first component of wisdom is a "universal, full, entire, generous, and seigneurial intellectual freedom."[24] This freedom is the essence, the proper right and privilege of the wise man. *Nisi sapiens liber nemo: stulti omnes et improbi serui.* It has two parts: freedom from the opinions of the herd and freedom to examine and judge all things without having to commit oneself to any of them. The first is the easier. Easy because one has only to recognize the mass of men for what they are, fools. Their opinions are base, vulgar, and generally false. Flee them, therefore, avoid their company and conversation, imitate the wisest men of every age and build a spiritual solitude where the soul, like a carte blanche, is free of popular vice

[22] *Sag.*, I, iii: I, 19.
[23] *Pensées*, 81 (75). *L'Œuvre de Pascal*, Jacques Chevalier, ed. (Paris, Bibliothèque de la Pléiade, 1950), 839.
[24] *Sag.*, II, ii: II, 26.

and error. Public opinion is "foolish, volatile, inconstant, uncertain, the guide of fools and of the herd." The wise man isolates himself from its contagion and follows reason only, the guide of all wise men. "It is true liberty and mastery to follow reason, the hardest servitude to be led by opinion."[25] This freedom is the first condition of wisdom.

The second is what Charron calls an *universelle et pleine liberté de l'esprit*, that skeptical freedom so praised in Cicero's *De Academica* and by Sextus. The pages he devotes to it are among his most amiable. It is not surprising that he was one of the Enlightenment's favorite authors. This freedom consists in a liberty to judge all things, to be bound by none of them, and to remain universally receptive to every point of view. It is a purely internal and "secret" freedom which does not involve one's external behavior in the world. On the contrary, one should conform details of dress, behavior, and usage to the laws, customs, and ceremonies of the country in which one lives. But in the secret solitude of one's own mind one must freely judge all things for what they are by the standards of "universal reason." The vulgar must content themselves with this external conformity to appearances. They "may rule my hand, my tongue as much as they please; but not my mind. It has another master. To prevent the free activity of the mind is impossible; to wish to do so is the most monstrous tyranny which can exist. The wise man will resist actively and passively. He will maintain his own liberty and not trouble that of others."[26] Charron gives the following example. We Christians bury our dead. To this practice the wise man living in a Christian society will conform. But he has a full, untrammelled freedom to examine, weigh, and judge this method of disposing of the dead, to compare it with other methods, and to conclude, as does Charron himself, that cremation is more rational, nobler, more befitting human dignity than putting a man in the ground, the coarsest of the elements, to rot, putrify, and feed the worms.[27]

[25] *Petit Traicté de Sagesse*, II, 3: *Sag.*, III, 275. Cf. *Sag.*, II, i: II, 12–16.
[26] *Sag.*, II, ii: II, 37–38.
[27] *Sag.*, II, ii: II, 40–41.

Within himself then the wise man has no invisible master. He seeks the truth with perfect freedom, clean of prejudice, independent of all authority and the opinion of the vulgar. He examines everything, doubts every answer, weighs and balances every reason. He accepts—but only provisionally and never dogmatically—what seems most probable, honorable, and useful. The wise man is indifferent. He considers all things coldly, without passion. He never says, this is so; but, this seems so, *ita videtur*; or, even more wisely, *Je ne sçay*.[28] Conscious always of uncertainty, he is always open to a better solution. For, after all, the wise man has examined the whole universe and imagined it as a giant picture, a living image of "our mother Nature in her undiminished majesty." He has meditated on the inequality and myriad differences among men; on the great diversity of laws, customs, religions, opinions, usages in the world; on the infinite number of conflicting philosophical solutions of basic problems—unity and plurality, the world's creation or eternity, the immortality or mortality of the soul. This is how he has learned "to know himself, admire nothing, find nothing new or strange in the world, strengthen and perfect himself."[29] Inevitably, reasonably, wisely he has come to the gentle skepticism of *Je ne sçay*.

One must be free to doubt, to judge all things, to remain indifferent and disengaged precisely because one can be certain of nothing. Sapiential freedom is "founded on the following proposition, so celebrated among wise men: nothing is certain; we know nothing; there is nothing in nature but doubt, nothing more certain than uncertainty, *solum certum nihil esse certi—hoc unum scio quod nil scio*; one can argue equally well about everything; all we do is seek, enquire, fumble with appearances, *scimus nihil, opinamur verisimilia*; truth and falsehood enter our minds by the same door, hold there an equal place and credit, maintain themselves by the same means; there is no opinion universally held by all men everywhere, none which is not debated and contested, none whose opposite is not held and supported."[30] In short, because the intellect cannot know

---

[28] *Sag.*, II, ii: II, 45. Cf. *Ibid.*, 50.
[29] *Sag.*, II, ii: II, 58. Cf. Sextus, *Pyrr. Hyp.*, III, 198 ff.
[30] *Sag.*, II, ii: II, 45–46.

the truth wisdom demands a universal liberty equivalent to a universal relativism, an inner, secret integrity equivalent to universal skepticism. This is "the modesty of the Academy" so necessary to the wise man; for his function is not to determine, proclaim, and then defend the truth—that is impossible—but only to seek the truth.

Wisdom, therefore, does not consist in a knowledge of the truth. It is an attitude of mind, which Charron calls liberty, based on the fact that intellectual certainty is unattainable. It is the absence of fanaticism and a tolerant skepticism. Safe from the danger of "participating in so many errors due to the fantasy of man," the wise man is free, open to all, master of all, tranquil, and full of modest repose.[31] Elyot, Sadoleto, and Bovillus defended wisdom as the highest kind of human knowledge. For Charron it has become an ironical and serene intellectual liberty, rooted in an acceptance of human ignorance.

IV

If the first characteristic of wisdom is liberty, a tolerant skepticism based on the conviction that the intellect is incapable of absolute truth, its second, and more important characteristic is a *preud'hommie* based on the fact that his will can love and do the good. In his first Preface to *De la Sagesse* Charron defines wisdom as *preude prudence, c'est à dire preud'hommie avec habilité, probité bien advisée.*[32] *Preud'hommie*, he emphasizes later, is the "first, principal, and fundamental part of wisdom," the "foundation and pivot of wisdom."[33] He associates it with *probité, droicture, bonté,* and *vertu.*[34] It is inseparable from *bien faire* and from the effort *à nous rendre meilleurs.*[35] The man who possesses it is an *homme de bien.* Charron defines it, finally, as *la vraye vertu,*[36] notes explicitly that is a function of the will,[37] and says that it "includes all the moral

---

[31] *Sag.*, II, ii: II, 52.   [32] *Sag.*, Preface (1601): I, xxxii.

[33] *Sag.*, II, iii: II, 74, 94.   [34] *Sag.*, II, iii: II, 74, 80, 95, 97.

[35] *Sag.*, III, xiv: III, 89. Cf. *Sag.*, II, iii: II, 75.

[36] *Sag.*, II, v: II, 149.

[37] *Petit Traicté de Sagesse*, II, 6: *Sag.*, III, 287. "Le sixiesme office et traict du sage qui regarde la volonté, est vne forte et ferme probité et preud'hommie."

virtues, but consists especially of justice, the ruler and mistress of them all, which is to render to each his own. The wise man will acquit himself well and devotedly of all his duties to everyone, God, himself, his neighbor."[38]

The source of *preud'hommie* is the Stoic law of nature; and its essence is to follow nature, the fundamental injunction of Stoic ethics. "The good, goal, and end of man, in which lies his tranquillity, freedom, contentment, in one word, his perfection in this world, is to live and act according to nature."[39] For the law of nature is sovereign, universal, and infallible. To live according to this law is to live well and blessedly, and that is the supreme good of this world. All the ancient sages confirm this. "If you follow the guide of nature, you will never err," said Cicero;[40] and Seneca confirms him: "The good is what is in harmony with nature; to live happily is to live in harmony with nature."[41] All our misfortunes come from our obstinate pursuit of things outside, against, or above nature. Even animals join their example to the precepts of the ancients. They let themselves be guided by the "simplicity of nature," and their lives are innocent and peaceful, full of tranquillity and repose, free of all the evils, vices, and derangements which men bring on themselves by refusing to believe nature and follow her. True

[38] *Sag.*, III, 289.

[39] *Sag.*, II, iii: II, 94. "Voyci donc la vraye preud'hommie (fondement et pivot de sagesse) suivre nature, c'est-à-dire la raison. Le bien, le but et la fin de l'homme auquel gist son repos, sa liberté, son contentement, et en un mot sa perfection en ce monde, est vivre et agir selon nature; quand ce qui est en luy le plus excellent commande, c'est-à-dire la raison, la vraye preud'hommie est une droite et ferme disposition de la volonté, à suivre le conseil de la raison."

[40] *De Off.*, I, xxviii, 100. "Officium autem, quod ab eo ducitur, hanc primam habet viam, quae deducit ad conventientiam, conservationemque naturae: quam si sequemur ducem, numquam aberrabimus: consequemurque et id, quod acutum et perspicax natura est; et id, quod ad hominum consociationem accommodatum: et id, quod vehemens atque forte."

[41] *Epist. Moral.*, XV, ep. 1 (ep. 118), 11. "Hanc quidam finitionem reddiderunt: Bonum est quod secundum naturam est." Cf. *De vita beata*, VIII, 1. "Natura enim duce utendum est; hanc ratio observat, hanc consulit. Idem est ergo beate vivere et secundum naturam."

preud'hommie, therefore, is "a firm and constant disposition of the will to follow the advice of reason." As the needle of a compass is never at rest until it finds the North, and in this way directs the navigator, so man is never an *homme de bien* if he does not direct his life, his manners, his judgments, and his will according to this fundamental law, which is his torch and an inner, personal illumination.[42] The essence of *preud'hommie* and the most important recommendation of wisdom is to follow nature.

The law of nature shines in each of us. It is a "natural light," our human participation in equity and universal reason, "that reason, equity, and natural illumination which God has inspired in every man (if he is not totally denatured) and which, like a flaming star, shines in him with perpetual brilliance."[43] For the law of nature is a shining ray of divinity, an emanation and dependence of eternal divine law.[44] Again Charron quotes his favorite author: "For what is nature but God and divine reason, which pervades the universe and all its parts?"[45] The man who follows nature follows the will of God. The law of nature is, in a sense, God. "It is God himself, the first, original, and fundamental law, being God and nature in the world like the king and his law in the state."[46]

[42] *Petit Traicté de Sagesse*, II, 7: *Sag.*, III, 290–291.

[43] *Ibid.*

[44] *Sag.*, II, iii: II, 78. "Or le ressort de cette preud'hommie, c'est loy de nature, c'est-à-dire l'equité et raison universelle, qui luict et esclaire et un chascun de nous. Qui agist par ce ressort, agist selon Dieu: car cette lumiere naturelle est un esclaire et rayon de la Divinité, une defluxion et dependence de la loy eternelle et divine. Il agist aussi selon soy, car il agist selon ce qu'il y a de plus noble et de plus riche en soy. Il est homme de bien."

[45] Seneca, *De Beneficiis*, IV, vii, 1. "Natura, inquit, haec mihi praestat. Non intelligis te, cum hoc dicis, mutare nomen Deo? Quid enim aliud est natura quam Deus et divina ratio, toti mundo et partibus eius inserta?" Cf. Seneca, *Natur. Quaest.*, II, xlv, 1–2. "... eundem quem nos Iovem intellegunt, custodem rectoremque universi, animum ac spiritum mundi, huius operis dominum et artificem, cui nomen omne convenit. ... Est enim, cuius consilio huic mundo providetur, ut inconfusus exeat, et actus suos explicet, vis illum naturam vocare, non peccabis."

[46] *Sag.*, II, iii: II, 82–83. "... qui agit selon elle, agist vrayement selon Dieu, car c'est Dieu, ou bien sa premiere, fondamentale et universelle loy

But Charron is no pantheist. He recalls the scholastic distinction: *Natura naturans est Deus*; but *natura naturata eius opus*. God is nature, God is even the law of nature; but the "natural light" which shines in man, the source of *preud'hommie* and wisdom, is a human participation in the divine and uncreated light. It is a dependence of the "eternal law which is God himself and His will." It is not God, but it is the necessary intermediary between His divine law and the particularities of human law. For all laws are only copies, some good some bad, of the law of nature imprinted on man's soul. The law of Moses—*une copie externe et publique*—the law of the Twelve Tables, Roman Law, the edicts and ordinances of kings, the moral teachings of theology and philosophy, all flow from the "invisible fountain" of the human soul.[47] If the greatest legislators have built their states on this basis, surely man has sufficient guidance, within himself, to lead a good and harmonious life.

This is all the more true because the light which illuminates man's soul is purely natural. Seeds of virtue are innate in every man, man is good by nature, and he has both a natural obligation to be wise and the power to become so. The light of nature, man's participation in equity and universal reason, "contains and hatches in itself the seeds of every virtue, probity, and justice."[48] Once more Seneca is his source: "We have implanted in us the seeds of all ages, of all arts, of all virtues, and God our master brings forth our intellects from obscurity."[49] Like Sir Thomas Elyot, who also posited innate "sedes of things," a "leme of science," a potential wisdom which,

---

qui l'a mis au monde, et qui la premiere est sortie de luy; car Dieu et nature sont au monde, comme en un estat, le roy son autheur et fondateur, et la loy fondamentale qu'il a bastie pour la conservation et regle dudit estat. C'est un esclat et rayon de la divinité, une defluxion et dependance de la loy eternelle qui est Dieu mesme, et sa volonté."

[47] *Sag.*, II, iii: II, 84–85.

[48] *Sag.*, II, iii: II, 87.

[49] *D Beneficiis*, IV, vi, 6. Cf. *Natur. Quaest.*, III, xxix, 3–4. "Ut in semine omnis futuri ratio hominis comprehensa est et legem barbae et canorum nondum natus infans habet: totius enim corporis, et sequentis aetatis in parvo occultoque liniamenta sunt."

properly cultivated, would flower to a clear and polished brilliance,[50] Charron's intention is to reinforce man's natural capacity for virtue and wisdom. Seeds of virtue are "naturally scattered and insinuated in our minds," and on them the mind can live joyfully and richly, as on its natural food. For the least cultivation causes them to push up into luxuriant growth, into a fully developed *preud'hommie*. Any contrary view is "injurious to God and nature." For "nature is a wise, learned, industrious, and sufficient mistress, who makes us apt for everything," fixes our sapiential end, and gives us the desire and innate natural capability to attain it.[51]

Because the light of nature hatches seeds of virtue in our minds and comes to us direct from a good and virtuous God, we must go on to say that nature is good and that man is good by nature. "Men are naturally good and follow evil only for its pleasure or profit. Legislators, therefore, in order to induce them to follow their own naturally good inclination, and not in order to force their wills, have proposed two contrary things, punishment and reward."[52] Wickedness, on the contrary, is against nature. It is ugly, difformed, incommodious, and an offense to all good judgment. Once known and understood, all men hate it.[53] From this it is evident that all things in nature are arranged as well as they can possibly be. Human nature has been endowed with the seeds of virtue and set in motion toward its end and good. Man naturally desires this end and good, and by following nature he is assured of its possession.[54] His end is wisdom, and it is to Seneca's equations that Charron points him: *Sapientia est in naturam converti*; or again: "True wisdom consists

---

[50] *The Boke named the Governour*, H. H. S. Croft, ed. (London, 1880), II, 363–364.

[51] *Sag.*, I, xiv: I, 112. "... les semences de toutes sciences et vertus sont naturellement esparses et insinuées en nos esprits, dont ils peuvent vivre riches et joyeux de leur propre; et pour peu qu'ils soyent cultivés, ils foisonnent et abondent fort." Cf. *Sag.*, I, viii: I, 71–72.

[52] *Sag.*, II, iii: II, 87.   [53] *Sag.*, II, iii: II, 103.

[54] *Sag.*, II, iii: II, 87. "Nature a disposé toutes choses au meilleur estat qu'elles puissent estre, et leur a donné le premier mouvement au bien et à la fin qu'elles doivent chercher, de sorte que qui la suyvra ne fauldra point d'obtenir et posseder son bien et sa fin."

in not departing from nature and in molding our conduct according to her laws and model."[55]

Man, finally, precisely because he is a man, has a natural obligation to be an *homme de bien*. Human nature, that natural law which is innate in him, is itself the cause, motive, and obligation of his *preud'hommie*. "Every man has a natural obligation, internal and universal, to be an *homme de bien*, full of probity according to the intention of his author and maker. Man should not expect or look for any other cause, obligation, driving force, or motive of his *preud'hommie*; nor can he ever have one more just or legitimate, more powerful, more ancient, for it is contemporary with man and born with him."[56] To be a man, to live like a man, in short, is exactly the same as being and living like an *homme de bien*. Anyone who does not care to be this is a monster, betrays his own nature, and ceases, in fact, to be a man at all. For *preud'hommie* must come to him by and from himself, from that inner driving force with which God has created him and not from any external source.[57] No concern for honor or reputation, no fears of laws or magistrates, no consideration of reward and punishment should externally force the natural probity of his will. Such *preud'hommie* would be fleeting, occasional, and accidental. But "I want my wise man to have an essential,

[55] *De vita beata*, III, 2–3. "Interim, quod inter omnes Stoicos convenit, rerum naturae adsentior; ab illa non deerrare et ad illius legem exemplumque formari sapientia est. Beata est ergo vita, conveniens naturae suae; quae non aliter contingere potest, quam si primum sana mens est, et in perpetua possessione sanitatis suae." Cf. *Epist. Moral.*, XV., ep. 2 (ep. 94), 69. "Hoc est enim sapientia, in naturam converti et eo restitui, unde publicus error expulerit."

[56] *Sag.*, II, iii: II, 79–80.

[57] *Sag.*, II, iii: II, 80. "Tout homme doibt estre et vouloir estre homme de bien, pource qu'il est homme: qui ne se soucie de l'estre est un monstre, renonce à soy-mesme, se desment, se destruit, par droict n'est plus homme, et debvroit par effect desister de l'estre, il l'est à tort. Il faut que la preud'hommie naisse en luy par luy-mesme, c'est-à-dire par le ressort interne que Dieu y a mis, et non par aucun autre externe estranger, par aucune occasion ou induction." Cf. *Petit Traicté de Sagesse*, II, 6: *Sag.*, III, 289. "Ie veux donc que ce soient choses inseparables estre et consentir de viure homme, estre et vouloir estre homme de bien."

invincible *preud'hommie,* owed to himself alone, rooted directly in himself, and one which can no more be taken or separated from him than humanity from man."[58]

The autonomy of wisdom is thus guaranteed by the nature of man. Because the law of nature is imprinted in him, he is endowed with innate seeds of virtue and is good by nature. Because he is naturally good, he can be, again by nature or "essentially," an *homme de bien.*[59] *Preud'hommie* is radical, fundamental, and essential. It is a seed of universal reason. It is in the soul like the spring in a clock or like natural heat in the body. It is perpetual, strong, and invincible. The man who has it is wise; and he lives and acts according to God, to himself, to nature, and to the universal order and government of the world.[60]

The general characteristics of wisdom are now clear. They are two: an intellectual liberty which commands an attitude of tolerant skepticism and *preud'hommie,* an imitation of the law of nature whose cause, motive, and sanction is human nature itself. Wisdom begins in self-knowledge, which reveals to man the weakness of his intellect and the power of his will. This insight into human nature determines Charron's double definition of wisdom as a firm disposition of the will to follow reason and the law of nature and a calm inclination of the intellect to universal doubt. By simultaneously denying the intellect a capacity for certain truth and attaching *preud'hommie* exclusively to the will, he thus concludes decisively the shift of wisdom from the intellect to the will. By then placing the essence of *preud'hommie* in an imitation of nature, he recreates a profoundly humanistic wisdom, a return to Seneca's *est enim sapientia in naturam converti,* a surrender to the tempting sequence of becoming wise by being natural. A final variety of revived classical wisdom thus finds its place beside those of Plato, Aristotle, and Cicero, an autonomous disposition of the will to follow nature

---

[58] *Sag.,* II, iii: II, 81. Cf. *Petit Traicté de Sagesse,* IV, 5: *Sag.,* III, 312.

[59] *Sag.,* II, iii: II, 83. "Ainsi est-il homme de bien essentiellement, et non par accident et occasion: car cette loy et lumiere est essentielle et naturelle en nous, dont aussi est appellée nature et loy de nature."

[60] *Sag.,* II, iii: II, 86.

beside the intellectual and contemplative knowledge of Ideas, first causes, and principles, or the universality of things divine and human and their causes. It is humanistic, too, in its emphasis on the dignity of man and his autonomous power to be wise. By following nature the wise man emphasizes the excellence of his own nature. He is good because he has innate possibilities of good, an *homme de bien* because he is a man, and wise because wisdom is the natural end and perfection of man as man.

v

How, specifically, does man become wise? There are two ways, says Charron, one natural, the other acquired. Some men are born with *preud'hommie*. They have it "naturally"—from the "temperament of their parents' seed," from their mothers' milk, or from their earliest education. We say of them that they are well-born. They have an innate goodness, a "strong, active, masculine, and efficacious goodness, which is a prompt, easy, and constant affection for what is good, upright, and just according to reason and nature."[61] Other men, on the contrary, are born with violent passions and a coarse and ugly nature. They must acquire *preud'hommie* and wisdom by laborious effort. This acquired wisdom is called virtue, and it consists in correcting and reforming one's *mauvais naturel* by the study and practice of moral philosophy, "which is the lamp, guide, and rule of our life, which explains and excellently illustrates the law of nature and instructs man in all things . . . , which sweetens and tames a rude and savage nature and forms and fashions it to wisdom." Moral philosophy defines the rules of acquired wisdom. It is "the true science of man; and all the rest, compared to it, is nothing but vanity, or at least unnecessary and of little use. For it teaches us to live well and die well and that is everything."[62]

[61] *Sag.*, II, iii: II, 95–96.

[62] *Sag.*, Preface (1604): I, xlviii. Cf. *Sag.*, II, iii: II, 96–97 and *Petit Traicté de Sagesse*, I, 6: *Sag.*, III, 269. "Voila les deux moyens de paruenir et obtenir la sagesse, le naturel et l'acquis: qui a esté heureux au premier, c'est à dire qui a esté fauorablement estrené de nature et est d'vn temperament bon et doux, lequel produit vne grande bonté et douceur de mœurs, a grand marché

Preud'hommie is an imitation of nature; but it is moral philosophy which explains the law of nature. If, therefore, the primary command of wisdom is to follow nature, its particular rules are reducible to a practice of the cardinal virtues, especially justice, which is to render each his own. In its highest form wisdom is a self-formation to justice so sovereign and perfect that every seed of vice has been uprooted. Virtue is then an essential *habitus* and complexion of the soul. This is man's perfection, a virtuous wisdom "acquired by long study and serious exercise of the rules of philosophy, joined to a handsome, strong, and rich nature; for both are necessary, the natural and the acquired."[63] Wisdom is thus the practice of justice, whose rules are practical applications of the general injunction to follow nature.[64]

Justice, and our duties in general, may be divided into three parts. "For man has three duties: to God, to himself, to his neighbor; above himself, to himself, and beside himself."[65] Man's first duty to himself is self-knowledge. This is the imperative of thought, "that solitary occupation and joyous conversation" of man with his own soul. From it flows the fundamental duty to "rule and regulate" his soul in its two parts, intellect and will. His duty to the intellect is to fill it with useful, serious things; nourish it on healthy, moderate, and natural opinions; regulate and order it with care, "for order and pertinence are effects of wisdom which give price to the soul." But above all man is just to his soul by doubting all things. "It is a lovely thing to know how to doubt and be ignorant; it is our one certainty, advised by the noblest philosophers; it is the principal effect and fruit of knowledge." His duty to the will, on the other hand, is to submit it always to "right reason, which is the duty of

---

du second, sans grande peine il se trouue tout porté et disposé à la sagesse; qui autrement, il doit auec grand et laborieux estude du second, rabiller et supleer ce qui luy defaut: comme Socrates, vn des plus sages, disoit de soy, que par estude de la Philosophie il auoit corrigé et redressé son mauuais naturel."

[63] *Sag.*, II, iii: II, 98.
[64] *Petit Traicté de Sagesse*, IV, 2: *Sag.*, III, 306. Cf. *Ibid.*, 289.
[65] *Sag.*, III, v: II, 436.

virtue," to regulate it "according to nature and reason," and to flee the mendacities of popular opinion. "An *homme de bien* owes it to himself to respect, fear, and submit himself to his reason and his conscience, which is his good genius."[66] By skepticism, therefore, and by virtue man is just to his intellect and his will.

Particular rules of justice to the will, which coalesce with the virtues of temperance and fortitude, are based on man's fundamental obligation to submit his passions to the regulations of right reason. "The beginning of justice," said Bodin, in a passage which Charron has adapted for his own use, "its first and oldest commandment, is the dominion of reason over sensuality. Before one can command others, one must learn to command oneself, giving reason the power to command and subject the appetites to its obedience. This is the first and original justice, internal and one's own; and it is the most beautiful."[67] The surest method to moderate the passions is to know them, their strength and nature, the power each has over us and we over it. Once known, we must oppose and fight against them with "a lively virtue and a firm resolution of the soul" to subjugate them. The sovereign remedy, finally, "is to let oneself be gently guided by reason and nature, which is the ripe, solid, and definitive guide of all wise men."[68]

An example of this struggle which defines the essential activity of the wise man is the effort to subdue the passion of anger. To combat it we should avoid occasions of anger, like the king who deliberately broke a gift of precious china so that he would not be angry if a servant later broke a plate, or like victorious Caesar who burned the captured letters of his enemies without reading them in order to avoid the fury their contents would have caused him.[69] Or we should avoid its causes. For example, since the opinion that one has been

---

[66] *Sag.*, III, vi: II, 443–445.

[67] *Sag.*, III, v: II, 431–432. Cf. Jean Bodin, *De la République*, I, iii. *De la République, traité de Jean Bodin, ou traité du gouvernement* (London, 1756), 28.

[68] *Sag.*, II, i: II, 21.

[69] *Sag.*, II, i: II, 19 and *Sag.*, III, xxxi: III, 205.

scorned or insulted is a frequent cause of anger, we must be impervious to the opinion of others, remembering that "the most glorious victory is to be master of oneself and insulated against any external provocation." Take as examples Agathocles and Antigonus. They laughed at those who insulted them and did not harm them later when they were in their power. Third, we should always keep the blood and humors cool, and, above all, keep silent. A very wise man once advised the enraged Augustus to pronounce all the letters of the alphabet before replying. Think, finally, of the ugliness of this passion, meditate philosophically on the beauties of moderation, and submit the will to the simple guidance of reason and nature.[70] These are particular rules of wisdom. Lived by, they will yield a sapiential nugget, the eradication of anger from the soul.

The second part of justice and man's second obligation is his duty to his neighbors. Our duties to others are as firmly based in nature as our duties to God and to ourselves. We have, for example, a natural obligation to do good to others. "God, nature, and all reason urges us to do good and merit the gratitude of our fellows." Similarly, friendship, because it is the nurse and cement of human society, is "the soul and life of the world, more necessary to us, say wise men, than fire or water." To keep one's word faithfully is also a bond of human society and the very foundation of justice. It too is a rule which should be religiously observed.[71] We have, in addition to these, more special duties to our fellow man. The husband is obliged to nourish, love, defend, and instruct his wife, the father to support, discipline, and educate his children, the aristocrat to defend his king and protect the oppressed.[72] We have, finally, and here wisdom merges imperceptibly with prudence, the duty to conduct our personal lives, insofar as they impinge on others, with honesty, modesty, and self-control.

Prudence, says Charron, "is the art of life, as medicine is the art

[70] *Sag.*, III, xxxi: III, 206–208.

[71] *Sag.*, III, xi: III, 38; *Sag.*, III, vii: III, 3; *Sag.*, III, viii: III, 16.

[72] *Sag.*, III, xii, xiv, xviii: III, 61, 68, 148.

of health."[73] Its sources are history and experience.[74] It teaches us how to behave in any difficult affair or dangerous accident. The character of its sapiential rules are nicely illustrated by the pattern of behavior Charron recommends to individuals caught up in civil war. The question had an immediate relevance for Frenchmen in the later years of the sixteenth century; and Charron, who had joined, then left the League, was well qualified to pose and answer it. From direct personal experience then, "from a knowledge of things which we ourselves have seen and handled,"[75] and from historical reflection, a passage on the horrors of civil war from one of Cicero's letters,[76] he derives his first proposition: "There is no evil more miserable nor more shameful than civil war. It is a sea of misfortunes."[77] What then should be the attitude of an *homme de bien*? Should he, for example, take sides or hold himself aloof? Certainly the latter; for civil divisions are illegitimate per se and the private individual cannot take part in them without inhumanity and injustice. He will therefore retire, if that is possible, to a safe and isolated place in the country and wait for the conclusion of hostilities. Furthermore, the wise man, at least in his public behavior, will be equally courteous to both sides, offend no one, and deplore the common misfortune. Like Atticus he will be a moderate, "famous for his modesty and prudence in such storms, considered by all to favor the right side, yet never taking arms and never offending the other."[78]

More coherently and more explicitly Charron has reached

---

[73] *Sag.*, III, i: II, 283. Cf. Cicero, *De Finibus*, V, vi, 16. "Quoniam igitur, ut medicina valitudinis, navigationis gubernatio, sic vivendi ars est prudentia. necesse est, eam quoque ab alia re esse constitutam et profectam."

[74] Charron, too (*Sag.*, III, i: II, 288), quotes the lines of Affranius: "Usus me genuit, mater peperit memoria." (Aulus Gellius, *Attic Nights*, XIII, viii, 1–3.)   [75] *Sag.*, III, i: II, 287.

[76] Cicero, *Epistol. ad Fam.*, IV, 9. "Omnia sunt misera in bellis civilibus, quae majores nostri ne semel quidem, nostra aetas saepe jam sensit: sed miserius nihil, quam ipsa victoria; quae etiamsi ad meliores venit, tamen eos ipsos ferociores impotentioresque reddit, ut, etiamsi natura tales non sint, necessitate esse cogantur."

[77] *Sag.*, III, iv, 11; II, 421.   [78] *Sag.*, III, iv, 12: II, 427.

conclusions similar to Cardan's. Wisdom, said Cardan, is *bene ac diu vivere*. Charron was not a physician; he omits *diu* and concentrates on *bene*. Wisdom, he says, is to live well and die well, for this is everything. Given this revision, the two men agree. Cardan defined wisdom as the pursuit of virtue and the insurance of an honest probity in every act. Charron says that wisdom is the constant, active practice of virtue, that the wise man conducts himself virtuously and well in the active life. Its first imperative is to follow reason and the law of nature. From this inner light man learns his natural obligations, his duties to himself, to others, and to God. Moral philosophy explains the obligations and supplies the specific rules of conduct by which they are fulfilled. These are the rules of justice, fortitude, temperance, and prudence. They teach man self-control and the mastery of his passions, how to conduct himself prudently and wisely in his family, in his business, toward his neighbor, toward the state, in good fortune and in bad. Wisdom is explicitly and precisely the practice of moral virtue. It is, as Cicero had said, an *ars vivendi*.[79]

The final duty of the wise man, and the third obligation of justice, is to God, "sovereign and absolute master of the world." This duty is piety or religion, and it is the first part of justice and the noblest of moral codes. Religion, therefore, is to be classified under *preud'hommie*, that is, under a part of *preud'hommie*. "For this reason my wise guardian of the law and of moral virtue will honor, fear, love, revere, and serve God in all things with body and soul and then render, according to the order and measure determined by the law, what he owes to his neighbor and himself."[80] Religion is thus a subdivision of *preud'hommie* and justice. But, emphasizes Charron, it is nevertheless distinct from them. This distinction of *preud'hommie* and religion guarantees the secular autonomy of wisdom.

Religion and *preud'hommie*, piety and probity, devotion and conscience are very different things. The entire and perfect man possesses both. He neither confuses them nor rejects one in favor of

[79] *De Finibus*, I, xii, 42   [80] *Petit Traicté de Sagesse*, II, 6: *Sag.*, III, 289.

the other. Some men observe only the cult and service of God and care nothing for true virtue or *preud'hommie*. Their religion is purely external. They are religious, but they are also bad. Other men, on the other hand, prize only virtue and *preud'hommie* and pay little attention to religion. Certain philosophers have this fault, and it can also be found among atheists. Both positions are vicious extremes. Still others confound religion and *preud'hommie*. They assert—this was the position of both Luther and Loyola—that "religion is a union of every good and every virtue, that all virtues are included in it and subjected to it. They recognize, therefore, no virtue and no *preud'hommie* but that which finds its origin and driving force in religion."[81] *Preud'hommie*, so they say, must follow and serve religion.

Such confusion is intolerable to Charron. By confounding religion and *preud'hommie*, they confound philosophy and theology, faith and reason, grace and nature. Between faith and reason, however, there is, and must be maintained, a clear, imperative distinction. Like Francis Bacon, Charron radically splits nature from the supernatural. Reason is excluded from the realm of faith; but faith is equally excluded from the realm of reason. Religion, he asserts, violates commonsense. It is far above the highest capacities of human intelligence, and its truths come to us solely by extraordinary and celestial revelations. To this Revelation men must submit simply and humbly, without discussion, heads bowed, and intellects captive, *captivantes intellectum ad obsequium fidei*.[82]

Preud'hommie, on the other hand, is in the realm of reason. It is purely human, an autonomous and natural wisdom with no necessary relation whatever with faith and the Christian religion. *Preud'hommie* is a "moral and human virtue, a part of justice, one of the four cardinal virtues"; and it can exist—the fact is proved by the lives of many good and virtuous philosophers—independently

[81] *Sag.*, II, v: II, 148–151.

[82] *Sag.*, II, v: II, 128–129; *Sag.*, II, ii: II, 34. Cf. II Cor. 10:5; Francis Bacon, *The Advancement of Learning*, G. W. Kitchin, ed. (Everyman's Library, 1915), 89; and John Owen, *The Skeptics of the French Renaissance* (London, 1893), 583 ff.

of all true religion. Its source is not religion, "but as we have proved, it must spring from nature, from that law and light which God has put in each of us at his creation."[83] We are good, virtuous, just, and wise, not because we are pious Christians, but because reason and our very nature demands these virtues of us. We cannot be anything else without violating nature, the general order of the world, ourselves, our being and our end.[84] Therefore, not only is *preud'hommie* not posterior to religion, it is prior to it. Far from religion engendering *preud'hommie*, it is "rather *preud'hommie* which should cause and engender religion; for it is primordial, older, and more natural." *Preud'hommie* is a universal, natural virtue; religion is particular, acquired, and frequently not virtuous at all.[85] Wisdom and Christianity, in short, are totally independent. They are not opposed. On the contrary, each should embellish and supplement the other.[86] But they are separate.

[83] *Sag.*, II, v: II, 151–152. "... car la religion qui est posterieure, est une vertu speciale et particuliere, distincte de toutes les autres vertus, qui peust estre sans elles et sans probité, comme a esté dict des Pharisiens, religieux et meschans: et elles sans religion comme en plusieurs philosophes, bons et vertueux, toutesfois irreligieux. Elle est aussi, comme enseigne toute la theologie, vertu morale, humaine, piece appartenante à la justice, l'une des quatre vertus cardinales, laquelle nous enseigne en general de rendre a chascun ce qui lui appartient, gardant à chascun son rang."

[84] *Sag.*, II, v: II, 153.

[85] *Sag.*, II, v (ed. of 1601): II, 157. "Je veux aussi la pieté et la religion, non qui fasse, cause ou engendre la preud'hommie ja née en toy, et avec toy, plantée de nature, mais qui l'approuve, l'authorise et la couronne. La religion est posterieure à la preud'hommie; c'est aussi chose apprinse, receue par l'ouye, *fides ex auditu et per verbum Dei*, par revelation et instruction, et ainsi ne la peust pas causer. Ce seroit plustost la preud'hommie qui debvroit causer et engendrer la religion; car elle est première, plus ancienne et naturelle; laquelle nous enseigne qu'il faut rendre à un chascun ce qui lui appartient, gardant à chascun son rang.... Ceux-là donc pervertissent tout ordre, qui font suyvre et servir la probité à la religion." Cf. F. Strowski, *Pascal et son temps* (Paris, 1907), I, 186 ff.

[86] *Sag.*, II, v: II, 156–158. "Je veux donc (pour finir tout ce propos) en mon sage une vraye preud'hommie et une vraye pieté jointes et mariées ensemble, et toutes deux complettes et couronnées de la grace de Dieu, laquelle il ne refuse à aucun qui la demande, *Deus dat spiritum bonum omnibus petentibus eum*, comme a esté dict."

By these firm distinctions Charron completes the Renaissance secularization of the idea of wisdom. Wisdom is an autonomous and naturally acquired moral virtue. Religion is a gift of grace, "a pure gift of God, which we must desire and ask for humbly and ardently, and prepare ourselves for as well as we can by the exercise of the moral virtues and an observation of the law of nature."[87] The Middle Ages had identified the quest for wisdom and the quest for God. Aquinas, precariously balancing the claims of grace and nature, might allow this search to proceed on two parallel lines, natural and revealed. More commonly, with Augustine or Nicholas of Cusa, the illuminations of Revelation were thought to light each step of the way. Wisdom was a specifically Christian insight, a knowledge of the Trinity, the *principium* of all things, which ordered all experience and hierarchized each love. Wisdom, indeed, was the Trinity. Charron, by his profound split of faith and reason, recreates in full the secular autonomy of the antique conception. Christianity had tamed an antique moral category by identifying it with the Second Person of the Trinity. Charron ends and makes explicit the transformation by which the Renaissance reconverted wisdom from its Christian service, stripped it of its transcendent meanings, and restored it to its earlier human associations. Charron's definition of religion is the medieval definition of wisdom. His definition of wisdom reproduces the fundamental characteristics of the antique cardinal virtues. Wisdom is again a moral virtue, open to all men by the sole exercise of their natural faculties, independent of any revealed religion.

VI

On the title page of the 1604 edition of *De la Sagesse* is an engraving of Léonard Gaultier, an *Allegory of Wisdom*. The iconography, supplied by Charron himself,[88] is a neat summary of his idea of

[87] *Petit Traicté de Sagesse*, IV, 6: *Sag.*, III, 313.

[88] Auvray, "Lettres de Pierre Charron a Gabriel Michel de la Rochemaillet," 326. "Au reste," Charron writes to la Rochemaillet on April 27th, 1603, "j'espère vous envoyer painct ce qu'il fauldra graver en taille doulce pour mettre au frontispice de mon livre, que sera le protraict de sagesse; c'est chose de quoy je me suis advisé depuis trois jours seulement; je y veux penser."

wisdom.[89] *Sagesse* is represented as a beautiful woman, naked, *quia puram naturam sequitur*, and standing firmly on the cube of Justice. Her face is healthy, joyful, and radiantly imposing. On her head are branches of laurel and olive, symbolizing the fruits of wisdom: victorious self-mastery and tranquillity. Around her is the empty space of sapiential liberty. Her arms are crossed as though she were embracing herself. This signifies the wise man's independence and self-sufficiency. Like *Sapientia* in the *Wisdom and Fortune* which illustrates Bovillus' *De sapiente*, she is looking at herself in a mirror, "because she always looks at and knows herself." To her right we read the devise, *Je ne sçay*; to the left, *Paix et peu*. Chained below her feet are four women: Passion, her face in a hideous grimace; wild-eyed Opinion, supported by the heads of the fickle and inconstant mob; Superstition, her hands clasped like a kitchen maid, trembling with fear; and Science, artificial, acquired, pedantic, and arrogant, the archenemy of wisdom, who reads in a book the words

---

[89] Charron has explained the allegory in *Sag.*, Preface (1604): I, xliv–xlvi. A sonnet which appears for the first time in the edition of 1606 adds certain details:

> La Sagesse est à nud, droicte et sans artifice,
> D'Oliue et de Laurier son chef est verdoyant.
> Son mirouër est tenu des doigs du foudroyant,
> Et s'eslesue au dessus du Cube de justice.
> Sous ses pieds au carcan, les meres de tout vice
> Forcenant de despit, grommelant, aboyant,
> Contr'elle en vain l'effort de leur rage employant,
> Tant de Sagesse est fort et ferme l'édifice.
> La Passion s'anime impetueusement;
> Le Peuple fauorise et porte obstinément
> La folle Opinion, sourde aveugle et perverse:
> Tremblante, sans sçauoir, la Superstition
> S'estrangle d'elle mesme; et la Presomption
> De la Pedanterie est mise à la renverse.

A more elaborate explanation was given by the Elzevirs in their editions of 1646, 1656, and 1662. It has been reproduced by Duval (*Sag.*, I, xliv–xlv) as a variant of Charron's own description.

OUY and NON—dogmatic knowledge crushed by the laughing skepticism of the wise *homme de bien*. This is Charron's wisdom, an imitation of nature whose imperatives are skepticism and *preud'hommie*, whose cause and obligation is man's own nature, whose method is the active practice of justice, whose fruits are constancy, tranquillity, and an imperturbable virtue.

Chapter 8

Tradition and Innovation in Renaissance Ideas of Wisdom

Renaissance wisdoms can be classified according to their objects and according to their modes of acquisition. Classified according to their objects there were three main varieties of wisdom current in the fifteenth and sixteenth centuries. Wisdom was defined as the knowledge of divine things; as the knowledge of human things; and as the knowledge of all things divine and human and their causes. Classified according to their modes of acquisition, there were again three varieties of wisdom: revealed; that acquired by reason only; and that acquired by both Revelation and reason.

Other definitions flow from the different ways in which divine and human things were understood. The general statement that wisdom is a knowledge of divine things was made specific by particular statements defining divine things. It was said that wisdom is the knowledge of the highest causes and principles, of the immaterial and constant forms of the intelligible word, of Ideas, of God. And since this God was a Christian God, wisdom became a knowledge of Christian doctrine or of Christ, the Wisdom and Word of God. More philosophically minded theologians understood by divine things the Ideas in the mind of God, Christ as infinite Form and First Cause, or the Trinity as the *principium* of all things.

A similar variety was caused by defining human things more concretely. Some writers meant the human soul and body and said that wisdom is self-knowledge. Others meant the particulars of sense experience and called physics the beginning of wisdom. A few humanists spoke of the human things of history. From the records of men active in history they drew lessons of governmental wisdom and private prudence. Finally, by human things were commonly meant the rules of morality and the human actions they guided. This defined wisdom as a moral virtue and an *ars vivendi*.

But these are purely technical classifications. It is legitimate and more interesting to speak of traditional and innovating varieties of wisdom and to classify them accordingly. The basis of such an historical classification must be the medieval norm: wisdom as a revealed knowledge of divine things understood in an explicitly Christian sense. Then any conception which asserts that wisdom is naturally acquired, which includes human things among the objects of wisdom, or which does not understand divine things in an explicitly Christian sense is an innovation. Traditional definitions, on the other hand, reassert the basic elements of medieval wisdom, its dependence on grace, and its exclusive preoccupation with divine and Christian things.

Innovation in Renaissance speculation on wisdom was the result of a process of secularization which humanized the object of wisdom and guaranteed the natural autonomy of its acquisition. Cardinal Sadoleto and Sir Thomas Elyot defined wisdom as a knowledge of divine things; but in spite of the esoteric elevation of its object, they insisted that such knowledge was acquired by natural reason. It "belongethe to understandynge," said Elyot; for the way to know divine things "is called raison, and the knowlage thereof is named understanding." Sadoleto called wisdom the end and good of human reason and emphasized that it was reason which grasped it. Bovillus and Conrad Celtis, although their conceptions of wisdom differed from Elyot's and Sadoleto's, were equally convinced that it was a naturally acquired virtue. Celtis gave travel, experience, observation, and reading in the Greek and Roman classics as its principal sources. For Bovillus *sapientia* was man's perfection, species, and act; and he described the passage from potency to act, from ignorance to wisdom, as an autonomous process within the realm of reason and nature. Cardan and Charron, finally, defined wisdom with the Stoics as an *ars vivendi* and identified it with prudence and justice. That very identification made it unnecessary to insist further on the natural, human character of its acquisition. Justice and prudence

8

were cardinal virtues, considered by all but the most ascetic as perfections outside and apart from the order of redemption. Wisdom, said Charron, is a matter of conscience, not of devotion. It deals with actions which are "simply, naturally, and ethically good," not with those which merit salvation. Wisdom, in short, is a "human, moral virtue" whose origin is nature and human reason.

Judged by the same standard, any wisdom which needs grace for its acquisition is traditional. Salutati defined wisdom as virtue, but insofar as he thought that man could not be good without the aid of grace he is a traditional thinker. The traditional element in Cusanus is his insistence that intellectual cognition, whose fruit is wisdom, is an amalgam of faith and reason. Luther equated wisdom and Christian theology and put its mode of acquisition wholly in the area of grace. In this, as in so much else, he represents a revival of medieval attitudes opposed to the classical revivals of his humanist contemporaries. When St. John of the Cross, finally, described that ascent of the soul to union with its bride, which is the Wisdom of God, he made it plain that the ascent was impossible without God's grace and that he "who shall labor to attain to union with the Wisdom of God in reliance on his own wisdom and skill is supremely ignorant and distant therefrom."

The Florentine Neo-Platonists present a subtler problem. Ficino speaks regularly of divine illumination and of the active role of God in human knowledge. He speaks relatively little of faith, grace, or Revelation. In certain texts he thus seems to be restating fundamental doctrines of Plotinus and Proclus, now directly known for the first time, reviving, so to speak, a pagan "grace" with no necessary relation to Christianity. This is structurally parallel to the medieval idea of wisdom, yet at the same time a clear break with tradition. Other texts, however, suggest that these Neo-Platonic conceptions are being given Augustinian meanings rather than their original ones. Ficino's doctrine of divine illumination then tends to become indistinguishable from Augustine's and his emphasis on the active role of God in human knowledge is imperceptibly transformed into a recognition of the indispensability of Christian grace. When this happens, the Florentine Neo-Platonists are working on the same medieval assumptions as Salutati and Cusanus.

Some Renaissance thinkers secularized wisdom in a second way: by humanizing its object, transferring it, in fact, from heaven to earth.

It is characteristic of the Middle Ages that its sapiential objects were divine, and it is understandable that pious laymen, mystics, and professional theologians of the Renaissance should retain this "divine" wisdom. Luther made the Second Person of the Trinity wisdom's exclusive object. The Catholic mystics, although some of them tended to abandon the abstract term in favor of a more intense devotion to the concrete person of Christ, did the same. Academic theologians understood divine Wisdom more philosophically, calling the object of wisdom an infinite Form or the First Cause. Many humanists, too, said that wisdom was a knowledge of divine things only: Ideas, disembodied forms, and the heavenly bodies, or, with Aristotle, the highest causes and principles. This was the position of Bruni and Pontano, Ficino and Sadoleto, for example. Their insistence that the object of wisdom is exclusively divine links them verbally with the Middle Ages; their "pagan" definition of divine things links them to ancient Aristotelianism, Platonism, and Neo-Platonism. But, whatever its background, this is an element in their conception of wisdom which comes to seem increasingly traditional when it is contrasted with the more novel tendency of thinkers under the influence of ancient systems dormant in the Middle Ages to make human things objects of wisdom.

For the beginnings of significant innovation came only with the increasing currency of the notion that wisdom's object included human things as well as divine. This was a significant enrichment and an explicit humanization. Not only universals, forms, and first causes, but particulars, concrete substances, secondary causes, and effects were then included in the content of wisdom; while to the traditional sapiential sciences of theology and metaphysics were added new ones: astronomy, physics, history, and even medicine. The identification of *sapientia* and ethics completed this humanizing process. From a knowledge of both divine and human things, wisdom became the active manipulation of human things alone; from solitary contemplation, action in the world; from a knowledge of the true, a pursuit of the good. The result was a wisdom rooted in and ruling man's most banal activities, his politics and business, his family and personal relations. Finally, the object of wisdom became man himself, and its fundamental command self-knowledge. The extent of these changes is the distance between the *Sapientia* on the North Portal of Chartres, who reads a holy book and points to heaven, and the Wisdoms which illustrate Charron and Bovillus' *De sapiente*. Their pedestal is the cube of justice, and they look, not toward heaven, but at their own reflections in a hand mirror, the *speculum sapientiae*.

Of course, innovating conceptions of wisdom did not supplant traditional varieties inherited from the Middle Ages. New and old coexisted. During the years immediately before and after 1400, for example, every important definition of wisdom was reproduced by Italian humanists. Wisdom was identified with Christian piety. It was called a knowledge of Plato's Ideas. Bruni repeated the Aristotelian and Stoic definitions, and Salutati defined it as *eruditio moralis*. A hundred years later John Colet was developing an essentially Augustinian idea of wisdom in his Oxford lectures on the Pauline Epistles, Lefèvre d'Etaples publicized the Thomist conception in a textbook on the *Metaphysics* of Aristotle, Tommaso Inghirami entertained his friends with his secular extremisms, Celtis and Johann Reuchlin defined wisdom as a knowledge of all things divine and human and their causes, and Erasmus, by his analysis of *sapientia* in the *Enchiridion*, strengthened humanism's tendency to make wisdom an active moral virtue. Similarly, the eleven years from 1533 to 1544 saw the publication of a series of important books, each defending a different and particular definition of wisdom: Elyot's *Disputacion Platonike* (1533), Calvin's *Institute* (1536), Sadoleto's *De laudibus philosophiae* (1538), and the *De sapientia* of Cardan (1544). There was hardly less variety at the end of the century. Montaigne, Guillaume du Vair, and Charron consolidated the moralized wisdom of the *homme de bien*, a natural *preud'hommie* got by an imitation of nature. But intellectualist and theological notions of wisdom survived intact. In his *De constantia* (1583) Justus Lipsius called wisdom a knowledge of divine things; Bodin's *Universae naturae theatrum* defined it as a knowledge of all things divine and human and their causes; and St. Robert Bellarmine adjured himself as follows: "But do thou, my soul, occupy thyself with drawing honey from the rock and oil from granite, that is, wisdom from foolishness, the wisdom of God from the folly of the Cross." It was in the name of this "divine wisdom," that Buffalo, the Papal nuncio, strongly attacked Charron. The *De la Sagesse*, he wrote to Cardinal Aldobrandini, was "a scandalous book, indistinguishable from the impious doctrine of Machiavelli and greatly harmful to the Christian religion."

New and traditional definitions of wisdom were even advanced by the same man. Filelfo revived the Augustinian formula *sapientia est pietas*; he supported the Platonic and Stoic conceptions; he said that wisdom was a moral virtue. In the *De asse* Budé spoke of wisdom in the same accents as Colet and Luther; while in the *De philologia*, he defined wisdom in two other ways: as the contemplation of divine, eternal, and immutable things and, with the Stoics, as a knowledge of all things divine and human. Cardan was even more eclectic. He called wisdom piety and identified it with theology. He called it the contemplation of God, who is the supreme essence. But he also defined it as the knowledge of intelligible forms, of things without any sensible accident, and as an *universa cognitio humana*. Finally, he transformed it into a moral virtue and a collection of medical and ethical precepts and summarized its meaning in the phrase *bene ac diu vivere*.

This coexistence, in time and in individuals, of tradition and innovation reflects the ideological confusion of a period of transition. But behind this confusion there is one intelligible pattern which includes all important changes in the idea of wisdom between the *De sapientia* of Petrarch and Charron: the gradual process by which wisdom was transformed from intellectual *eruditio* to a moral virtue, from theoretical knowledge to probity in action. If there is one idea of wisdom peculiarly characteristic of the Renaissance, it is this of

Erasmus: *sapientia est virtus cum eruditione liberali coniuncta*. It is also a common definition of *humanitas*.

The process which resulted in this ethical conception of wisdom was not a simple, continuous evolution. It was far advanced in Florentine humanism at the beginning of the fifteenth century. But it lost its momentum later in the century, and only began to regain it early in the sixteenth century in the active moralism of Erasmus and his circle. It is fair to say that from Bovillus to Sadoleto, that is, until about 1540, the majority of advanced intellectuals considered wisdom a kind of elevated, esoteric knowledge, remarkable either for the splendor and remoteness of its object or for its encyclopedic contents. Even in them, of course, there is often latent a moralized wisdom. On an anonymous woodcut illustrating the *De sapiente*, for example, and based on Bovillus' text, the wise man is pictured saying: "Put your trust in virtue; fortune is fickler than the waves of the sea." Celtis was haunted by the sapiential encyclopedia, but he made prudence his motto. By 1532 Budé was conscious that neither erudition nor virtue necessarily implied the other, and Sadoleto took pains to point out that a knowledge of divine things was indispensable for the virtuous regulation of things human. But it was only after the *De sapientia* of Cardan and Le Caron's *Dialogues* (1556) that a fundamentally ethical understanding of wisdom became dominant. By the time of Montaigne, du Vair's *Philosophie morale des Stoïques*, and Charron it was as characteristic of the later Renaissance as Bovillus' Promethean sage had been of an earlier period.

In this perspective Charron's *De la Sagesse* becomes peculiarly representative. It summarizes what happened to the idea of wisdom during the Renaissance. It marks the term of a temporal evolution within the fifteenth and sixteenth centuries and so defines the relation of innovating varieties of wisdom to each other. Precisely because of this, it is a legitimate archetype which can be used to define the relation between new and traditional concepts of wisdom. It is, in fact, humanism's conclusion from all its speculation on the meaning of wisdom and the modes of its acquisition: the notion that wisdom was an intrinsic perfection of the natural man and that this perfection was best understood as a moral virtue. This conclusion is a revival of the central meaning of antique wisdom and a return to the ethical preoccupations of a *prisca sapientia* whose source, function, and end were purely human. At the same time it is a clear break with the medieval idea of wisdom, with any Christian *sapientia* centred exclusively on divine things and acquired by faith and divine illumination. The idea of wisdom elaborated in Charron's *De la Sagesse* is, therefore, not only one of several varieties of wisdom current during the Renaissance. It is the most characteristic variety of Renaissance wisdom and the one which embodies its completed contribution. With respect to antique wisdom this contribution was a form of humanism. Behind the verbal formulas of a classical definition it recovered its original, human meanings. With respect to medieval notions of wisdom it was a form of secularism. It disassociated wisdom from its Christian assumptions and transcendent meanings. With respect to earlier innovating varieties of wisdom —the Renaissance revivals of the Platonic, Aristotelian, and Stoic definitions—it was a form of moralism and an emphasis on the useful, active life. The result was a conception of wisdom which remained a European ideal until the collapse of the humanistic tradition in the later nineteenth century: an autonomous and active moral virtue which defined man's dignity and described the highest degree of perfection of which human nature is capable.

Index

Afranius, 99
Agathocles, 200
Alberti, Leon Battista, 46 ff., 69 ff.
Albertus Magnus, 14, 96
Aldobrandini, Cardinal Pietro, 213
Alexander of Hales, 2, 14–15, 27
Alexander the Great, 101
Alfonso I, King of Naples, 47
Anaxagoras, 46, 52, 55, 84, 151, 153
Anselm, St., 37
Antigonus, 200
Apelles, 95, 168
Apollo, 9, 34, 109, 186
Aquinas, St. Thomas, 1, 14, 15–18, 27, 30, 55, 60, 83 n., 90 f., 134, 137, 141, 146, 205, 212
Argyropulos, Joannes, 68
Aristotle, 1 f., 6 ff., 10 f., 13 f., 17, 19, 37 f., 41, 43 f., 46, 48, 53, 55 f., 59 ff., 78 f., 84, 101, 115, 118, 134 f., 141, 151, 167, 196, 211 f.
Atticus, 201
Augustine, St., 1 ff., 4–13, 14, 17, 19 ff., 30 f., 37, 39, 41, 43, 50, 59, 61, 66, 83 n., 93 f., 103, 105, 124, 127 f., 135, 138 f., 145, 205, 210, 212 f.
Augustus, 200
Aulus Gellius, 99 f.
Ausonius, 9 n.
Averroës, 172

Bacon, Francis, 2, 203
Baldus de Ubaldis, Petrus, 56
Bartolus of Sassoferrato, 56
Bellarmine, St. Robert, 213
Benedetto da Maiano, 58
Bernard, St., 37
Boccaccio, Giovanni, 32 n., 33, 67
Bodin, Jean, 93, 178, 199, 213
Boethius, 59 n., 102

Bonaventura, St., 27, 37
Botticelli, Sandro, 58, 95
Bovillus, Carolus, 2, 94, 106–123, 149, 153, 155, 168, 176, 190, 206, 209, 212, 214
Brant, Sebastian, 130, 163, 164
Briçonnet, Guillaume, 126 n.
Brunelleschi, Filippo, 58
Bruni, Leonardo, 1, 44–49, 51 ff., 56, 58, 68, 70, 77, 93, 103, 107 f., 156, 181, 211 f.
Bruno, Giordano, 62 n.
Budé, Guillaume, 2, 94, 148, 150 ff., 163, 182, 213 f.

Caesar, 75, 199
Calvin, John, 125, 143–147, 186, 212
Camillus, 69
Caraffa, Cardinal Giampietro, 73
Cardano, Gerolamo, 2, 93, 165–176, 177, 179, 202, 209, 212 ff.
Cato, 33 f., 69, 155
Celtis, Conrad, 2, 94, 95–105, 118, 154, 162 f., 168, 209, 212, 214
Charron, Pierre, 1 f., 18, 90 f., 148 n., 149, 156, 178–207, 209 f., 212 ff.
Cicero, 2, 7 f., 30, 32, 39, 40 n., 42, 44, 46, 48, 70, 79 n., 84, 85 n., 93, 95, 103, 110, 140, 150 n., 151, 162, 171, 184 n., 188, 191, 196, 201 f.
Cleobulus, 9
Clichtove, Josse, 89 f., 176
Colet, John, 27, 43, 119 f., 124 f., 127, 130 f., 134, 146 f., 162, 163 n., 176, 212 f.
Contarini, Cardinal Gaspare, 72

Dante, 30, 46
Democritus, 84
Des Periers, Bonaventure, 164, 186

Harvard Historical Monographs

* Out of print